3 9082 07867 5025

D0872673

VISUAL QUICKSTART GUIDE

WORD 2000

FOR WINDOWS

Maria Langer

 Peachpit Press

	DATE
FEB 2 7 2002	
APR 1 9 2003	
APR 0 7 2004	
MAR 3 1 2008	
OCT 0 5 2009	

29/2001

Visual QuickStart Guide
Word 2000 for Windows
Maria Langer

Peachpit Press
1249 Eighth Street
Berkeley, CA 94710
510-524-2178 · 800-283-9444
510-524-2221 (fax)

Find us on the World Wide Web at: http://www.peachpit.com/

Peachpit Press is a division of Addison Wesley Longman

Copyright © 1999 by Maria Langer

Editor: Nancy Davis
Indexer: Emily Glossbrenner
Cover Design: The Visual Group
Production: Maria Langer, Kate Reber

Colophon

This book was produced with Adobe PageMaker 6.5 on a Power Macintosh G3/300. The fonts used were Kepler Multiple Master, Meta Plus, and PIXymbols Command. Screenshots were created using Hijaak Capture on a Gateway 2000 GP6-266.

Notice of Rights

Notice of Liability

Trademarks

ISBN 0-201-35428-4

9 8 7 6 5 4 3 2 1

Printed and bound in the United States of America.

 Printed on recycled paper.

Dedication

To Spot,
the Wonderdog

Thanks!

To Nancy Davis, for her long-distance editing skills. As usual, it's a pleasure to work with you, Nancy!

To Nancy Ruenzel, for continuing to let me write new titles in the *Visual QuickStart Guide* series.

To Kate Reber, for letting me get a little closer to a "moving target" but not forcing *me* to bulls-eye it. I appreciate your efforts (and your patience) on this project. But I really think you folks should let me develop the layout for *Visual QuickStart Guides*—heck, I write enough of them!

To the rest of the folks at Peachpit Press— especially Gary-Paul, Trish, Hannah, Paula, Zigi, Jimbo, and Keasley—for doing what they do so well.

To Emily Glossbrenner for applying her indexing skills. Anyone who's ever done an index can tell you what a pain in the neck it is. Yet Emily continues to do them for me—and she does a far better job than I ever could!

To Microsoft Corporation's Office development team, for putting together a great revision to the world's best word processor.

And to Mike, for the usual reasons.

http://www.gilesrd.com/mlanger/

TABLE OF CONTENTS

INTRODUCTION TO WORD 2000

Introduction

Word, a component of Microsoft Office, is the most popular word processing application for Windows users. Now more powerful and user friendly than ever, Word 2000 enables users to create a wide range of documents, ranging in complexity from simple, one-page letters to complex, multi-file reports with figures, table of contents, and index.

This Visual QuickStart Guide will help you learn the basics of Word 2000 by providing step-by-step instructions, plenty of illustrations, and a generous helping of tips. On these pages, you'll find everything you need to know to get up and running quickly with Word 2000—and more!

This book was designed for page flipping. Use the thumb tabs, index, or table of contents to find the topics for which you need help. If you're brand new to Word or word processing, however, I recommend that you begin by reading at least the first two chapters. **Chapter 1** provides basic information about Word's interface while **Chapter 2** introduces word processing concepts and explains exactly how they work in Word.

If you've used other versions of Word and are interested in information about new Word 2000 features, be sure to browse through this **Introduction**. It'll give you a good idea of the new things Word has in store for you.

START HERE

New & Improved Features in Word 2000

Places bar — *Back button*

Figure 1 The Open dialog box has a whole new look.

Word 2000 includes many brand new features, as well as major improvements to some existing features.

✔ Tip

- This book covers most—but not all—of these features.

File management

- The Open (**Figure 1**) and Save dialog boxes now display 50 percent more files.

- The Open (**Figure 1**) and Save dialog boxes include a Places bar, which provides quick and easy access to commonly used folders, files, and locations.

- The History folder on the Places bar in the Open (**Figure 1**) and Save dialog boxes contains links to the last 20 documents on which you have worked.

- The Back button in the Open (**Figure 1**) and Save dialog boxes makes it easy to backtrack through recently visited folders.

- Quick file switching makes each open document accessible via the Windows Taskbar (**Figure 2**).

Editing

- Word's new Collect and Paste feature enables you to copy multiple selections from Office 2000 documents and paste any combination of them, in any order, into your document.

- Word's new Click and Type feature makes it possible to position text anywhere on a page in Print Layout view by simply clicking and typing.

- Table editing has been improved, making it easier to create and edit tables.

Figure 2 Each open document appears in the Taskbar.

Figure 3 Commonly used commands appear on a personalized menu...

Figure 4 ...but you can always display the full version of the menu.

Figure 5 The most commonly used toolbar buttons on the Standard and Formatting toolbar appear in a single row as personalized toolbars.

Figure 6 You can click a button to display the rest of a toolbar's buttons.

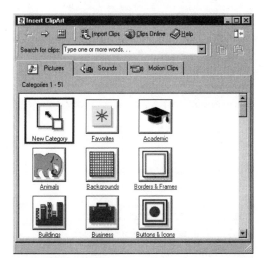

Figure 7 The Clip Art Gallery has many improvements.

Figure 8 Themes make it easy to create nice looking, consistently formatted Web pages.

Customization

◆ Word automatically tracks the menu commands you use most and displays them on short, personalized menus (**Figure 3**), which can be expanded to show all commands (**Figure 4**).

◆ Word automatically tracks the toolbar buttons you use most and displays them in a single row on the screen (**Figure 5**). Other toolbar buttons can be displayed when needed (**Figure 6**).

◆ It's now quicker and easier to customize toolbars.

Clip Art

◆ The Clip Art Gallery (**Figure 7**) is now searchable and includes more art and AutoShapes.

◆ Clip art can be organized into custom groups (**Figure 7**).

◆ Clip art can be dragged from the Clip Art Gallery window (**Figure 7**) into a Word document.

◆ You can now leave the Clip Art Gallery window (**Figure 7**) open while working with Word documents.

◆ Native clip art file formats are now passed to Word when art is pasted or inserted into a Word document.

Internet

◆ Word can read and save to HTML format with greater fidelity than ever before.

◆ Documents can be saved in HTML format directly to the Web.

◆ Themes (**Figure 8**) provide an easy way to create appealing, consistent looking Web pages.

Continued on next page...

NEW & IMPROVED FEATURES IN WORD 2000

Continued from previous page.

◆ An improved interface for the Insert Hyperlink dialog box (**Figure 9**) makes it easier to insert hyperlinks into Word documents.

◆ Word automatically checks and attempts to repair broken hyperlinks when you save a document.

◆ Word automatically selects the correct graphic format (GIF or JPEG) based on a graphic's contents when saving a graphic that's part of an HTML document.

◆ Word now includes many new and advanced Internet-based collaboration features.

Year 2000 Compliance

◆ Word 2000 is Year 2000 compliant.

◆ Word now includes advanced tools that system administrators can use to manage Year 2000 issues.

Online Help

◆ The Office Assistant no longer resides within its own window. Instead, it floats over the document window (**Figure 10**) to be less distracting.

◆ You can ask the Office Assistant for help in your own words (**Figure 11**).

◆ The Office Assistant now provides links to additional information on the Web.

◆ The Office Assistant can now be turned off.

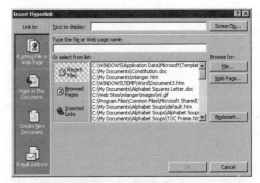

Figure 9 The Insert Hyperlink dialog box makes it easier than ever to insert hyperlinks into documents.

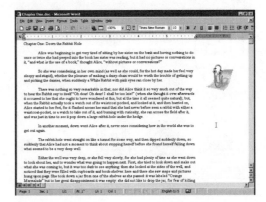

Figure 10 The Office Assistant now floats over the document window and does its best to stay out of your way.

Figure 11 You can ask the Office Assistant for help in your own words.

THE WORD WORKPLACE

Meet Microsoft Word

Microsoft Word is a full-featured word processing program that you can use to create all kinds of text-based documents—letters, reports, form letters, mailing labels, envelopes, flyers, and even Web pages.

Word's interface combines common Windows screen elements with buttons, commands, and controls that are specific to Word. To use Word effectively, you must have at least a basic understanding of these elements.

This chapter introduces the Word workplace by illustrating and describing the following elements:

◆ The Word screen, including window elements.

◆ Menus, shortcut keys, toolbars, and dialog boxes.

◆ Views and document navigation techniques.

◆ Word's online help feature, including the Office Assistant.

✔ Tips

■ If you're brand new to Windows, don't skip this chapter. Many of the interface elements discussed in this chapter apply to all Windows programs, not just Word.

■ If you've used previous versions of Word, browse through this chapter to learn about some of the interface elements that are new to this version of Word.

The Word Screen

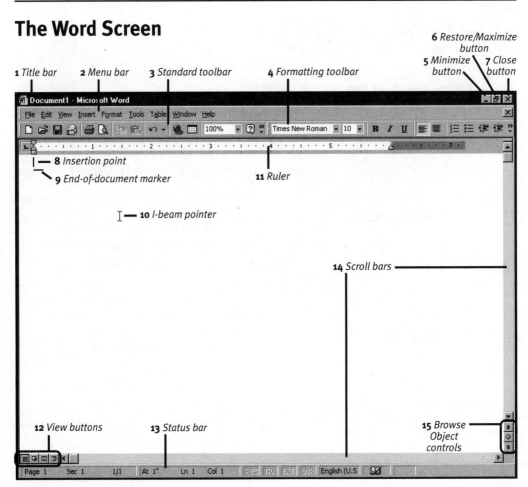

Figure 1 The Word screen in Normal view.

Key to the Word Screen

1 *Title bar*
The title bar displays the name of the active program and document.

2 *Menu bar*
The menu bar appears near the top of the window and offers access to Word's commands.

3 *Standard toolbar*
The Standard toolbar (shown here as a personal toolbar) offers buttons for many basic Word commands. This toolbar is very similar in other Office 2000 programs.

4 *Formatting toolbar*

The Formatting toolbar (shown here as a personal toolbar) offers buttons for formatting commands.

5 *Minimize button*

The minimize button enables you to reduce the window to a button at the bottom of the screen. Clicking the button for a minimized window restores it to its normal size.

6 *Restore/Maximize button*

The restore button (shown here) resizes the window to a custom size that is smaller than the full size of the screen. (You can resize a window by dragging any of its edges when it is not maximized.) The maximize button increases the window's size so it fills the screen.

7 *Close button*

The close button offers one way to close the window.

8 *Insertion point*

The blinking insertion point indicates where text will appear when typed or inserted with the Paste command.

9 *End-of-document marker*

The end-of-document marker indicates the end of the document.

10 *I-beam pointer*

The I-beam pointer enables you to position the insertion point or to select text. This pointer, which is controlled by the mouse, turns into various other pointers depending on its position and the Word view.

11 *Ruler*

The horizontal ruler (shown here) enables you to set paragraph formatting options such as tabs and indentation. A vertical ruler that offers additional formatting options appears in Page Layout view.

12 *View buttons*

View buttons enable you to switch between various Word views.

13 *Status bar*

The status bar displays information about the document.

14 *Scroll bars*

Scroll bars enable you to shift the window's contents to view different parts of the document.

15 *Browse Object controls*

These buttons enable you to navigate among various document elements.

THE WORD SCREEN

The Mouse

As with most Windows programs, you use the mouse to select text, activate buttons, and choose menu commands.

Mouse pointer appearance

The appearance of the mouse pointer varies depending on its location and the item it is pointing to. Here are some examples:

◆ In the document window, the mouse pointer usually looks like an I-beam pointer (**Figure 1**).

◆ On a menu name, the mouse pointer appears as an arrow pointing up and to the left (**Figure 2**).

◆ In the selection bar between the left edge of the document window and the text, the mouse pointer appears as an arrow pointing up and to the right (**Figure 3**).

◆ On selected text, the mouse pointer appears as an arrow pointing up and to the left (**Figure 4**).

To use the mouse

There are four basic mouse techniques:

◆ **Pointing** means to position the mouse pointer so that its tip is on the item to which you are pointing (**Figure 2**).

◆ **Clicking** means to press the mouse button once and release it. You click to position the insertion point or to activate a button.

◆ **Double-clicking** means to press the mouse button twice in rapid succession. You double-click to open an item or to select a word.

■ **Dragging** means to press the mouse button down and hold it while moving the mouse. You drag to resize windows, select text, choose menu commands, or draw shapes.

Figure 2
The mouse pointer on a menu name.

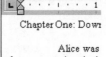

Figure 3
The mouse pointer in the selection bar.

Chapter One: Down

Alice was
once or twice she h
it, "and what is the

So she was conside
and stupid), whethe
picking the daisies,

Chapter One: Down

Alice was
once or twice she h
it, "and what is the

Figure 4
The mouse pointer pointing to a selected word.

✔ Tip

■ Throughout this book, when I instruct you to simply *click*, press the left mouse button. When I instruct you to *right-click*, press the right mouse button.

THE MOUSE

Figure 5
A personalized menu version of the Edit menu.

Figure 6
The Edit menu with all commands displayed.

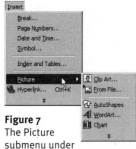

Figure 7
The Picture submenu under the Insert menu. In this example, both the menu and submenu are displayed as personalized menus.

Menus

All of Word's commands are accessible through its menus. Word has three types of menus:

◆ **Personalized menus** appear on the menu bar near the top of the window. These menus automatically track and display only the commands you use most (**Figure 5**).

◆ **Full menus** also appear on the menu bar near the top of the window, but only when you either double-click the menu name, pause while displaying the menu, or click the arrows at the bottom of the menu. **Figure 6** shows the menu in **Figure 5** as a full menu with all commands displayed.

◆ **Shortcut menus** appear at the mouse pointer when you right-click on an item (**Figure 7**).

Here are some rules to keep in mind when working with menus:

◆ A menu command that appears in gray cannot be selected.

◆ A menu command followed by an ellipsis (...) displays a dialog box.

◆ A menu command followed by a triangle has a submenu. The submenu displays additional commands when the main command is chosen (**Figure 7**).

◆ A menu command followed by one or more keyboard characters can be chosen with a shortcut key.

✔ Tips

■ Commands that appear on both personalized and full menus have a dark gray background while those that appear only on full menus have a light gray background. You can see this by comparing **Figures 5** and **6**.

■ I discuss dialog boxes and shortcut keys later in this chapter.

MENUS

To use a menu

1. Click on the name of the menu from which you want to choose a command. The personalized version of the menu appears (**Figure 5**).

2. If necessary, click the menu name again to display the full menu version of the menu (**Figure 6**).

3. If the command you want is on a submenu, click the name of the submenu to display it (**Figure 7**). Repeat this step if necessary to display submenus on submenus.

4. Click the command you want.

✔ Tips

■ Throughout this book I use the following notation to indicate menu commands: *Menu Name > Submenu Name* (if necessary) > *Command Name*. For example, to instruct you to choose the Word Art command on the Picture submenu under the Insert menu (**Figure 7**), I'd say, "choose Insert > Picture > Word Art."

■ You can also use mouseless menus. Press Alt , then use the letter and arrow keys to display and select menus and commands. Press Enter to activate a selected command.

To use a shortcut menu

1. Point to the item on which you want to use the shortcut menu.

2. Right-click to display the shortcut menu (**Figure 8**).

3. Click to choose the command you want.

✔ Tips

■ The shortcut menu only displays the commands that can be applied to the item to which you are pointing.

■ Shortcut menus are sometimes referred to as *context-sensitive* or *contextual menus*.

Figure 8
A shortcut menu appears at the mouse pointer when you right-click on an item.

Shortcut Keys

Shortcut keys are combinations of keyboard keys that, when pressed, choose a menu command without displaying the menu. For example, the shortcut key for the Select All command under the Edit menu (**Figures 5** and **6**) is Ctrl A. Pressing this key combination chooses the command.

✔ Tips

- All shortcut keys use at least one of the following modifier keys:

Key Name	Keyboard Key
Control	Ctrl
Shift	Shift
Alt	Alt

- A menu command's shortcut key is displayed to its right on the menu (**Figures 5** and **6**).

- Many shortcut keys are standardized from one application to another. The Open, Save, and Print commands are three good examples; they're usually Ctrl O, Ctrl S, and Ctrl P.

- **Appendix A** includes a list of shortcut keys.

To use a shortcut key

1. Hold down the modifier key for the shortcut (normally Ctrl).

2. Press the letter or number key for the shortcut.

For example, to choose the Select All command, hold down Ctrl and press A.

Toolbars

Word includes a number of toolbars for various purposes. Each toolbar has buttons or menus you can use to activate menu commands or set options.

By default, Word automatically displays both the Standard and Formatting toolbars in a single row right beneath the menu bar (**Figure 1**):

■ The **Standard toolbar** (**Figure 9**) offers buttons for a wide range of commonly used commands.

■ The **Formatting toolbar** (**Figure 10**) offers buttons for formatting selected items.

By default, Word displays toolbars using its personalized toolbar feature. This feature keeps track of the buttons and options you use and displays the ones you use most on the toolbar. The other toolbar buttons are hidden; you can display them by clicking More Buttons at the end of the toolbar (**Figures 9** and **10**).

✔ Tips

■ Other toolbars may appear automatically depending on the task you are performing with Word.

■ Toolbar buttons that are gray (for example, Redo in **Figure 9**) cannot be selected.

■ Toolbar buttons that have a light gray background (for example, Align Left in **Figure 10**) are "turned on."

■ A toolbar button that includes a triangle (for example, Undo and Zoom in **Figure 9**) displays a menu.

■ You can identify a toolbar button by its ScreenTip.

■ A toolbar can be *docked* or *floating*. A docked toolbar (**Figures 9** and **10**) is positioned against any edge of the screen. A floating toolbar can be moved anywhere within the screen.

More Buttons

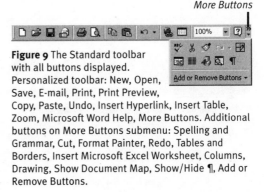

Figure 9 The Standard toolbar with all buttons displayed. Personalized toolbar: New, Open, Save, E-mail, Print, Print Preview, Copy, Paste, Undo, Insert Hyperlink, Insert Table, Zoom, Microsoft Word Help, More Buttons. Additional buttons on More Buttons submenu: Spelling and Grammar, Cut, Format Painter, Redo, Tables and Borders, Insert Microsoft Excel Worksheet, Columns, Drawing, Show Document Map, Show/Hide ¶, Add or Remove Buttons.

More Buttons

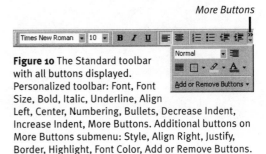

Figure 10 The Standard toolbar with all buttons displayed. Personalized toolbar: Font, Font Size, Bold, Italic, Underline, Align Left, Center, Numbering, Bullets, Decrease Indent, Increase Indent, More Buttons. Additional buttons on More Buttons submenu: Style, Align Right, Justify, Border, Highlight, Font Color, Add or Remove Buttons.

TOOLBARS

Figure 11
A ScreenTip appears when you point to a button.

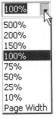

Figure 12
The Zoom menu appears when you click the triangle that's part of the Zoom button.

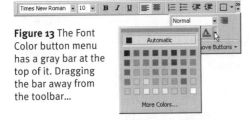

Figure 13 The Font Color button menu has a gray bar at the top of it. Dragging the bar away from the toolbar...

Figure 14
...displays the menu as a floating toolbar.

Figure 15 You can also change the setting in a button that has a text box by clicking the contents of the text box to select it,...

Figure 16 ...typing in a new setting, and pressing [Enter].

To view more buttons

Click the More Buttons button at the far right end of the toolbar. Additional buttons for the toolbar appear (**Figures 9** and **10**).

To view ScreenTips

Point to a toolbar button. A tiny yellow box containing the name of the button appears (**Figure 11**).

To use a toolbar button

1. Point to the button for the command or option that you want (**Figure 11**).

2. Click once on the toolbar button to activate the command or select the option.

To use a toolbar menu

1. Point to the triangle to the right of the button.

2. Press the mouse button down to display the menu (**Figure 12**).

3. Choose an option from the menu.

✔ Tips

- Toolbar menus that display a gray bar along the top edge (**Figure 13**) can be "torn off" and used as floating menus or palettes. Simply display the menu, point to the gray bar, and drag it away from the toolbar. When the menu appears in a separate window, release the mouse button. The menu is displayed as a floating toolbar with a title bar that displays its name (**Figure 14**).

- Toolbar menus that display text boxes (**Figure 12**) can be changed by typing a new value into the text box. Just click the contents of the text box to select it (**Figure 15**), then type in the new value and press [Enter] (**Figure 16**).

USING TOOLBARS

To float a docked toolbar

Drag the toolbar's move handle (**Figure 17**) away from the toolbar's docked position (**Figure 18**).

✔ Tip

■ Floating a docked toolbar will change the appearance and position of other toolbars docked in the same row (**Figure 18**).

To dock a floating toolbar

Drag the toolbar's title bar to the edge of the screen (**Figure 19**).

✔ Tip

■ You can dock a toolbar against the top (**Figure 17**), either side (**Figure 19**), or the bottom of the screen. Buttons may change appearance when the toolbar is docked on the side of the screen.

To move a toolbar

◆ If the toolbar is docked, drag it by its move handle to a new position on the screen.

◆ If the toolbar is floating, drag it by its title bar to a new position on the screen.

To display or hide a toolbar

Choose the name of the toolbar that you want to display or hide from the Toolbars submenu under the View menu (**Figure 20**).

If the toolbar name has a check mark to its left, it is currently displayed and will be hidden.

or

If the toolbar name does not have a check mark to its left, it is currently hidden and will be displayed.

✔ Tip

■ If a toolbar is floating (**Figure 18**), you can click its close button to hide it.

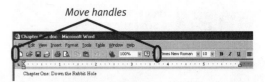

Move handles

Figure 17 By default, the Standard and Formatting toolbars are docked.

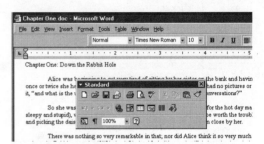

Figure 18 When you float the Standard toolbar, the Formatting toolbar expands to occupy some of the vacated space.

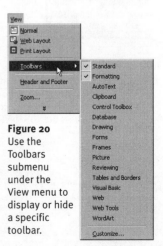

Figure 19
When you drag a toolbar to the edge of the screen, it becomes docked there. In this example, the Standard toolbar is docked on the left side of the screen.

Figure 20
Use the Toolbars submenu under the View menu to display or hide a specific toolbar.

Figure 21
The Word Count dialog box just displays information.

Dialog Boxes

Like most other Windows programs, Word uses dialog boxes to communicate with you.

Word can display many different dialog boxes, each with its own purpose. There are two basic types of dialog boxes:

◆ Dialog boxes that simply provide information (**Figure 21**).

◆ Dialog boxes that offer options to select (**Figure 22**) before Word completes the execution of a command.

✔ Tip

■ Often, when a dialog box appears, you must dismiss it by clicking OK or Cancel before you can continue working with Word.

Anatomy of a Word dialog box

Here are the components of many Word dialog boxes, along with information about how they work.

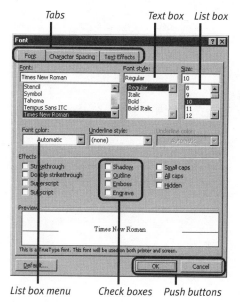

Tabs   Text box   List box

List box menu   Check boxes   Push buttons

Figure 22 The Font dialog box offers menu options.

◆ **Tabs** (**Figure 22**), which appear at the top of some dialog boxes, let you move from one group of dialog box options to another. To switch to another group of options, click its tab.

◆ **Text boxes** (**Figures 22** and **23**) let you enter information from the keyboard. You can press ⌞Tab⌟ to move from one text box to the next or click in a text box to position the insertion point within it. Then enter a new value.

◆ **List boxes** (**Figure 22**) offer a number of options to choose from. Use the scroll bar to view options that don't fit in the list window. Click an option to select it; it becomes highlighted and appears in the text box.

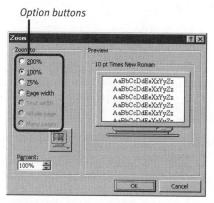

Option buttons

Figure 23 The Zoom dialog box also offers a few options.

Continued on next page...

Continued from previous page.

◆ **Check boxes (Figure 22)** let you turn options on or off. Click in a check box to toggle it. When a check mark or X appears in the check box, its option is turned on.

◆ **Option buttons (Figure 23)** let you select only one option from a group. Click on an option to select it; the option that was selected before you clicked is deselected.

◆ **List box menus (Figure 22)** also let you select one option from a group. Display a list box menu as you would any other menu (**Figure 24**), then choose the option that you want.

◆ **Preview areas (Figures 22** and **23)**, when available, illustrate the effects of your changes before you finalize them by clicking the OK button.

◆ **Push buttons (Figures 21**, **22**, and **23)** let you access other dialog boxes, accept the changes and close the dialog box (OK), or close the dialog box without making changes (Cancel). To select a button, click it once.

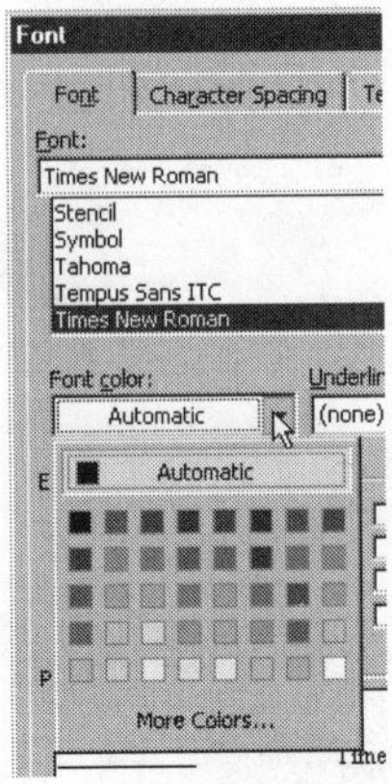

Figure 24
Displaying a menu within a dialog box.

✔ Tips

■ When the contents of a text box are selected, whatever you type will replace the selection.

■ Word often uses text boxes and list boxes together (**Figure 22**). You can use either one to make a selection.

■ If a pair of tiny triangles appear to the right of a text box (**Figure 23**), you can click a triangle to increase or decrease the value in the text box.

■ In some list boxes, double-clicking an option selects it and dismisses the dialog box.

■ You can turn on any number of check boxes in a group, but you can select only one option button in a group.

■ The Word 2000 documentation and online help system sometimes refer to list box menus as *drop-down lists* or *pop-up menus*.

■ A push button with a black border around it is the button that will be "clicked" if you press (Enter).

■ You can usually "click" the Cancel button by pressing (Esc).

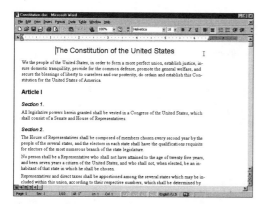

Figure 25 Normal view.

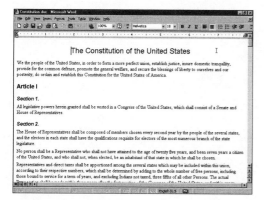

Figure 26 Web Layout view.

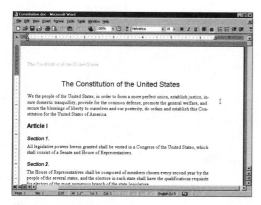

Figure 27 Print Layout view.

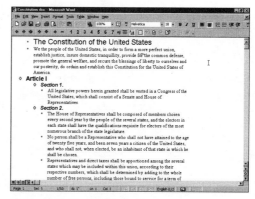

Figure 28 Outline view.

Views

Word offers several different ways to view the contents of a document window.

◆ **Normal view (Figure 25)** shows continuously scrolling text. It is the fastest view for entering and editing text but does not show page layout elements.

◆ **Web Layout view (Figure 26)** displays the contents of a document so they are easier to read on screen. Text appears in a larger font size and wraps to fit the window rather than margins or indentations.

◆ **Print Layout view (Figure 28)** displays the objects on a page positioned as they will be when the document is printed. This is a good view for working with documents that include multiple column text or positioned graphics, such as a newsletter or flyer.

◆ **Outline view (Figure 27)** displays the document's structure—headings and body text—in a way that makes it easy to rearrange the document. Headings can be collapsed to hide detail and simplify the view. I discuss working with Outline view in **Chapter 9**.

Continued on next page...

VIEWS

Continued from previous page.

✔ Tips

- Although each view is designed for a specific purpose, you can use almost any view to work with a document.

- The illustrations throughout this book display windows in Normal view, unless otherwise indicated.

To switch to another view

Choose the desired view option from the View menu (**Figure 29**).

or

Click the appropriate view button at the bottom of the window (**Figure 30**).

✔ Tip

- By default, the Outline View command appears only on the full version of the View menu (**Figure 29**). If you use it often enough, however, it should switch to the personalized version of the menu. I tell you more about personalized and full menus earlier in this chapter.

Figure 29
Document view options can be found under the View menu.

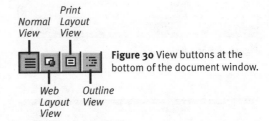

Figure 30 View buttons at the bottom of the document window.

Normal View

Print Layout View

Web Layout View

Outline View

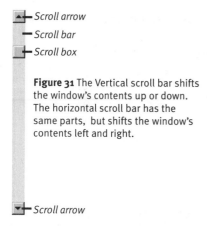

—Scroll arrow

—Scroll bar

—Scroll box

Figure 31 The Vertical scroll bar shifts the window's contents up or down. The horizontal scroll bar has the same parts, but shifts the window's contents left and right.

—Scroll arrow

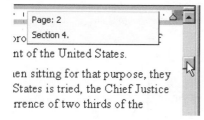

nt of the United States.

ien sitting for that purpose, they States is tried, the Chief Justice rrence of two thirds of the

Figure 32 When you drag the scroll box, a yellow box with the page number and heading appears.

✔ Tip

- Having trouble remembering which scroll arrow to click? Just remember this: click up to see up, click down to see down, click left to see left, and click right to see right.

Document Navigation

Word offers a variety of ways to view different parts of a document.

- **Scroll bars** let you shift the contents of the document window.

- The **Go To command** lets you view a specific document element, such as a certain page.

- **Browse Object buttons** let you browse a document by its elements.

- The **Document Map** lets you move quickly to a specific heading.

✔ Tip

- Although some keyboard keys change the portion of the document being viewed, they also move the insertion point. I tell you about these keys in **Chapter 2**.

To scroll the contents of the document window

Click the scroll arrow (**Figure 31**) for the direction that you want to view. For example, to scroll down to view the end of a document, click the down arrow.

or

Drag the scroll box (**Figure 31**) in the direction that you want to view. As you drag, a yellow box appears on screen (**Figure 32**). It indicates the page and, if applicable, the heading that will appear on screen when you release the mouse button. Release the mouse button to view the indicated part of the document.

or

Click in the scroll bar above or below the scroll box (**Figure 31**). This shifts the window contents one screenful at a time.

To use the Go To command

1. Choose Edit > Go To (**Figure 6**) or press
   Ctrl G. The Find and Replace dialog box
   appears with its Go To tab displayed
   (**Figure 33**).

2. In the Go to what list box, select the type of
   document element that you want to view.

3. Enter the appropriate reference in the text
   box.

4. Click Next to go to the next reference.

5. Click the dialog box's Close button to
   dismiss it.

For example, to go to page 5 of a document,
select Page in step 2 and enter the number 5 in
step 3.

To browse a document by its elements

1. Point to the Select Browse Object button
   (**Figure 34**).

2. Click and, if necessary, hold down the
   mouse button to display the Select Browse
   Object menu.

3. Choose the element by which you want to
   browse (**Figure 35**).

4. Use the Next and Previous navigation
   buttons to view the next or previous
   element.

✔ Tips

- The name of the object that a button
  represents appears at the top of the Select
  Browse Object menu when you point to the
  button (**Figure 35**).

- Some of the buttons on the Select Browse
  Object menu (**Figure 35**) display dialog
  boxes that you can use for browsing.

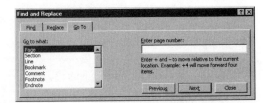

Figure 33 The Go To tab of the Find and Replace
dialog box.

Figure 34 The Browse Object buttons at
the bottom of the vertical scroll bar.

Figure 35 This menu appears when you
click the Select Browse Object button.

- When you choose an element from the
  Select Browse Object menu (**Figure 35**),
  the navigation buttons (**Figure 34**) may
  turn blue to indicate that an element has
  been selected.

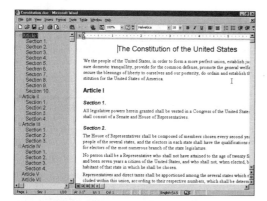

Figure 36 The Document Map in Normal view.

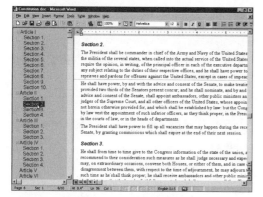

Figure 37 Clicking a heading in the Document Map shifts the view to display that part of the document.

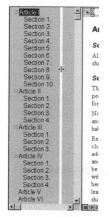

Figure 38 You can resize the Document Map's pane by dragging its right border.

Figure 39 Click the minus sign to the left of a heading to hide its subheadings.

To use the Document Map

1. Choose View > Document Map (**Figure 29**).

   or

   Click the Document Map button 🔍 on the Standard toolbar.

   The Document Map appears in a pane on the left side of the window (**Figure 36**).

2. Click the heading that you want to view. The main window pane's view shifts to show the heading that you clicked (**Figure 37**).

✔ Tips

- Navigating with the Document Map also moves the insertion point. I tell you more about moving the insertion point in **Chapter 2**.

- You can change the width of the Document Map's pane by dragging the border between it and the main window pane (**Figure 38**). When you release the border, both panes resize.

- You can collapse and expand the headings displayed in the Document Map by clicking the minus or plus signs to the left of the heading names (**Figure 39**).

- To hide the Document Map when you are finished using it, choose View > Document Map or click the Document Map button 🔍 on the Standard toolbar.

USING THE DOCUMENT MAP

Windows

Word allows you to open more than one document window at a time.

✔ Tips

- The active document window is the one that is currently visible.

- I explain how to create and open documents in **Chapter 2**.

To activate a different window

Choose the name of the window that you want to view from the list at the bottom of the Window menu (**Figure 40**).

or

Click the name of the document in the Windows Taskbar (**Figure 41**).

The window you selected becomes the active window.

To neatly arrange windows

Choose Window > Arrange All (**Figure 40**).

The windows are resized and repositioned so you can see into each one (**Figure 42**).

To close a window

1. If necessary, activate the window that you want to close.

2. Choose File > Close (**Figure 43**) or press ⌃Ctrl W.

✔ Tip

- If the document contains unsaved changes, Word warns you (**Figure 44**). I tell you about saving documents in **Chapter 2**.

Figure 40
You can find a list of all open documents at the bottom of the Window menu.

Figure 41 Each Word document is listed separately in the Windows Taskbar.

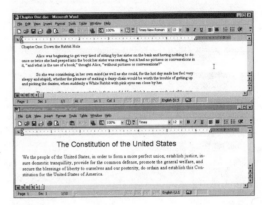

Figure 42 Arranged windows.

Figure 43
The File menu.

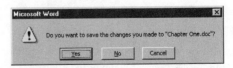

Figure 44 A dialog box like this appears when you close a document window that contains unsaved changes.

Figure 45
The Office Assistant.

Figure 46
The Help menu.

Figure 47
The Office Assistant, with a tip.

The Office Assistant

The Office Assistant is an animated character (**Figure 45**) that appears on screen. It can provide tips and assistance while you work.

To display the Office Assistant

Choose Help > Show the Office Assistant (**Figure 46**).

or

Click the Microsoft Word Help button 🔲 on the Standard toolbar. (This technique will only work if the Office Assistant has not been disabled.)

To hide the Office Assistant

Choose Help > Hide the Office Assistant.

To move the Office Assistant

1. Position the mouse pointer on the Office Assistant.

2. Press the mouse button down and drag the Office Assistant to a new position on the screen.

✔ Tip

- The Office Assistant will automatically move out of the way if necessary as you work.

To get tips

1. Click the light bulb that appears near the Office Assistant's head (**Figure 45**) when the Office Assistant has a tip for you. The tip appears in a balloon near the Office Assistant (**Figure 47**).

2. When you are finished reading the tip, click the OK button.

USING THE OFFICE ASSISTANT

To ask a question

1. If necessary, click the Office Assistant to get its attention. A balloon with a text box containing instructions appears (**Figure 48**).

2. Type your question into the text box and click the Search button. A list of possible topics appears in another balloon (**Figure 49**).

3. Click a topic that interests you. The Microsoft Word Help window appears (**Figure 50**). It provides detailed information and clickable links for the topic you selected.

4. When you are finished reading help information, click the Microsoft Word Help window's close button to dismiss it.

To disable the Office Assistant

1. Display the Office Assistant and click it to display its balloon (**Figure 48**).

2. Click the Options button.

3. In the Office Assistant dialog box that appears (**Figure 51**), turn off the Use the Office Assistant check box.

4. Click OK. The Office Assistant disappears.

✔ Tips

■ Once the Office Assistant has been disabled, it will not reappear unless you choose Help > Show the Office Assistant (**Figure 46**).

■ You can also use the Office Assistant dialog box (**Figure 51**) to customize the way the Office Assistant looks and works.

Figure 48 The Office Assistant asks you what you want to do.

Figure 49 When you click Search, the Office Assistant displays a list of help topics.

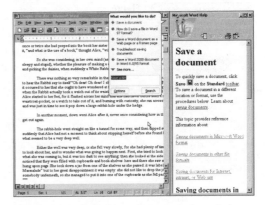

Figure 50 Detailed information appears in a window beside the document.

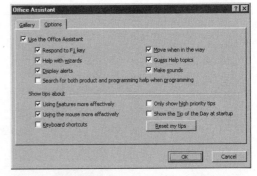

Figure 51 The Office Assistant dialog box lets you set its options—and disable it.

Figure 52
The Microsoft Word
Help window with the
help tabs hidden...

Microsoft Word Help

Word has an extensive online help feature that provides information about using Word to complete specific tasks. You access Microsoft Word Help via the Office Assistant (as discussed on the previous page) or by using commands under the Help menu (**Figure 46**).

To open Microsoft Word Help

1. If the Office Assistant is enabled, follow the steps on the previous page to display the Microsoft Word Help window (**Figure 50**).

    or

    If the Office Assistant is disabled, choose Help > Microsoft Word Help (**Figure 46**), press F1 , or click the Microsoft Word Help button 🔲 on the Standard toolbar to display the Microsoft Word Help window (**Figure 51** or **52**).

2. If necessary, click the Show button at the top of the window to expand the window and view the help tabs (**Figure 52**).

✔ Tip

■ The Microsoft Word Help window includes hyperlinks—blue, underlined words and phrases that, when clicked, display related information.

To ask a question

1. Open the Microsoft Word Help window as instructed above.

2. If necessary, click the Answer Wizard tab (**Figure 53**).

3. Enter your question in the text box at the top of the tab and click Search. A list of help topics appears in the Select topic to display box.

4. Click a topic that interests you. Detailed information and instructions appear on the right side of the window.

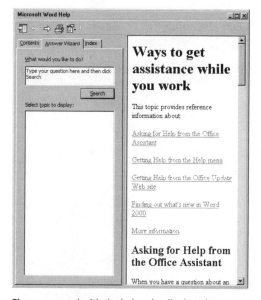

Figure 53 ...and with the help tabs displayed.

To use the Table of Contents

1. Open the Microsoft Word Help window as instructed on the previous page.

2. If necessary, click the Contents tab (**Figure 54**).

3. Click the plus sign to the left of a main topic to display its subtopics (**Figure 55**).

4. Click a subtopic that interests you. Detailed information and instructions appear on the right side of the window.

To use the Index

1. Open the Microsoft Word Help window as instructed on the previous page.

2. If necessary, click the Index tab (**Figure 56**).

3. Type one or more keywords in the text box near the top of the window. Then click Search.

   or

   Scroll through the keywords list and click one that interests you.

   A list of topics appears in the Choose a topic box (**Figure 57**).

4. Click a topic. Detailed information and instructions appear on the right side of the window.

Figure 54 The Contents tab of the Microsoft Word Help window.

Figure 55 Clicking the plus sign to the left of a topic displays subtopics.

Figure 56 The Index tab of the Microsoft Word Help window.

Figure 57 Use keywords to find topics that interest you.

WORD BASICS 2

Word Processing Basics

Word processing software has revolutionized the way we create text-based documents. Rather than committing each character to paper as you type—as you would do with a typewriter—word processing enables you to enter documents on screen, edit and format them as you work, and save them for future reference or revision. Nothing appears on paper until you use the Print command.

If you're brand new to word processing, here are a few concepts you should understand before you begin working with Word or any other word processing software:

◆ Words that you type that do not fit at the end of a line automatically appear on the next line. This feature is called *word wrap.*

◆ Do not press Enter at the end of each line as you type. Doing so inserts a Return character, which signals the end of a paragraph, not the end of a line. Press Enter only at the end of a paragraph or to skip a line between paragraphs.

◆ Do not use Spacebar to indent text or position text in simple tables. Instead, use Tab in conjunction with tab settings on the ruler.

◆ Text can be inserted or deleted anywhere in the document.

✔ Tip

■ I tell you more about all of these concepts in this chapter and throughout this book.

Running Word

To use Word, you must run the Word application.

To run Word from the Taskbar

Click Start > Programs > Microsoft Word.

The Word splash screen appears briefly (**Figure 1**), then an empty document window named *Document1* appears (**Figure 2**).

To run Word by opening a Word document

1. In Windows Explorer, locate the icon for the document that you want to open (**Figure 3**).

2. Double-click the icon.

The Word splash screen appears briefly (**Figure 1**), then a document window containing the document that you opened appears (**Figure 4**).

Exiting Word

When you're finished using Word, you should exit it.

To exit Word

Choose File > Exit (**Figure 5**). Here's what happens:

◆ If any documents are open, they close.

◆ If an open document contains unsaved changes, a dialog box appears (**Figure 6**) so you can save the changes.

◆ The Word program closes.

✔ Tips

■ Exiting Word also instructs Word to save preference settings and any changes to the Normal template.

■ As you've probably guessed, Word automatically exits when you restart or shut down your computer.

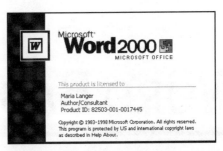

Figure 1 The Word 2000 splash screen.

Figure 2 When you run Word from the Taskbar, it displays an empty document window.

Figure 3
A Word
document icon.

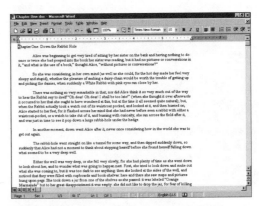

Figure 4 When you run Word by opening a Word document icon, it displays the document that you opened.

Figure 5
Word's File menu offers a variety of commands for working with files.

Figure 6 A dialog box like this appears when a document with unsaved changes is open when you exit Word.

Contemporary
Letter.dot

Figure 7
A Word template icon.

Letter
Wizard.wiz

Figure 8
A Word wizard icon.

Word Documents, Templates, & Wizards

The documents you create and save using Word are Word document files. These files contain all the information necessary to display the contents of the document as formatted using Microsoft Word.

All Word document files are based on *templates*. A template is a collection of styles and other formatting features that determine the appearance of a document. Templates can also include default text, macros, and custom toolbars.

For example, you can create a letterhead template that includes your company's logo and contact information or is designed to be printed on special paper. The template can include styles that utilize specific fonts. It can also include custom toolbars with buttons for commands commonly used when writing letters.

Wizards take templates a step further. They are special Word document files that include Visual Basic commands to automate the creation of specific types of documents. Word comes with many wizards you can explore on your own.

✔ Tips

- A Word document icon (**Figure 3**), template icon (**Figure 7**), and wizard icon (**Figure 8**) are very similar in appearance.

- Word can open and save files in formats other than Word document format. I tell you more about file formats later in this chapter.

- When no other template is specified for a document, Word applies the default template, *Normal*.

- I cover styles in **Chapter 4**. Macros, custom toolbars, and Visual Basic, however, are advanced features that are beyond the scope of this book.

Creating Documents

To create a new document, you use the New command.

To create a blank document

1. Choose File > New (**Figure 5**).

2. In the New dialog box that appears (**Figure 9**), make sure the Blank Document icon is selected. (You may have to click the General tab to display it.) Then click OK.

or

Press Ctrl N.

or

Click the New button ☐ on the Standard toolbar.

A blank document based on the Normal template appears (**Figure 2**).

To create a document based on a template other than Normal

1. Choose File > New (**Figure 5**).

2. In the New dialog box that appears (**Figure 9**), select the tab that includes the template you want to use.

3. Select the icon for the template that you want to use (**Figure 10**).

4. Click OK.

A document based on the template that you selected appears (**Figure 11**). Follow the instructions in the template to replace placeholder text with your text.

✔ Tip

■ The Preview area in the New dialog box (**Figure 10**) gives you an idea of what the template looks like.

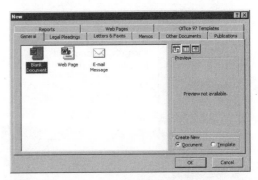

Figure 9 The General tab of the New dialog box.

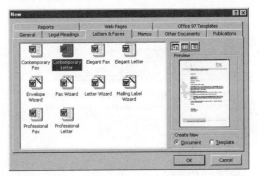

Figure 10 Selecting a template in the Letters & Faxes tab of the New dialog box.

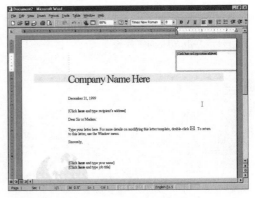

Figure 11 A document based on a template.

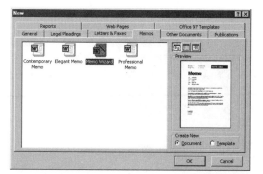

Figure 12 Selecting a wizard in the Memos tab of the New dialog box.

Figure 13 An introduction to the Memo Wizard.

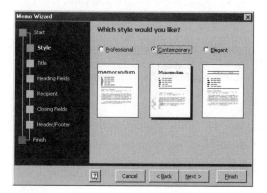

Figure 14 Step 1 of the Memo Wizard prompts you to select a memo style.

To create a document with a wizard

1. Choose File > New (**Figure 5**).

2. In the New dialog box that appears (**Figure 9**), select the tab that includes the wizard you want to use.

3. Select the icon for the wizard that you want to use (**Figure 12**).

4. Click OK.

5. Follow the steps in the Wizard dialog boxes that appear (**Figures 13** through **20** on this page and the next page) to create the document.

When the wizard is finished, the basic document appears (**Figure 21**).

✔ Tips

- When the wizard is finished, you can customize the document it creates to meet your own specific needs.

- **Figures 13** though **21** show just one wizard example. Other wizards will prompt you for other information. Explore Word's wizards on your own to see what they can do for you.

Figures continued on next page...

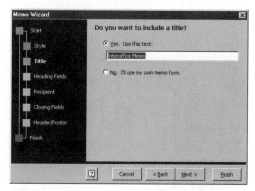

Figure 15 Step 2 of the Memo Wizard prompts you for a title for the memo.

CREATING DOCUMENTS WITH WIZARDS

27

Figures continued from previous page.

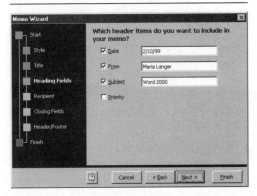

Figure 16 Step 3 of the Memo Wizard prompts you for information to be included in the memo's header.

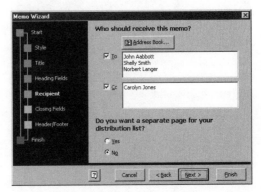

Figure 17 Step 4 of the Memo Wizard prompts you for the names of the people who should receive the memo.

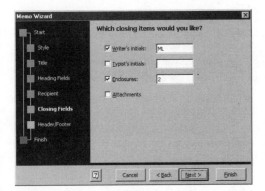

Figure 18 Step 5 of the Memo Wizard prompts you for information that should appear at the end of the memo.

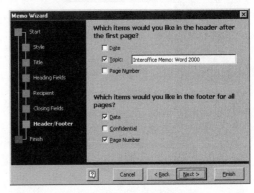

Figure 19 Step 6 of the Memo Wizard prompts you for header and footer contents for additional memo pages.

Figure 20 The last Memo Wizard screen tells you you're all done.

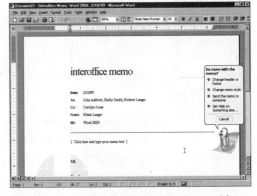

Figure 21 Here's what the Memo Wizard created for me based on information in **Figures 13** through **20**.

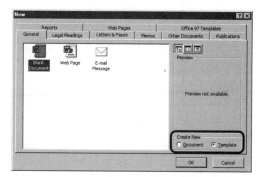

Figure 22 To create a template, be sure to select the Template option button in the New dialog box.

To create a template

1. Choose File > New (**Figure 5**).

2. In the New dialog box that appears, select the icon for Blank Document in the General tab (**Figure 9**) or any other template on which you want to base the new template.

3. Select the Template option button in the Create New section of the dialog box (**Figure 22**).

4. Click the OK button.

5. A document window based on the template you selected appears. Add text, styles, or other features to the document as discussed throughout this book.

✔ Tip

- When you save the document, it is automatically saved as a template. I tell you how to save documents and templates later in this chapter.

Opening Existing Documents

Once a document has been saved on disk, you can reopen it to read it, modify it, or print it.

To open an existing document

1. Choose File > Open (**Figure 5**) or press [Ctrl][O].

   or

   Click the Open button 📂 on the Standard toolbar.

2. Use the Open dialog box that appears (**Figure 23**) to locate the file that you want to open:

   ◆ Use the Look in menu near the top of the dialog box (**Figure 24**) to go to another location.

   ◆ Double-click a folder to open it.

3. Select the file that you want to open and click the Open button.

   or

   Double-click the file that you want to open.

✔ Tips

■ The Places bar, a series of buttons along the left side of the Open dialog box (**Figure 23**), enables you to quickly go to certain locations:

   ▲ **History** maintains a list of the 20 most recent locations where you accessed files.

   ▲ **My Documents** opens the My Documents folder on your hard disk.

   ▲ **Desktop** displays items on your Windows desktop.

   ▲ **Favorites** displays items you added to your Favorites.

   ▲ **Web Folders** displays folders you access on the Web.

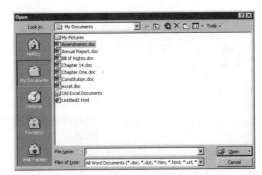

Figure 23 Word's Open dialog box.

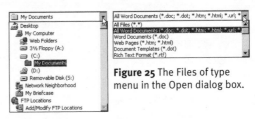

Figure 25 The Files of type menu in the Open dialog box.

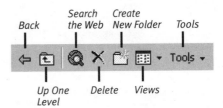

Figure 24 The Look in menu in the Open dialog box.

Back   Search the Web   Create New Folder   Tools

Up One Level   Delete   Views

Figure 26 The command bar in the Open dialog box.

■ To view only specific types of files in the Open dialog box, select a format from the Files of type menu at the bottom of the dialog box (**Figure 25**).

■ If you select All Files from the Files of type menu (**Figure 25**), you can open just about any kind of file. Be aware, however, that a document in an incompatible format may not appear the way you expect when opened.

■ You can use buttons on the command bar (**Figure 26**) in the Open dialog box to work with listed files and folders.

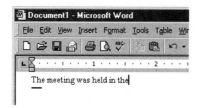

Figure 27 Text characters appear at the blinking insertion point as you type.

Figure 28 Word wrap automatically occurs when the text you type won't fit on the current line.

Figure 29 Press [Enter] to start a new paragraph.

Figure 30 Press [Shift][Enter] to start a new line in the same paragraph.

Entering Text

In most cases, you will enter text into a Word document using the keyboard.

✔ Tip

- A wavy red or green line beneath text indicates that the text has a possible spelling or grammar error. I tell you about spelling and grammar checking in **Chapter 5**.

To type text

Type the characters, words, or sentences that you want to enter into the document. Text appears at the blinking insertion point as you type it (**Figure 27**).

✔ Tip

- Do not press [Enter] at the end of a line. A new line automatically begins when a word can't fit on the current line (**Figure 28**).

To start a new paragraph

At the end of a paragraph, press [Enter]. This inserts a paragraph break or return character that ends the current paragraph and begins a new one (**Figure 29**).

To start a new line

To end a line without ending the current paragraph, press [Shift][Enter]. This inserts a line break character within the current paragraph (**Figure 30**).

✔ Tip

- Use a line break instead of a paragraph break if you want to begin a new line without beginning a new paragraph. This makes it easy to apply paragraph formatting to a group of lines that belong together. I tell you more about paragraph formatting in **Chapters 4** and **5**.

Formatting Marks

Every character you type is entered into a Word document—even characters that normally can't be seen, such as space, tab, return, line break, hidden text, and optional hyphen characters.

Word enables you to display these *formatting marks* as black marks (**Figure 31**), making it easy to see all the characters in a document.

✔ Tips

- Formatting marks are sometimes referred to as *nonprinting* or *invisible* characters.

- By displaying formatting marks, you can get a better understanding of the structure of a document. For example, **Figure 31** clearly shows the difference between the return and line break characters entered in **Figure 30**.

To show or hide formatting marks

Click the Show/Hide ¶ button ¶ on the Standard toolbar. This toggles the display of formatting marks.

To specify which formatting marks should be displayed

1. Choose Tools > Options (**Figure 32**).

2. In the Options dialog box that appears, click the View tab (**Figure 33**).

3. Turn on the check boxes in the Formatting marks area of the dialog box to specify which characters should appear.

4. Click OK.

✔ Tip

- To display all formatting marks, turn on the All check box in step 3.

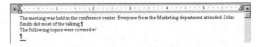

Figure 31 Text with nonprinting characters displayed. This example shows space, return, and line break characters.

Figure 32
The Tools menu.

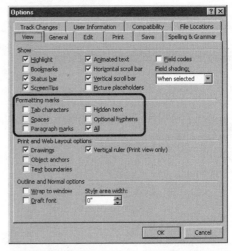

Figure 33 The View tab of the Options dialog box enables you to pick and choose which formatting marks appear on screen.

Press:	To move the insertion point:
←	one character to the right
→	one character to the left
↑	one line up
↓	one line down
Ctrl ←	one word to the right
Ctrl →	one word to the left
Ctrl ↑	one paragraph up
Ctrl ↓	one paragraph down
End	to the end of the line
Home	to the beginning of the line
Ctrl End	to the end of the document
Ctrl Home	to the beginning of the document
Page Up	up one screen
Page Down	down one screen
Ctrl Page Up	to the top of the previous page
Ctrl Page Down	to the top of the next page
Ctrl Alt Page Up	to the top of the window
Ctrl Alt Page Down	to the bottom of the window
Shift F5	to the previous edit

Table 1 Keystrokes for moving the insertion point.

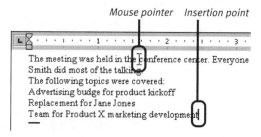

Figure 34 Position the mouse pointer where you want the insertion point to move.

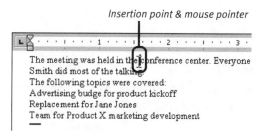

Figure 35 Click to move the insertion point.

The Insertion Point

The blinking insertion point indicates the position in which the information you type or paste will be inserted. There are two main ways to move the insertion point: with the keyboard and with the mouse.

✔ Tip

- The insertion point also moves when you use the Document Map to navigate within a document. I tell you about the Document Map in **Chapter 1**.

To move the insertion point with the keyboard

Press the appropriate keyboard key(s) (**Table 1**).

✔ Tip

- There are additional keystrokes that work within cell tables. I tell you about them in **Chapter 10**, where I discuss tables.

To move the insertion point with the mouse

1. Position the mouse's I-beam pointer where you want to move the insertion point (**Figure 34**).

2. Click the mouse button once. The insertion point moves (**Figure 35**).

✔ Tips

- Simply moving the I-beam pointer is not enough. You must click to move the insertion point.

- Do not move the mouse while clicking. Doing so will select text.

MOVING THE INSERTION POINT

Inserting & Deleting Text

You can insert or delete characters at the insertion point at any time.

◆ When you insert characters, any text to the right of the insertion point shifts to the right to make room for new characters (**Figures 36** and **37**).

◆ When you delete text, any text to the right of the insertion point shifts to the left to close up space left by deleted characters (**Figures 38** and **39**).

◆ When you insert or delete text, word wrap adjusts if necessary to comfortably fit characters on each line (**Figures 37** and **39**).

To insert text

1. Position the insertion point where you want to insert the text (**Figure 36**).

2. Type the text that you want to insert (**Figure 37**).

✔ Tip

■ You can also insert text by pasting the contents of the Clipboard at the insertion point. I tell you about using the Clipboard to copy and paste text later in this chapter.

To delete text

1. Position the insertion point to the right of the character(s) that you want to delete (**Figure 38**).

2. Press Backspace to delete the character to the left of the insertion point (**Figure 39**).

or

1. Position the insertion point to the left of the character(s) that you want to delete.

2. Press Delete to delete the character to the right of the insertion point.

Figure 36 Position the insertion point.

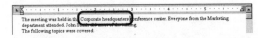

Figure 37 Type the text that you want to insert.

Figure 38 Position the insertion point to the right of the character(s) you want to delete.

Figure 39 Press Backspace to delete the characters, one at a time.

✔ Tip

■ You can also delete text by selecting it and pressing Backspace or Delete. I tell you how to select text next.

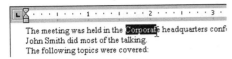

Figure 40 Drag over text to select it.

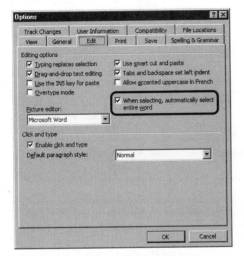

Figure 41 The Edit tab of the Options dialog box allows you to disable the automatic word selection feature.

Selecting Text

You can select one or more characters to delete, replace, copy, cut, or format it. Selected text appears with a colored background or in inverse type.

✔ Tip

- There are many ways to select text. This section provides just a few of the most useful methods.

To select text by dragging

1. Position the mouse I-beam pointer at the beginning of the text.

2. Press the mouse button down and drag to the end of the text you want to select (**Figure 40**).

3. Release the mouse button.

All characters between the starting and ending points are selected.

✔ Tips

- This is the most basic text selection technique. It works for any amount of text.

- By default, Word automatically selects entire words. You can disable this feature by choosing Tools > Options (**Figure 32**), clicking the Edit tab in the Options dialog box that appears (**Figure 41**), and turning off the check box for When selecting, automatically select entire word.

To select text by clicking

Click as instructed in **Table 2** to select specific amounts of text.

✔ Tips

- You can combine techniques in **Table 2** with dragging to select multiple lines and paragraphs.

- When you select an entire word by double-clicking it, Word also selects any spaces after it.

To select the contents of a document

Choose Edit > Select All (**Figure 43**) or press Ctrl A.

Editing Selected Text

Once you select text, you can delete it or replace it with other text.

To delete selected text

Press Backspace or Delete. The selected text disappears.

To replace selected text

With text selected, type the replacement text. The selected text disappears and the replacement text is inserted in its place.

To select:	Do this:
a word	double-click the word
a sentence	hold down Ctrl and click in the sentence
a line	click in the selection bar to the left of the line (Figure 42)
a paragraph	triple-click in the paragraph or double-click in the selection bar to the left of the paragraph
the document	hold down Ctrl and double-click in the selection bar to the left of any line
any amount of text	position the insertion point at the beginning of the text, then hold down Shift and click at the end of the text

Table 2. Techniques for selecting text by clicking.

Figure 42 Click in the selection bar beside a line to select the entire line.

Figure 43
Word's Edit menu.

Copying & Moving Text

Word offers two ways to copy or move text:

◆ Use the Copy, Cut, and Paste commands (or their shortcut keys) to place text on the Clipboard and then copy it from the Clipboard to another location.

◆ Use drag-and-drop editing to copy or move selected text.

You can copy or move text to the following locations:

◆ To a different location within the same document.

◆ To a different Word document.

◆ To a document created with a program other than Word.

✔ Tips

■ Copying and moving text makes it possible to reuse text and reorganize a document without a lot of retyping.

■ The *Clipboard* is a place in RAM that is used to temporarily store selected items that are copied or cut. Word supports two Clipboards:

   ▲ The *Windows Clipboard* is shared among all Windows applications that support the copy and paste commands.

   ▲ The *Office Clipboard* is shared among all Microsoft Office applications. It offers additional features, such as Collect and Paste, which I discuss later in this chapter.

■ Text copied or cut to the Clipboard remains on the Clipboard until you use the Copy or Cut command again or restart your computer. This enables you to use Clipboard contents over and over.

■ These techniques also work with objects such as graphics. I tell you more about working with objects in **Chapter 8**.

To copy text with Copy & Paste

1. Select the text that you want to copy (**Figure 44**).

2. Choose Edit > Copy (**Figure 43**) or press `Ctrl` `C`.

   or

   Click the Copy button 🖹 on the Standard toolbar.

   The selected text is copied to the Clipboard. The document does not change.

3. Position the insertion point where you want the text copied (**Figure 45**).

4. Choose Edit > Paste (**Figure 43**) or press `Ctrl` `V`.

   or

   Click the Paste button 🖺 on the Standard toolbar.

   The text in the Clipboard is copied into the document at the insertion point (**Figure 46**).

To move text with Cut & Paste

1. Select the text that you want to move (**Figure 47**).

2. Choose Edit > Cut (**Figure 43**) or press `Ctrl` `X`.

   or

   Click the Cut button ✂ on the Standard toolbar.

   The selected text is copied to the Clipboard and removed from the document.

3. Position the insertion point where you want the text moved (**Figure 48**).

4. Choose Edit > Paste (**Figure 43**) or press `Ctrl` `V`.

   or

   Click the Paste button 🖺 on the Standard toolbar.

   The text in the Clipboard is copied into the document at the insertion point (**Figure 49**).

Figure 44 Select the text that you want to copy.

Sincerely,

John Aabbott
Product Manager

Figure 45 Position the insertion point where you want the copied text to appear.

John Aabbott
Product Manager
Alphabet Soup

Figure 46 When you use the Paste command, the Clipboard contents appear at the insertion point.

Thanks for your very kind letter regarding Alphabet Squares, the newest edition to our Alphabet Soup product line. We're glad to know that there are many hungry soup eaters out there who appreciate the variety of letters we include in every can. Your report that you use our soup to help you solve crossword puzzles is fascinating!

I've included a coupon for 75 cents off your next purchase of Alphabet Squares. Please enjoy your next can "on us."

make the appropriate adjustments to assure that these letters are more properly represented.

Sincerely,

Figure 47 Select the text that you want to move.

variety of letters we include in every can. Your report that you use our soup to help you solve crossword puzzles is fascinating!

I'll send your comments regarding the overabundance of Qs and Zs to our production department. They'll make the appropriate adjustments to assure that these letters are more properly represented.

Sincerely,

John Aabbott
Product Manager
Alphabet Soup

Figure 48 Position the insertion point where you want the cut text to appear.

I'll send your comments regarding the overabundance of Qs and Zs to our production department. They'll make the appropriate adjustments to assure that these letters are more properly represented.

I've included a coupon for 75 cents off your next purchase of Alphabet Squares. Please enjoy your next can "on us."

Sincerely,

John Aabbott
Product Manager
Alphabet Soup

Figure 49 When you use the Paste command, the Clipboard contents appear at the insertion point.

ur Alphabet Soup
ho appreciate the
you solve crossword

Figure 50
Point to the selection.

Sincerely,

John A abbott
Product Manager

Figure 51
Hold down Ctrl and drag
to copy the selection.

puzzles is fascinating!

I've included a coupon for 75 cents off your next purchase of Alphabet Squares. Please enjoy your next can on us.

I'll send your comments regarding the overabundance of Qs and Zs to our production department. They'll make the appropriate adjustments to assure that these letters are more properly represented.

Sincerely,

Figure 52 Point to the selection.

I've included a coupon for 75 cents
"on us."

I'll send your comments regarding
make the appropriate adjustments t

Sincerely,

John A abbott
Product Manager
Alphabet Soup

Figure 53 Drag to move the selection.

To copy text with drag-and-drop editing

1. Select the text that you want to copy (**Figure 44**).

2. Position the mouse pointer on the selected text (**Figure 50**).

3. Hold down Ctrl, press the mouse button down, and drag. As you drag, a tiny box and vertical line move with the mouse pointer, which has a plus sign beside it to indicate that it is copying (**Figure 51**).

4. When the vertical line at the mouse pointer is where you want the text copied, release the mouse button and Ctrl. The selected text is copied (**Figure 46**).

To move text with drag-and-drop editing

1. Select the text that you want to move (**Figure 47**).

2. Position the mouse pointer on the selected text (**Figure 52**).

3. Press the mouse button down and drag. As you drag, a tiny box and vertical line move with the mouse pointer (**Figure 53**).

4. When the vertical line at the mouse pointer is where you want the text moved, release the mouse button. The selected text is moved (**Figure 49**).

DRAG-AND-DROP EDITING

Collect and Paste

Collect and Paste enables you to copy up to 12 selections at a time and paste any combination of them—or all of them—into a document. This feature utilizes the Clipboard toolbar (**Figure 54**), which gives you access to the Microsoft Office Clipboard.

Copy   Paste   Clear
All   Clipboard

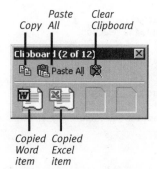

Figure 54
The Microsoft Office Clipboard with two items copied.

Copied Copied
Word   Excel
item   item

✔ Tip

■ The Microsoft Office Clipboard is shared by all Office 2000 programs. This means you can use Collect and Paste to copy selections in multiple documents created with any combination of Office programs and paste them in any other Office document.

To open the Clipboard toolbar

Choose View > Toolbars > Clipboard (**Figure 55**).

To use Collect and Paste

1. Select the first item you want to collect.

2. Click the Copy button 🗐 on the Clipboard toolbar. An icon for the current application appears in one of the wells at the bottom of the toolbar (**Figure 56**).

3. Repeat steps 1 and 2 for each item you want to collect. You can collect up to 12 items.

4. Position the insertion point where you want to paste one or more collected items.

5. To paste in one item, click its icon in the Clipboard toolbar. You can repeat this step to paste multiple items in any order.

 or

 To paste in all items in the order in which they were collected, click the Paste All button 🗐 Paste All on the Clipboard toolbar.

6. Repeat steps 4 and 5 to paste in items as desired.

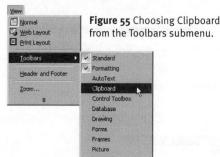

Figure 55 Choosing Clipboard from the Toolbars submenu.

Figure 56 When you click the Copy button on the Clipboard toolbar, an icon for the selection appears on the toolbar.

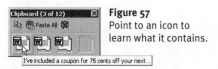

Figure 57
Point to an icon to learn what it contains.

✔ Tips

■ To learn what's in a collected item, point to its icon. The beginning of its contents appears as a screen tip below it (**Figure 57**).

■ To clear all collected items from the Microsoft Office Clipboard, click the Clear Clipboard button 🗐 on the Clipboard toolbar.

USING COLLECT AND PASTE

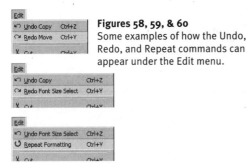

Figures 58, 59, & 60
Some examples of how the Undo, Redo, and Repeat commands can appear under the Edit menu.

Undoing, Redoing, & Repeating Actions

Word offers a trio of commands that enable you to undo, redo, or repeat the last thing you did.

◆ **Undo** reverses your last action. Word supports multiple levels of undo, enabling you to reverse more than just the very last action.

◆ **Redo** reverses the Undo command. This command is only available if the last thing you did was use the Undo command.

◆ **Repeat** performs your last action again. This command is only available when you performed any action other than use the Undo or Redo command.

✔ Tips

■ The exact wording of these commands on the Edit menu (**Figure 43**) varies depending on the last action performed. The Undo command is always the first command under the Edit menu; the Redo or Repeat command (whichever appears on the menu) is always the second command under the Edit menu. **Figures 58**, **59**, and **60** show some examples.

■ The Redo and Repeat commands are never both available at the same time.

■ Think of the Undo command as the Oops command—anytime you say "Oops," you'll probably want to use it.

■ The Repeat command is especially useful for applying formatting to text scattered throughout your document. I tell you more about formatting in **Chapters 3** and **4**.

To undo the last action

Choose Edit > Undo (**Figures 43, 58, 59,** or **60**) or press Ctrl Z.

or

Click the Undo button ↶ ▾ on the Standard toolbar.

Figure 61 Use the Undo button's menu to select actions to undo.

To undo multiple actions

Choose Edit > Undo or press Ctrl Z repeatedly.

or

Click the triangle beside the Undo button on the Standard toolbar to display a menu of recent actions. Drag down to select all the actions that you want to undo (**Figure 61**). Release the mouse button to undo all selected actions.

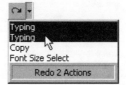

Figure 62 Use the Redo button's menu to select actions to redo.

To reverse the last undo

Choose Edit > Redo (**Figures 58** and **59**) or press Ctrl Y.

or

Click the Redo button ↷ ▾ on the Standard toolbar.

To reverse multiple undos

Choose Edit > Redo or press Ctrl Y repeatedly.

or

Click the triangle beside the Redo button on the Standard toolbar to display a pop-up menu of recently undone actions. Drag down to select all the actions that you want to redo (**Figure 62**). Release the mouse button to reverse all selected undos.

To repeat the last action

Choose Edit > Repeat (**Figures 43** and **60**) or press Ctrl Y.

UNDOING, REDOING, & REPEATING ACTIONS

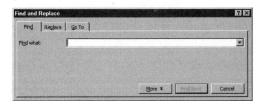

Figure 63 The Find tab of the Find and Replace dialog box.

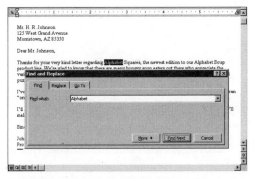

Figure 64 Word selects each occurrence of the text that it finds.

Figure 65 When Word has finished showing all occurrences of the search text, it tells you.

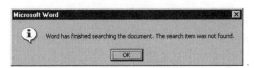

Figure 66 Word also tells you when it can't find the search text at all.

Find & Replace

Word has a very powerful find and replace feature. With it, you can search a document for specific text strings and, if desired, replace them with other text.

✔ Tip

■ By default, the Find and Replace commands search the entire document, beginning at the insertion point.

To find text

1. Choose Edit > Find (**Figure 43**) or press Ctrl F.

2. In the Find tab of the Find and Replace dialog box that appears (**Figure 63**), enter the text that you want to find.

3. Click the Find Next button. One of two things happens:

   ▲ If Word finds the search text, it selects the first occurrence that it finds (**Figure 64**). Repeat step 3 to find all occurrences, one at a time. When the last occurrence has been found, Word tells you with a dialog box (**Figure 65**) or an Office Assistant balloon.

   ▲ If Word does not find the search text, it tells you with a dialog box (**Figure 66**) or an Office Assistant balloon. You can repeat steps 2 and 3 to search for different text.

4. When you're finished, dismiss the Find and Replace dialog box by clicking its Cancel or close button.

✔ Tip

■ If desired, you can fine-tune search criteria. I tell you how a little later in this chapter.

FINDING TEXT

To replace text

1. Choose Edit > Replace (**Figure 43**) or press
   Ctrl H. The Replace tab of the Find and
   Replace dialog box appears (**Figure 67**).

2. Enter the text that you want to find in the
   Find what box.

3. Enter the text that you want to replace the
   found text with in the Replace with box.

4. Click the Find Next button to start the
   search. One of two things happens:

   ◆ If Word finds the search text, it selects
   the first occurrence that it finds (**Figure 68**). Continue with step 5.

   ◆ If Word does not find the search text, it
   tells you with a dialog box (**Figure 66**)
   or an Office Assistant balloon. You can
   repeat steps 2 and 4 to search for
   different text.

5. Do one of the following:

   ◆ To replace the selected occurrence and
   automatically find the next occurrence,
   click the Replace button (**Figure 69**).
   You can repeat this step until Word has
   found all occurrences (**Figure 65**).

   ◆ To replace all occurrences, click the
   Replace All button. Word tells you how
   many changes it made (**Figure 70**).

   ◆ To skip the current occurrence and
   move on to the next one, click the Find
   Next button. You can repeat this step
   until Word has found all occurrences
   (**Figure 65**).

6. When you're finished, dismiss the Find and
   Replace dialog box by clicking its Close
   button.

✔ Tip

■ If desired, you can fine-tune search criteria.
I tell you how on the next page.

Figure 67 The Replace tab of the Find and Replace
dialog box.

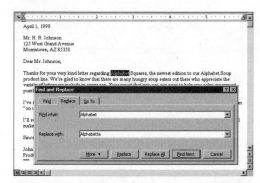

Figure 68 Word selects each occurrence of the search
text that it finds.

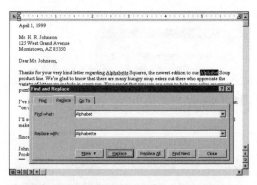

Figure 69 Clicking the Replace button replaces the
selected occurrence and finds the next one.

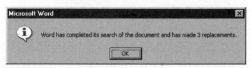

Figure 70 Clicking the Replace All button replaces all
occurrences. Word tells you how many replacements
it made.

REPLACING TEXT

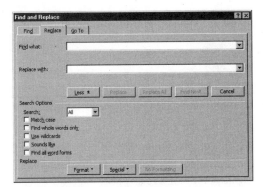

Figure 71 The Replace tab of the Find and Replace dialog box expanded to show additional search criteria options.

Figure 72
The Search menu in the Find and Replace dialog box.

Figure 73
Clicking the Format button in the Find and Replace dialog box displays a menu of formatting options.

Figure 74
Clicking the Special button in the Find and Replace dialog box displays a menu of special characters.

To fine-tune criteria

1. In the Find or Replace tab of the Find and Replace dialog box, click the More button. The dialog box expands to show additional search criteria options (**Figure 71**).

2. Click in the Find what or Replace with box to indicate which criterion you want to fine-tune.

3. Set search criteria options as desired:
   ◆ The **Search** menu lets you specify how you want to search (**Figure 72**).
   ◆ The **Match case** check box exactly matches capitalization.
   ◆ The **Find whole words only** check box finds the search text only when it is a separate word or phrase.
   ◆ The **Use wildcards** check box lets you include wildcard characters (such as ? for a single character and * for multiple characters).
   ◆ The **Sounds like** check box finds homonyms—words that sound alike but are spelled differently.
   ◆ The **Find all word forms** check box searches for all verb, noun, or adjective forms of the search text.

4. Set search or replace critera options as desired:
   ◆ The **Format** menu (**Figure 73**) lets you specify formatting options. Choosing one of these options displays the corresponding dialog box. I explain how to use these dialog boxes in **Chapters 3 and 4**.
   ◆ The **Special** menu (**Figure 74**) lets you find and replace special characters.

Saving Documents

When you save a document, you put a copy of it on disk.

Figure 75 The Save As dialog box.

✔ Tips

- Until you save a document, its information is stored only in your computer's RAM. Your work on the document could be lost in the event of a power outage or system crash.

- It's a very good idea to save documents frequently as you work. This ensures that the most recent versions are always saved to disk.

Figure 76 You can use the New Folder dialog box to create a new folder within the current location.

To save a document for the first time

1. Choose File > Save or File > Save As (**Figure 5**) or press Ctrl S.

   or

   Click the Save button 💾 on the Standard toolbar.

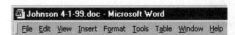

Figure 77 The name you give a document appears in the title bar after you save it.

2. Use the Save As dialog box that appears (**Figure 75**) to navigate to the folder (and disk, if necessary) in which you want to save the file:

   - Use the Save in menu near the top of the dialog box (**Figure 24**) to go to another location.

   - Double-click a folder to open it.

   - Click the Create New Folder button 📁 on the command bar to create a new folder within the current folder. Enter a name for the folder in the New Folder dialog box (**Figure 76**) and click OK.

3. Enter a name for the file in the File name box.

4. Click the Save button.

The file is saved to disk. Its name appears on the document window's title bar (**Figure 77**).

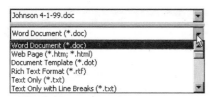

Figure 78 You can use the Save as type menu in the Save As dialog box to select a different file format.

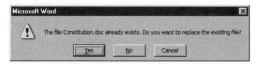

Figure 79 This dialog box appears when you attempt to save a file with the same name and same disk location as another file.

✔ Tips

- The Places bar, a series of buttons along the left side of the Save As dialog box (**Figure 75**), enables you to quickly go to certain locations. I tell you more about the Places bar earlier in this chapter.

- You can use buttons on the command bar (**Figure 26**) in the Save As dialog box to work with listed files and folders.

- You can use the Save as type menu at the bottom of the Save As dialog box (**Figure 78**) to specify a format for the file. This enables you to save the document in a format that can be opened and read by other versions of Word or other applications.

- Windows file names can be almost any length, as long as the complete path to the file (including drive letter, all folder names, and the file name) does not exceed 255 characters. File names cannot include any of the following characters: /, \, >, <, *, ?, ", |, :, or ;. It is not necessary to include the three-character extension when you enter a file name; Word does it for you based on the file type selected from the Save as type menu (**Figure 78**).

- If you save a file with the same name and same disk location as another file, a dialog box appears, asking if you want to replace the file (**Figure 79**).

  - ▲ Click Yes to replace the file already on disk with the file you are saving.

  - ▲ Click No to return to the Save As dialog box where you can enter a new name or specify a new location.

  - ▲ Click Cancel to dismiss the Save As dialog box.

To save changes to a document

Choose File > Save (**Figure 5**) or press Ctrl S.

or

Click the Save button 🖫 on the Standard toolbar.

The document is saved with the same name in the same location on disk.

To save a document with a different name or in a different disk location

1. Choose File > Save As (**Figure 5**).

2. Follow steps 2 and/or 3 on page 46 to select a new disk location and/or enter a different name for the file.

3. Click the Save button.

To save a document as a template

1. Choose File > Save As (**Figure 5**).

2. Enter a name for the file in the File name box.

3. Choose Document Template from the Save as type menu (**Figure 78**). The directory portion of the dialog box automatically displays the contents of the Templates folder (**Figure 80**).

4. To store the template in a specific folder, double-click the name of the folder to open it.

5. Click the Save button.

The file is saved as a template. Its name appears in the document title bar.

✔ Tips

■ To begin using a template right after you created it, close it, then follow the instructions near the beginning of the chapter to open a new file based on a template. The template appears in the New dialog box (**Figure 81**).

■ I tell you more about templates near the beginning of this chapter.

Figure 80 The Save As dialog box when you save a document as a template.

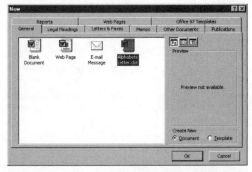

Figure 81 When a file has been saved as a template in the Templates folder, it appears in the New dialog box.

FORMATTING BASICS

Formatting Basics

Word offers a wide range of formatting options that you can use to make your documents more interesting and readable. Most formatting can be broken down into three types:

◆ **Font** or **character formatting** applies to individual characters of text. Examples include bold, italic, underline, and font color. The actual *font* or typeface used to display characters is also a part of font formatting.

◆ **Paragraph formatting** applies to entire paragraphs of text. Examples are indentation, justification, and line spacing.

◆ **Page formatting** applies to entire document pages or document sections. Examples include margins and vertical alignment of text on the page.

In this chapter, I introduce you to the most basic kinds of formatting—the formatting you'll probably use most often.

✔ Tips

■ When properly applied, formatting can make the document easier to read, as illustrated in **Figures 1** and **2**.

■ Don't get carried away with formatting— especially font formatting. Too much formatting distracts the reader, making the document difficult to read.

■ Page formatting is sometimes referred to as *document formatting*.

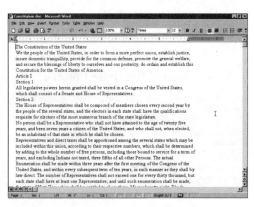

Figure 1 A document with no formatting.

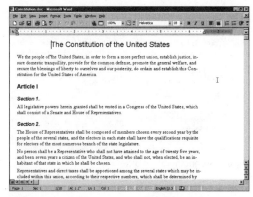

Figure 2 The same document with font, paragraph, and page formatting applied.

Learning about Applied Formats

Word offers an easy way to see what kind of formatting is applied to text: the What's This? command (**Figure 3**). This command enables you to display a window that tells you exactly what kind of formatting is applied to the text characters on which you click (**Figures 5** and **6**).

To learn about applied formats

1. Choose Help > What's This? (**Figure 3**) or press Shift F1 . A question mark appears beside the mouse pointer (**Figure 4**).

2. Click on a character for which you want to learn about applied formats. A box appears around the character you clicked. A window indicating the formatting applied to the character appears (**Figures 5** and **6**).

3. Repeat step 2 for each character for which you want to learn about applied formats.

4. When you have finished learning about formats applied to text, press Esc or choose Help > What's This? again to turn off the feature. The mouse pointer returns to normal and you can continue working with the document.

✔ Tips

- What's This? shows the formatting applied to the paragraph in which a character resides as well as the character itself.

- This feature distinguishes between formatting applied as part of a style and formatting that is directly applied. I cover styles in **Chapter 4**.

Figure 3
Choose What's This? from the Help menu.

Figure 4 A question mark appears beside the mouse pointer.

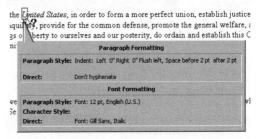

Figure 5 Here's one example of what you can learn about formatting applied to a character...

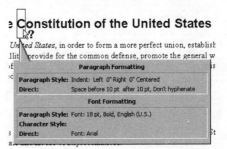

Figure 6 ...and here's another example.

Arial
Bookman Old Style
Century Gothic
Courier New
Forte
Garamond
Impact
Συμβολ
Verdana
Times New Roman
✦⌘■℣♫⌘■℣•

Figure 7 Some font examples using fonts installed on my system. Your system's fonts may differ.

Regular
Bold
Italic
Bold Italic

Figure 8 The basic font styles offered by Word.

10 points
12 points
14 points
18 points
24 points
36 points

Figure 9 Examples of font sizes. This illustration is not at actual size.

No Underline
Words Only
Single
Double
Thick
Dotted
Dash
Dot Dash
Wave

Figure 10 Some of the Underline options offered by Word.

Strikethrough
Double Strikethrough
Superscript
Subscript
Shadow
Outline
Emboss
Engrave
Small Caps
ALL CAPS

Figure 11 Examples of effects that can be applied to text.

Font Formatting

Font formatting, which is sometimes referred to as character formatting, can be applied to individual characters of text. Word offers a wide variety of options.

◆ **Font** (**Figure 7**) is the typeface used to display characters.

◆ **Font style** (**Figure 8**) is the appearance of font characters: regular, italic, bold, or bold italic.

◆ **Size** (**Figure 9**) is the size of characters, expressed in points.

◆ **Underline** (**Figure 10**) options allow you to apply a variety of underline styles beneath characters.

◆ **Underline** color is the color of any applied underline.

◆ **Color** is the color applied to text characters.

◆ **Highlight** is the color applied to the background of text.

◆ **Effects** (**Figure 11**) are special effects that change the appearance of characters. Options include strikethrough, double strikethrough, superscript, subscript, shadow, outline, emboss, engrave, small caps, all caps, or hidden.

✔ Tips

■ Although some fonts come with Microsoft Office, Word enables you to apply *any* font that is properly installed in your system.

■ A point is 1/72 inch. The larger the point size, the larger the characters.

■ Hidden characters do not show on screen unless formatting marks are displayed. I tell you about formatting marks in **Chapter 2**.

■ Word offers additional font formatting options not covered here; I tell you about them in **Chapter 4**.

Applying Font Formatting

Font formatting is applied to selected characters or, if no characters are selected, to the characters you type at the insertion point after applying formatting. Here are two examples:

◆ To apply a bold font style to text that you have already typed, select the text (**Figure 12**), then apply the formatting. The appearance of the text changes immediately (**Figure 13**).

◆ To apply a bold font style to text that you have not yet typed, position the insertion point where the text will be typed (**Figure 14**), apply the bold formatting, and type the text. The text appears in bold (**Figure 15**). You must remember, however, to "turn off" bold formatting before you continue to type (**Figure 16**).

Word offers several methods of applying font formatting:

◆ The Formatting toolbar enables you to apply font, size, some font styles, highlight, and font color formatting.

◆ Shortcut keys enable you to apply some font formatting.

◆ The Font dialog box enables you to apply all kinds of font formatting.

✔ Tips

■ In my opinion, it's easier to type text and then apply formatting than to format as you type.

■ I explain how to select text in **Chapter 2**.

We the people of the United States, in orde sure domestic tranquillity, provide for the secure the blessings of liberty to ourselves

Figure 12 Select the text that you want to format,...

We the people of the United States, in orc sure domestic tranquillity, provide for the secure the blessings of liberty to ourselves

Figure 13 ...then apply the formatting.

We the people of the|

Figure 14 Position the insertion point where you want the formatted text to appear,...

We the people of the United States|

Figure 15 ...then "turn on" the formatting and type the text.

We the people of the United States, in order to|

Figure 16 Be sure to "turn off" the formatting before continuing to type.

Figures 17 & 18 The Font (left) and Font Size (right) menus on the Formatting toolbar.

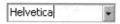

Figure 19 Select the contents of the Font box...

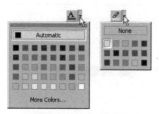

Figure 20 ...then type in the name of the font you want to apply.

Figures 21 & 22 The Font Color (left) and Highlight (right) menus on the Formatting toolbar.

![Microsoft Word dialog: The font 'Zapf Dingbats' is not available on your system. Do you want to use it anyway? Yes / No]

Figure 23 Word tells you when you've entered a font that is not installed.

To apply font formatting with the Formatting toolbar

Choose the font or size that you want to apply from the Font or Font Size toolbar menu (**Figures 17** and **18**).

or

1. Click the Font (**Figure 19**) or Font Size box on the toolbar to select its contents.

2. Enter the name of the font (**Figure 20**) or the size that you want to apply.

3. Press Enter.

or

Click the Bold **B**, Italic **I**, or Underline **U** button.

or

Click the Font Color button **A** to apply the currently selected color or choose another color from the Font Color toolbar menu (**Figure 21**).

or

Click the Highlight button to apply the currently selected color or choose another color from the Highlight toolbar menu (**Figure 22**).

✔ Tips

■ Font names appear on the Font menu in their typefaces (**Figure 17**).

■ Recently applied fonts appear at the top of the Font toolbar menu (**Figure 17**).

■ If you enter the name of a font that is not installed on your system, Word warns you (**Figure 23**). If you use the font anyway, the text appears in the document in the default paragraph font. The text will appear in the applied font after it is installed on your system or when the document is opened on a system on which the font is installed.

APPLYING FONT FORMATTING

To apply font formatting with shortcut keys

Press the shortcut key combination (**Table 1**) for the formatting that you want to apply.

✔ Tip

■ The shortcut keys to change font or font size require that you press the first key combination, enter the name of the font or size desired, then press Enter. These commands activate the edit boxes on the Font and Font Size menus on the Formatting toolbar.

To apply font formatting with the Font dialog box

1. Choose Format > Font (**Figure 24**) or press Ctrl D.

2. Set formatting options as desired in the Font tab of the Font dialog box that appears (**Figure 25**).

3. Click OK.

✔ Tip

■ The Preview area of the Font dialog box illustrates what text will look like with the selected formatting applied.

Formatting	Keystroke
Font	Ctrl Shift F *Font Name* Enter
Symbol font	Ctrl Shift Q
Font size	Ctrl Shift P *Size* Enter
Grow font	Ctrl Shift .
Grow font 1 point	Ctrl]
Shrink font	Ctrl Shift ,
Shrink font 1 point	Ctrl [
Bold	Ctrl B or Ctrl Shift B
Italic	Ctrl I or Ctrl Shift I
Underline	Ctrl U or Ctrl Shift U
Word underline	Ctrl Shift W
Double underline	Ctrl Shift D
Superscript	Ctrl Shift =
Subscript	Ctrl =
All caps	Ctrl Shift A
Small caps	Ctrl Shift K
Hidden	Ctrl Shift H

Table 1 Shortcut keys for font formatting.

Figure 24 The Format menu.

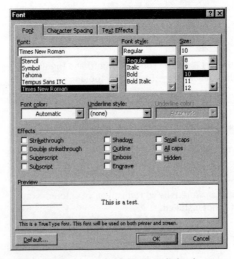

Figure 25 The Font tab of the Font dialog box.

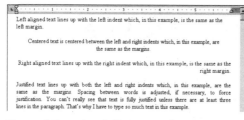

Figure 26 Examples of alignment options.

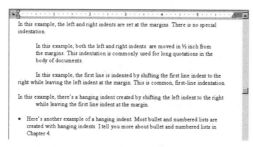

Figure 27 Examples of indentation options. The ruler, in this example, shows the indent marker settings for the first paragraph.

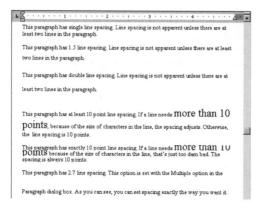

Figure 28 Examples of line spacing options.

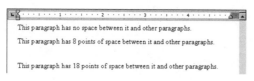

Figure 29 Examples of paragraph spacing options.

Paragraph Formatting

Paragraph formatting is applied to entire paragraphs of text. Word offers a variety of options:

◆ **Alignment** (**Figure 26**) is the way lines of text line up between the indents.

◆ **Indentation** (**Figure 27**) is the spacing between text and margins. Word allows you to set left and right margins, as well as special indentation for first line and hanging indents.

◆ **Line spacing** (**Figure 28**) is the amount of space between lines. Spacing can be set as single, 1.5 lines, double, at least a certain amount, exactly a certain amount, or multiple lines.

◆ **Paragraph spacing** (**Figure 29**) is the amount of space before and after the paragraph.

✔ Tip

■ Word offers additional paragraph formatting options not covered in this section. I tell you about tabs later in this chapter and about other paragraph formatting options in **Chapter 4**.

Applying Paragraph Formatting

Paragraph formatting is applied to selected paragraphs (**Figure 30**) or, if no paragraphs are selected, to the paragraph in which the insertion point is blinking (**Figure 31**).

Word offers several methods of applying paragraph formatting:

- The Formatting toolbar enables you to apply alignment and some indentation formats.

- Shortcut keys enable you to apply some paragraph formatting.

- The ruler enables you to apply indentation formatting.

- The Paragraph dialog box enables you to apply most kinds of paragraph formatting.

✔ Tips

- Paragraph formatting applies to the entire paragraph, even if only part of the paragraph is selected (**Figure 32**).

- A paragraph is the text that appears between paragraph marks. You can see paragraph marks when you display formatting marks (**Figures 30**, **31**, and **32**). I tell you about formatting marks in **Chapter 2**.

- When you press Enter, the formatting of the current paragraph is applied to the new one.

- I explain how to select text in **Chapter 2**.

To apply paragraph formatting with toolbar buttons

Click the Align Left ≣, Center ≣, Align Right ≣, or Justify ≣ button on the Formatting toolbar to apply desired alignment (**Figure 26**).

or

Click the Decrease Indent ≣ or Increase Indent ≣ button on the Formatting toolbar to adjust indentation (**Figure 27**).

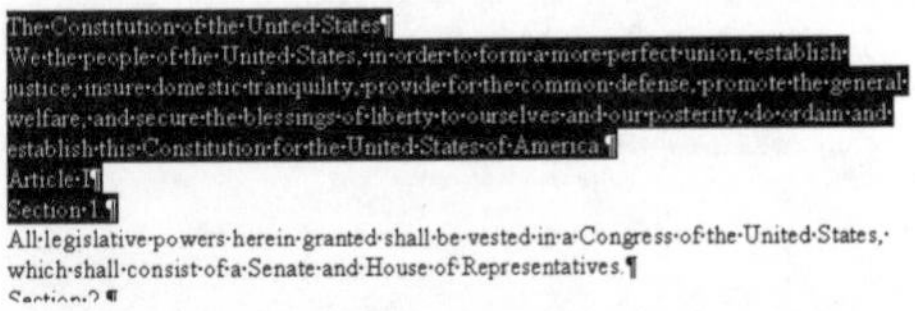

Figure 30 In this example, the first four paragraphs are complete selected and will be affected by any paragraph formatting applied.

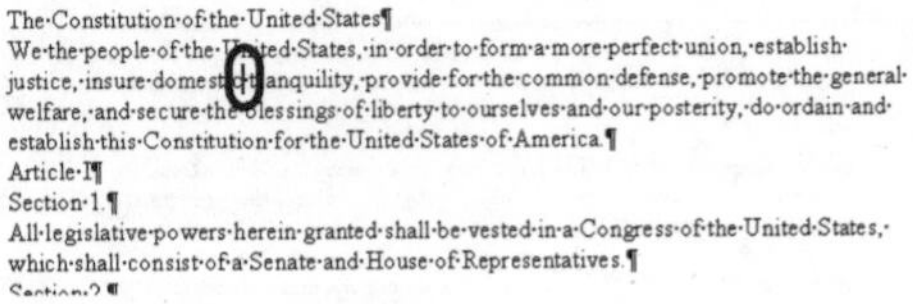

Figure 31 In this example, the insertion point is in the second paragraph. That entire paragraph will be affected by any paragraph formatting applied.

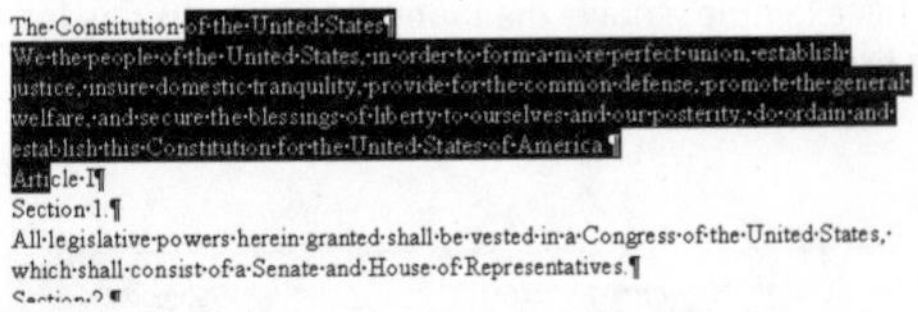

Figure 32 In this example, only part of the first and third paragraphs are selected, along with all of the second paragraph. All three paragraphs will be affected by any paragraph formatting applied.

Formatting	Keystroke
Align Left	Ctrl L
Center	Ctrl E
Align Right	Ctrl R
Justify	Ctrl J
Indent	Ctrl M
Unindent	Ctrl Shift M
Hanging Indent	Ctrl T
Unhang Indent	Ctrl Shift T
Single Line Space	Ctrl 1
1.5 Line Space	Ctrl 5
Double Line Space	Ctrl 2
Double underline	Ctrl Shift D
Open/Close Up Paragraph	Ctrl 0 (zero)

Table 2 Shortcut keys for paragraph formatting.

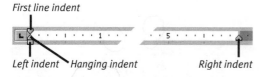

First line indent

Left indent   Hanging indent   Right indent

Figure 33 Indent markers on the ruler.

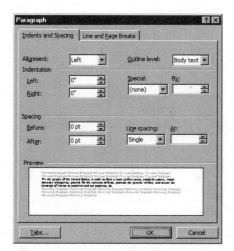

Figure 34 The Indents and Spacing tab of the Paragraph dialog box.

To apply paragraph formatting with shortcut keys

Press the shortcut key combination (**Table 2**) for the formatting that you want to apply.

To set indentation with the ruler

Drag the indent markers (**Figure 33**) to set indentation as desired:

◆ **First Line Indent** sets the left boundary for the first line of a paragraph.

◆ **Hanging Indent** sets the left boundary for all lines of a paragraph other than the first line.

◆ **Left Indent** sets the left boundary for all lines of a paragraph. (Dragging this marker moves the First Line Indent and Hanging Indent markers.)

◆ **Right Indent** sets the right boundary for all lines of a paragraph.

✔ Tips

■ Dragging the First Line Indent marker to the right creates a standard indent.

■ Dragging the Hanging Indent marker to the right creates a hanging indent.

To apply paragraph formatting with the Paragraph dialog box

1. Choose Format > Paragraph (**Figure 24**).

2. Set formatting options as desired in the Indents and Spacing tab of the Paragraph dialog box that appears (**Figure 34**).

3. Click OK.

✔ Tip

■ The Preview area of the Paragraph dialog box illustrates what text will look like with formatting applied.

APPLYING PARAGRAPH FORMATTING

Tabs

Tab stops determine the position of the insertion point when you press Tab.

By default, a blank document includes tab stops every half inch. They appear as gray marks on the bottom of the ruler (**Figure 35**). You can use the ruler or the Tabs dialog box to set tabs that override the defaults.

Word supports five kinds of tabs (**Figure 36**):

- **Left tab** aligns tabbed text to the left against the tab stop.

- **Center tab** centers tabbed text beneath the tab stop.

- **Right tab** aligns tabbed text to the right against the tab stop.

- **Decimal tab** aligns the decimal point (or period) of tabbed numbers beneath the tab stop. When used with text, a decimal tab works just like a right tab.

- **Bar tab** isn't a tab at all. It's a vertical line that appears beneath the tab stop.

Word also supports four types of *tab leaders* (**Figure 37**)—characters that appear in the space otherwise left by a tab: none, periods, dashes, and underscores.

✔ Tips

- Tabs are a type of paragraph formatting; when set, they apply to an entire paragraph.

- Tabs are often used to create simple tables.

- When trying to align text in a simple table, use tabs, not spaces. Tabs always align to tab stops while text positioned with space characters may not align properly due to the size and spacing of characters in a font.

- It's a good idea to display formatting marks when working with tabs (**Figure 38**). This enables you to distinguish tabs from spaces. I tell you about formatting marks in **Chapter 2**.

Figure 35 Default tab stops appear as tiny gray lines on the ruler.

Figure 36 Word's five tab stops in action. In order, they are: left, bar, right, center, and decimal. Examine the ruler to see how they're set.

Figure 37 Word's tab leader options: none, dotted, dashed, and underscored.

Figure 38 Displaying formatting marks enables you to see the tab characters.

TABS

Figure 39 The tab marker icons for left, center, right, decimal, and bar tabs.

To set tab stops with the ruler

1. Click the tab marker icon at the far-left end of the ruler (**Figure 35**) until it displays the icon for the type of tab stop that you want to set (**Figure 39**).

2. Click on the ruler where you want to position the tab stop to set it there.

3. Repeat steps 1 and 2 until all desired tab stops have been set (**Figure 38**).

✔ Tips

- When you set a tab stop, all default tab stops to its left disappear (**Figures 36** and **38**).

- You cannot set tab leaders with the ruler. Instead, use the Tabs dialog box. I tell you how on the next page.

To move a tab stop with the ruler

1. Position the mouse pointer on the tab stop that you want to move.

2. Press the mouse button down and drag the tab stop to its new position.

✔ Tip

- Don't click on the ruler anywhere except on the tab stop that you want to move. Doing so will set another tab stop.

To remove a tab stop from the ruler

1. Position the mouse pointer on the tab stop that you want to remove.

2. Press the mouse button down and drag the tab stop down into the document. When you release the mouse button, the tab stop disappears.

To open the Tabs dialog box

Choose Format > Tabs (**Figure 24**).

or

Click the Tabs button in the Paragraph dialog box (**Figure 34**).

or

Double-click a tab stop on the ruler (**Figure 36**).

To set tab stops with the Tabs dialog box

1. Open the Tabs dialog box (**Figure 40**).

2. In the Alignment area, select the option button for the type of tab that you want.

3. In the Leader area, select the option button for the type of leader that you want the tab stop to have.

4. Enter a measurement in the Tab stop position box.

5. Click the Set button. The tab stop is added to the tab list (**Figure 41**).

6. Repeat steps 2 through 5 for each tab stop that you want to set (**Figure 42**).

7. Click OK.

To remove tab stops with the Tabs dialog box

1. In the Tabs dialog box, select the tab stop that you want to remove.

2. Click the Clear button. The tab stop is removed from the list and added to the list of Tab stops to be cleared near the bottom of the dialog box (**Figure 43**).

3. Click OK.

✔ Tip

■ To remove all tab stops, click the Clear All button in the Tabs dialog box (**Figure 43**), then click OK.

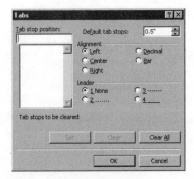

Figure 40 The Tabs dialog box.

Figure 41 When you add a tab, it appears in the list in the Tabs dialog box.

Figure 42 The tab stop settings for Figure 36.

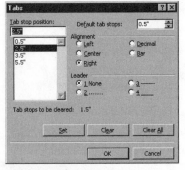

Figure 43 When you click Clear to remove a tab, it is removed from the list.

Figure 44 Position the insertion point in the paragraph for which you have set tab stops.

Figure 45 Press Tab to type at the first tab stop, then type. In this example, text is typed at a left-aligned tab stop.

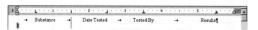

Figure 46 When you are finished typing a line, press Enter to start a new paragraph with the same tab stops.

Figure 47 Here's the completed table.

To change the default tab stops

1. In the Tabs dialog box, enter a new value in the Default tab stops edit box.

2. Click OK.

✔ Tip

■ Remember, tab stops that you set manually on the ruler or with the Tabs dialog box override default tab stops to their left.

To create a simple table with tab stops

1. Position the insertion point in the paragraph in which you set tabs (**Figure 44**).

2. To type at a tab stop, press Tab, then type (**Figure 45**).

3. Repeat step 2 to type at each tab stop.

4. Press Enter or Shift Enter to end the paragraph or line and begin a new one. The tab stops in the paragraph are carried forward (**Figure 46**).

5. Repeat steps 2 through 4 to finish typing your table (**Figure 47**).

✔ Tips

■ You can move tabs at any time—even after you have begun using them. Be sure to select all the paragraphs that utilize the tabs *before* you move them. Otherwise, you may only adjust tabs for part of the table.

■ Another way to create tables is with Word's table feature, which is far more flexible than using tab stops. I tell you about it in **Chapter 10**.

CREATING A TABLE WITH TAB STOPS

Page Formatting

Page formatting is applied to all pages in a document or document section. Word offers several options, two of which are covered in this chapter:

◆ **Margins (Figure 48)** and **gutter** refers to the spacing between the edge of the paper and the indents.

◆ **Vertical alignment (Figure 49)** is the vertical position of text on a page. Options include top, center, justified, and bottom.

✔ Tip

■ Word offers additional page formatting options not covered here. I tell you about working with header, footer, and section break options in **Chapter 4**.

Setting Page Formatting

Page formatting can be applied in four ways:

◆ To the entire document.

◆ To the document from the insertion point forward. This creates a section break at the insertion point.

◆ To selected text. This creates a section break before and after the selected text.

◆ To selected document sections. This requires that section breaks already be in place and that you either select the sections or position the insertion point in a section.

You apply page formatting with the Page Setup dialog box (**Figure 51**).

✔ Tip

■ I explain how to create and use section breaks in **Chapter 4**. Be sure to read about section breaks before using the Page Setup dialog box to format a section.

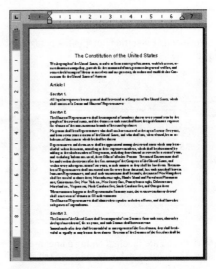

Figure 48 A margin is the space between the edge of the paper and the indent.

Figure 49 Examples of vertical alignment. From left to right: top, center, justified, and bottom.

Figure 50
The File menu.

To open the Page Setup dialog box

Choose File > Page Setup (**Figure 50**).

To set margins

1. Open the Page Setup dialog box and display the Margins tab (**Figure 51**).

2. Enter values in the Top, Bottom, Left, and Right boxes.

3. To set a gutter width, enter a value in the Gutter box. Then select one of the Gutter position option buttons.

4. To apply your changes to the entire document, make sure Whole document is selected from the Apply to menu. Otherwise, choose the desired option from the Apply to menu; I tell you more about that in **Chapter 4**.

5. Click OK.

✔ Tips

- The *gutter* is the amount of extra space on the inside margin of a document (**Figure 52**). It is designed to account for space used in binding.

- If you turn on the Mirror margins check box, the dialog box changes for double-sided pages (**Figure 52**).

- If you turn on the 2 pages per sheet check box, the page layout changes to print two pages on each sheet of paper.

- The Preview area of the Page Setup dialog box illustrates margin and gutter settings (**Figures 51** and **52**).

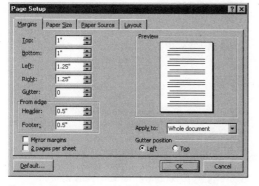

Figure 51 The Margins tab of the Page Setup dialog box.

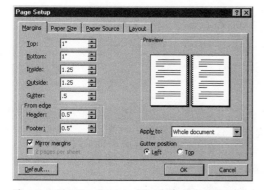

Figure 52 The Margins tab of the Page Setup dialog box with Mirror margins turned on and a half-inch gutter.

To set vertical alignment

1. Open the Page Setup dialog box and display the Layout tab (**Figure 53**).

2. Choose the alignment option that you want from the Vertical alignment menu (**Figure 54**).

3. To apply your changes to the entire document, make sure Whole document is selected from the Apply to menu. Otherwise, choose the desired option from the Apply to menu; I tell you more about that in **Chapter 4**.

4. Click OK.

✔ Tips

- Vertical alignment is only apparent on pages that are less than a full page in length.

- On screen, you can only view vertical alignment in Print Layout view and Print Preview. I tell you about Print Preview in **Chapter 6**.

To set default page formatting

1. Open the Page Setup dialog box.

2. Set options as desired in the Margins and Layout tabs (**Figures 51** and **53**).

3. Click the Default button.

4. Word asks if you want to change the default settings for the document (**Figure 55**). Click Yes only if you want the settings to apply to all new documents that you create based on the Normal (Blank Document) template.

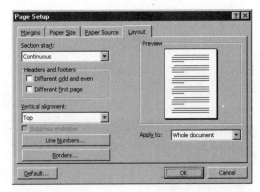

Figure 53 The Layout tab of the Page Setup dialog box.

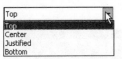

Figure 54 The Vertical alignment menu in the Layout tab of the Page Setup dialog box.

Figure 55 Word confirms that you really want to change the default document settings.

ADVANCED FORMATTING

Advanced Formatting

Word offers a number of formatting options and techniques in addition to those I discuss in **Chapter 3**:

- ◆ **Character spacing** includes the spacing, position, and kerning of characters.

- ◆ **Drop Caps** enlarges the first character(s) of a paragraph and wraps text around it.

- ◆ **Change Case** changes the case of characters.

- ◆ **Bullets and numbering** instructs Word to automatically insert bullet characters or numbers at the beginning of paragraphs.

- ◆ **Borders and shading** enable you to place borders around text, and color or shades of gray within text areas.

- ◆ **Format Painter** enables you to copy font and paragraph formats from one selection to another.

- ◆ **Styles** enables you to define and apply named sets of formatting options for individual characters or paragraphs.

- ◆ **AutoFormat** instructs Word to automatically format text you type.

- ◆ **Breaks** determines the end of a page, section, or column.

- ◆ **Multiple-column text** enables you to use newspaper-like columns in documents.

- ◆ **Headers and footers** enables you to specify text to appear at the top and bottom of every page in the document.

✔ Tip

- ■ It's a good idea to have a solid understanding of the concepts covered in **Chapter 3** before you read this chapter.

Character Spacing

Word offers several more advanced font formatting options:

◆ **Scale** determines the horizontal size of the characters, enabling you to stretch or compress them (**Figure 1**).

◆ **Spacing** determines the amount of space between each character of text. Spacing can be normal or can be expanded or condensed by the number of points you specify (**Figure 2**).

◆ **Position** determines whether text appears above or below the baseline. Position can be normal or can be raised or lowered by the number of points you specify (**Figure 3**).

◆ **Kerning** determines how certain combinations of letters "fit" together (**Figure 4**).

✔ Tips

■ Like any other type of font formatting, you can apply character spacing to characters as you type them or to characters that have already been typed. Check **Chapter 3** for details.

■ The *baseline* is the invisible line on which characters sit.

■ Don't confuse character position with superscript and subscript. Although all three of these font formatting options change the position of text in relation to the baseline, superscript and subscript also change the size of characters. I tell you about superscript and subscript in **Chapter 3**.

■ The effect of kerning varies based on the size and font of characters to which kerning is enabled. Kerning is more apparent at larger point sizes and requires that the font contain *kerning pairs*—predefined pairs of letters to kern. In many instances, you may not see a difference in spacing at all.

This is an example of character scale.
This is an example of character scale.
This is an example of character scale.

Figure 1 Three examples of character scale: 100% (top), 150% (middle), and 80% (bottom).

This is an example of character spacing.
This is an example of character spacing.
This is an example of character spacing.

Figure 2 Three examples of character spacing: normal (top), expanded by 1 point (middle), and condensed by 1 point (bottom).

This is an example of normal position.
This is an example of raised position.
This is an example of lowered position.

Figure 3 Three examples of character position: normal (top), raised 3 points (middle), and lowered 3 points (bottom).

To We
To We

Figure 4 Two common kerning pairs without kerning enabled (top) and with kerning enabled (bottom).

Figure 5
The Format menu.

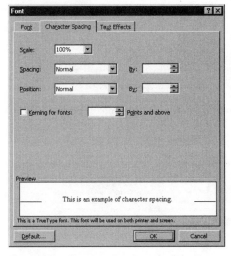

Figure 6 The Character Spacing tab of the Font dialog box.

Figure 7
The Scale menu.

Figure 8
The Spacing menu.

Figure 9
The Position menu.

To apply character spacing

1. Choose Format > Font (**Figure 5**).

2. In the Font dialog box that appears, click the Character Spacing tab to display its options (**Figure 6**).

3. To change scale, choose an option from the Scale menu (**Figure 7**).

4. To change spacing, choose an option from the Spacing menu (**Figure 8**). Then enter a value in its By text box.

5. To change position, choose an option from the Position menu (**Figure 9**). Then enter a value in its By text box.

6. To enable kerning, turn on the Kerning for fonts check box. Then enter a value in the Points and above text box to specify the minimum point size of fonts to which kerning should be applied.

7. Click OK.

✔ Tip

- The Preview area of the Font dialog box (**Figure 6**) shows what selected characters will look like when you apply settings by clicking OK.

APPLYING CHARACTER SPACING

Drop Caps

A drop cap is an enlarged and/or repositioned character at the beginning of a paragraph. Word supports two types of drop caps (**Figure 10**):

◆ **Dropped** enlarges the character and wraps the rest of the text in the paragraph around it.

◆ **In Margin** enlarges the character and moves it into the margin.

✔ Tips

■ Word creates drop caps using frames, a feature that enables you to precisely position text on a page or in relation to a paragraph. Frames is an advanced feature of Word that is beyond the scope of this book.

■ To see drop caps, you must be in Print Layout view or Print Preview. A drop cap appears as an enlarged character in its own paragraph in Normal view (**Figure 11**).

■ A drop cap can consist of more than just the first letter of a paragraph (**Figure 12**).

Alice was beginning to get very tired of sitting by her sister on the bank and having nothing to do: once or twice she had peeped into the book her sister was reading, but it had no pictures or conversations in it, "and what is the use of a book," thought Alice, "without pictures or conversations?"

A lice was beginning to get very tired of sitting by her sister on the bank and having nothing to do: once or twice she had peeped into the book her sister was reading, but it had no pictures or conversations in it, "and what is the use of a book," thought Alice, "without pictures or conversations?"

A lice was beginning to get very tired of sitting by her sister on the bank and having nothing to do: once or twice she had peeped into the book her sister was reading, but it had no pictures or conversations in it, "and what is the use of a book," thought Alice, "without pictures or conversations?"

Figure 10 The same paragraph three ways: without a drop cap (top), with a drop cap (middle), and with an in margin drop cap (bottom).

A lice was beginning to get very tired of sitting by her sister on the bank and having nothing to do: once or twice she had peeped into the book her sister was reading, but it had no pictures or conversations in it, "and what is the use of a book," thought Alice, "without pictures or conversations?"

Figure 11 A paragraph with a drop cap when viewed in Normal view.

Alice was beginning to get very tired of sitting by her sister on the bank and having nothing to do: once or twice she had peeped into the book what is the use of a book," thought Alice, "without pictures or conversations?"

Figure 12 A drop cap can consist of more than just one character.

Figure 13 The Drop Cap dialog box with the Dropped position selected.

To create a drop cap

1. Position the insertion point anywhere in the paragraph for which you want to create a drop cap.

2. Choose Format > Drop Cap (**Figure 5**).

3. In the Drop Cap dialog box that appears (**Figure 13**), click the position icon for the type of drop cap that you want to create.

4. Choose a font for the drop cap from the Font menu.

5. Enter the number of lines for the size of the drop cap character in the Lines to drop box.

6. Enter a value for the amount of space between the drop cap character and the rest of the text in the paragraph in the Distance from text box.

7. Click OK.

The first character of the paragraph appears as a drop cap (**Figure 10**).

✔ Tips

- After step 7, if you are not in Print Layout view, Word automatically switches to it so you can see the drop cap you created.

- To create a drop cap with more than one character (**Figure 12**), select the characters that you want to appear as drop caps, then follow steps 2 through 7 above.

To remove a drop cap

Follow the steps above, but select the icon for None in step 3.

CREATING & REMOVING DROP CAPS

Changing Case

You can use the Change Case dialog box (**Figure 14**) to change the case of selected characters. There are five options (**Figure 15**):

- **Sentence case** capitalizes the first letter of a sentence.

- **lowercase** changes all characters to lowercase.

- **UPPERCASE** changes all characters to uppercase.

- **Title Case** capitalizes the first letter of every word.

- **tOGGLE cASE** changes uppercase characters to lowercase and lowercase characters to uppercase.

✔ Tips

- Technically speaking, changing the case of characters with the Change Case dialog box does not format the characters. Instead, it changes the actual characters that were originally entered into the document.

- To change the case of characters without changing the characters themselves, use the All Caps or Small Caps option in the Font tab of the Font dialog box (**Figure 16**). I tell you how in **Chapter 3**.

To change the case of characters

1. Select the characters whose case you want to change.

2. Choose Format > Change Case (**Figure 5**).

3. In the Change Case dialog box that appears (**Figure 14**), select the option you want.

4. Click OK.

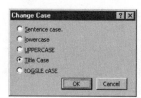

Figure 14
The Change Case dialog box.

You can use the Change Case dialog box to change the case of typed characters.
You can use the Change Case dialog box to change the case of typed characters.
you can use the change case dialog box to change the case of typed characters.
YOU CAN USE THE CHANGE CASE DIALOG BOX TO CHANGE THE CASE OF TYPED CHARACTERS.
You Can Use The Change Case Dialog Box To Change The Case Of Typed Characters.
yOU CAN USE THE cHANGE cASE DIALOG BOX TO CHANGE THE CASE OF TYPED CHARACTERS.

Figure 15 Change Case in action—from top to bottom, original text, Sentence case, lowercase, UPPERCASE, Title Case, and tOGGLE cASE.

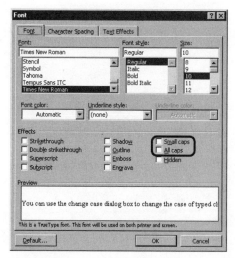

Figure 16 The "case" options in the Font tab of the Font dialog box.

The following topics were covered:
- Advertising budget for product kickoff
- Replacement for Jane Jones
- Team for Product X marketing development

The following topics were covered:
1. Advertising budget for product kickoff
2. Replacement for Jane Jones
3. Team for Product X marketing development

Figure 17 Three paragraphs with bullets (top) and numbering (bottom) formats applied.

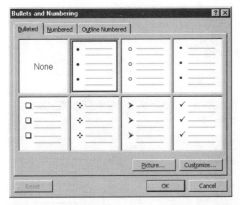

Figure 18 The Bulleted tab of the Bullets and Numbering dialog box.

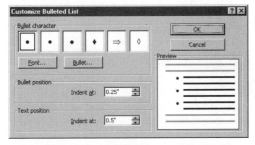

Figure 19 The Customize Bulleted List dialog box.

Bullets & Numbering

Word automatically includes bullets or numbers at the beginning of paragraphs to which you apply a bulleted or numbered list format (**Figure 17**).

✔ Tips

- You can apply bulleted or numbered list formats as you type or to paragraphs that have already been typed. Check **Chapter 3** for details.

- The bullet and number formats include hanging indents. I explain Word's indentation options in **Chapter 3**.

- If you use Word's numbering format, Word will automatically increment the number for each consecutive paragraph.

To apply bulleted list formatting

Click the Bullet button ⫶≣ on the Formatting toolbar.

or

1. Choose Bullets and Numbering from the Format menu (**Figure 5**).

2. In the Bullets and Numbering dialog box that appears, click the Bulleted tab to display its options (**Figure 18**).

3. Click the box that displays the type of bullet character that you want.

4. Click OK.

✔ Tips

- Clicking the Bullet button on the Formatting toolbar applies the last style of bullet used.

- To further customize a bullet list, after step 3 above, click the Customize button in the Bullets and Numbering dialog box (**Figure 18**). Set options in the Customize Bulleted List dialog box that appears (**Figure 19**), and click OK.

To apply numbered list formatting

Click the Numbering button ⊞ on the Formatting toolbar.

or

1. Choose Bullets and Numbering from the Format menu (**Figure 5**).

2. In the Bullets and Numbering dialog box that appears, click the Numbered tab to display its options (**Figure 20**).

3. Click the box that displays the numbering format that you want.

4. Click OK.

✔ Tips

- Clicking the Numbering button on the Formatting toolbar applies the last style of numbering used.

- To further customize a numbered list, after step 3 above, click the Customize button in the Bullets and Numbering dialog box (**Figure 20**). Set options in the Customize Numbered List dialog box that appears (**Figure 21**), and click OK.

To remove bulleted or numbered list formatting

1. Choose Bullets and Numbering from the Format menu (**Figure 5**).

2. In the Bullets and Numbering dialog box (**Figure 18** or **20**), click the None box.

3. Click OK.

or

To remove bulleted list formatting, click the Bullet button ⊞ on the Formatting toolbar.

or

To remove numbered list formatting, click the Numbering button ⊞ on the Formatting toolbar.

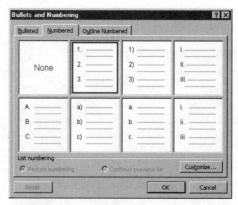

Figure 20 The Numbered tab of the Bullets and Numbering dialog box.

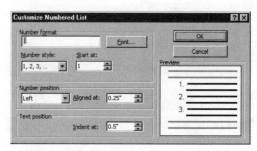

Figure 21 The Customize Numbered List dialog box.

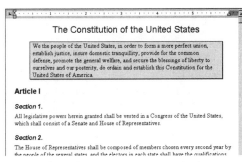

Figure 22 Borders and shading can emphasize text.

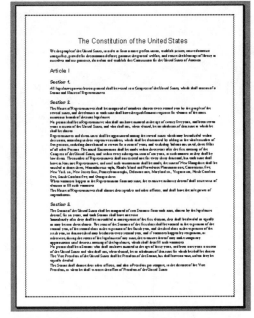

Figure 23 Page borders can make a page look fancy.

Borders & Shading

Borders and shading are two separate features that can work together to emphasize text:

◆ **Text borders** enables you to place lines above, below, to the left, or to the right of selected characters or paragraphs (**Figure 22**).

◆ **Page borders** enables you to place simple or graphic borders at the top, bottom, left, or right sides of document pages (**Figure 23**).

◆ **Shading** enables you to add color or shades of gray to selected characters or paragraphs (**Figure 22**).

✔ Tips

■ How borders or shading are applied depends on how text is selected:

▲ To apply borders or shading to characters, select the characters.

▲ To apply borders or shading to a paragraph, click in the paragraph or select the entire paragraph.

▲ To apply borders or shading to multiple paragraphs, select the paragraphs.

▲ To apply page borders to all pages in a document, click anywhere in the document.

▲ To apply page borders to a specific document section, click anywhere in that section.

■ When applying borders to selected text characters (as opposed to selected paragraphs), you must place a border around each side, creating a box around the text.

To apply text borders with the Border button

1. Select the text to which you want to apply borders.

2. Click the Border button 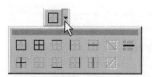 on the Formatting toolbar to apply the currently selected border.

or

Choose a border from the Border menu on the Formatting toolbar (**Figure 24**).

✔ Tips

- You can apply more than one border on the Borders menu to selected paragraphs. For example, if you want a top and bottom border, select the top border and then select the bottom border. Both are applied.

- Some border options on the Borders menu apply more than one border. For example, the Outside Border option (top-left button) applies the outside border as well as the top, bottom, left, and right borders.

To apply text borders with the Borders and Shading dialog box

1. Select the text to which you want to apply borders.

2. Choose Format > Borders and Shading (**Figure 5**).

3. Click the Borders tab in the Borders and Shading dialog box that appears to display its options (**Figure 25**).

4. Click a Setting icon to select the type of border. All options except None and Custom place borders around each side of the selected text.

5. Click a style in the Style list to select a line style.

6. Choose a line color from the Color menu (**Figure 26**).

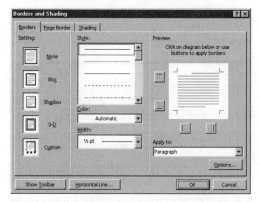

Figure 24 The Border menu on the Formatting toolbar. Each button illustrates where it will place a border (or multiple borders) when you select it.

Figure 25 The Borders tab of the Borders and Shading dialog box.

Figure 26 The Color menu in the Borders and Shading dialog box enables you to apply a specific color to a border.

APPLYING TEXT BORDERS

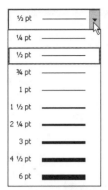

Figure 27
The Width menu in the Borders and Shading dialog box enables you to choose a border width.

Figure 28 The Apply to menu in the Borders and Shading dialog box offers two options when text is selected.

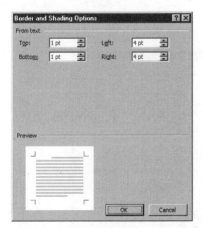

Figure 29 You can further customize a paragraph border with the Border and Shading Options dialog box.

7. Choose a line thickness from the Width menu (**Figure 27**).

8. If necessary, choose an option from the Apply to menu (**Figure 28**). The Preview area changes accordingly.

9. To apply custom borders, click the buttons in the Preview area to add or remove a line using the settings in the dialog box.

10. When the Preview area illustrates the kind of border that you want to apply, click OK.

✔ Tips

- You can repeat steps 5 through 7 and step 9 to customize each border of a custom paragraph border.

- You can further customize a paragraph border by clicking the Options button to display the Border and Shading Options dialog box (**Figure 29**). Set options as desired and click OK to return to the Borders and Shading dialog box.

To remove text borders

1. Select the text from which you want to remove borders.

2. Choose No Borders (the bottom-right option) from the Borders menu on the Formatting toolbar (**Figure 24**).

   or

   Choose Format > Borders and Shading (**Figure 5**), click the Borders tab in the Borders and Shading dialog box that appears (**Figure 25**), and click the None icon. Then click OK.

To apply page borders

1. If necessary, position the insertion point in the section of the document to which you want to apply page borders.

2. Choose Format > Borders and Shading (**Figure 5**).

3. Click the Page Border tab in the Borders and Shading dialog box that appears to display its options (**Figure 30**).

4. Click a Setting icon to select the type of border. All options except None and Custom place borders around each side of the page.

5. Click a style in the Style scrolling list to select a line style. Then choose a line color from the Color menu (**Figure 26**) and a line thickness from the Width menu (**Figure 27**).

6. If necessary, choose an option from the Apply to menu (**Figure 31**).

7. To apply custom borders, click the buttons in the Preview area to add or remove a line using the settings in the dialog box.

8. When the Preview area illustrates the kind of border that you want to apply, click OK.

✔ Tips

- You can repeat steps 5 and 7 to customize each border of a custom border.

- You can further customize a border by clicking the Options button to display the Border and Shading Options dialog box (**Figure 32**). Set options as desired and click OK to return to the Borders and Shading dialog box.

- If border art has been installed, you can use the Art menu in the Borders and Shading dialog box (**Figure 30**) to select a graphic border. Border art is not installed as part of a Typical Word or Office installation.

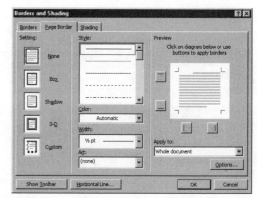

Figure 30 The Page Border tab of the Borders and Shading dialog box.

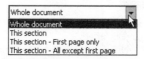

Figure 31 The Apply to menu in the Page Border tab of the Borders and Shading dialog box.

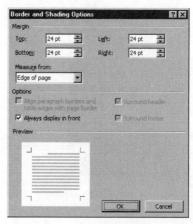

Figure 32 You can further customize a page border with the Border and Shading Options dialog box.

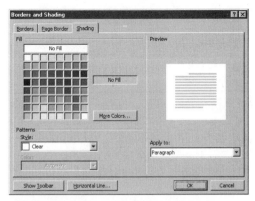

Figure 33 The Shading tab of the Borders and Shading dialog box.

Figure 34
The Style menu in the Patterns area. The first bunch of options are for shading percentages; the rest (not shown here) are for shading patterns.

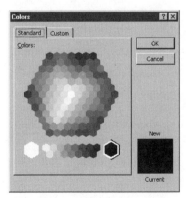

Figure 35 The Colors dialog box appears when you click the More Colors button.

To remove page borders

1. Position the insertion point in the section from which you want to remove borders.

2. Choose Format > Borders and Shading (**Figure 5**), click the Page Borders tab in the Borders and Shading dialog box that appears (**Figure 30**), and click the None icon. Then click OK.

To apply shading

1. Select the text to which you want to apply shading.

2. Choose Format > Borders and Shading (**Figure 5**).

3. Click the Shading tab in the Borders and Shading dialog box that appears to display its options (**Figure 33**).

4. Click a Fill color or shade to select it.

5. To create a pattern, choose an option from the Style menu (**Figure 34**) and then choose a color from the Color menu (**Figure 26**).

6. If necessary, choose an option from the Apply to menu (**Figure 28**). The Preview area changes accordingly.

7. When the Preview area illustrates the kind of shading that you want to apply, click OK.

✔ Tip

- You can choose from additional colors in step 4 by clicking the More Colors button to display the Colors dialog box (**Figure 35**).

To remove shading

1. Select the text from which you want to remove shading.

2. Choose Format > Borders and Shading (**Figure 5**), click the Shading tab in the Borders and Shading dialog box that appears (**Figure 33**), and click None. Then click OK.

PAGE BORDERS & TEXT SHADING

The Format Painter

The Format Painter enables you to copy the font or paragraph formatting of selected text and apply it to other text. This can save time and effort when applying the same formatting in multiple places throughout a document.

✔ Tip

■ Another way to apply the same formatting in various places throughout a document is with styles. I begin my discussion of Word's styles feature on the next page.

To use the Format Painter

1. Select the text whose formatting you want to copy (**Figure 36**).

2. Click the Format Painter button ✎ on the Standard toolbar. The Format Painter button is selected and the mouse pointer turns into an I-beam pointer with a tiny paint brush beside it (**Figure 37**).

3. Use the mouse pointer to select the text to which you want to copy the formatting (**Figure 38**).

When you release the mouse button, the formatting is applied (**Figure 39**) and the mouse pointer returns to normal.

✔ Tips

■ To copy paragraph formatting, be sure to select the entire paragraph in step 1, including the Return character formatting mark at the end of the paragraph. I tell you about formatting marks in **Chapter 2**.

■ To copy the same formatting to more than one selection, double-click the Format Painter button ✎. The mouse pointer remains a Format Painter pointer (**Figure 37**) until you press [Esc] or click the Format Painter button ✎ again.

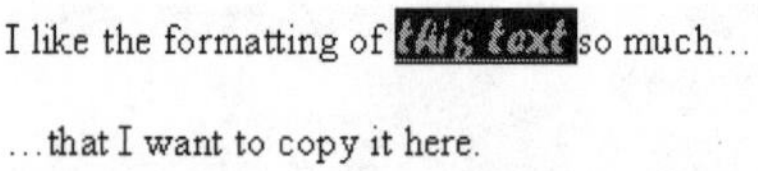

I like the formatting of this text so much…

…that I want to copy it here.

Figure 36 Select the text whose formatting you want to copy.

Figure 37 When you click the Format Painter button, the mouse pointer turns into a Format Painter pointer.

I like the formatting of *this text* so much…

…that I want to copy it here.

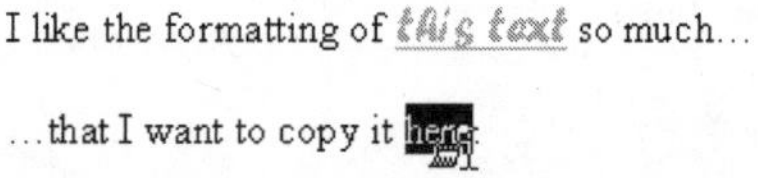

Figure 38 Use the Format Painter pointer to select the text to which you want to apply the formatting.

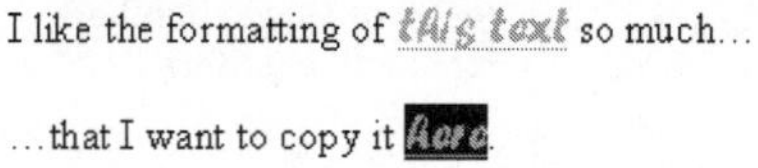

I like the formatting of *this text* so much…

…that I want to copy it here.

Figure 39 When you release the mouse button, the formatting is applied.

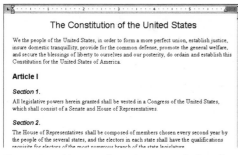

Figure 40 In this example, styles are applied to all text for consistent formatting.

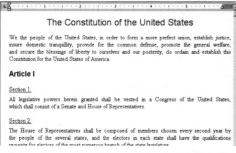

Figure 41 When two of the styles are modified, the formatting of all text with those styles applied changes automatically. In this example, Normal style's paragraph formatting was changed from align left to justified and Heading 2 style's font formatting was changed from bold italic Helvetica to underlined Times New Roman.

Styles

Word's *styles* feature enables you to define and apply sets of paragraph and/or font formatting to text throughout a document. This offers two main benefits over applying formatting using the basic techniques covered up to this point in the book:

- ◆ **Consistency.** All text with a particular style applied will have the same formatting (**Figure 40**)—unless additional formatting has also been applied.

- ◆ **Flexibility.** Changing a style's *definition*— the formatting that makes up the style—is relatively easy. Once changed, the change automatically applies to all text formatted with that style (**Figure 41**).

There are two kinds of styles:

- ◆ **Character styles** affect the formatting of characters. The default character style is called Default Paragraph Font and is based on the font formatting of the currently applied paragraph style.

- ◆ **Paragraph styles** affect the formatting of entire paragraphs. The default paragraph style is called Normal.

✔ Tips

- ■ Like font or paragraph formatting, you can apply character or paragraph styles as you type or to text that has already been typed. Check **Chapter 3** for details.

- ■ Styles are sometimes referred to as *style sheets*.

- ■ Word includes a number of predefined styles that you can apply to text.

- ■ Word's outline feature automatically applies predefined Heading styles as you create an outline. You can learn more about outlines in **Chapter 9**.

STYLES

To apply a style with the Style menu

Choose a style from the Style menu on the Formatting toolbar (**Figure 42**).

or

1. Click the name of the style in the Style menu's text box to select it (**Figure 43**).

2. Type in the exact name of the style that you want to apply (**Figure 44**).

3. Press ⎣Enter⎦.

✔ Tips

■ The Style menu displays the styles that have been applied in the document, the first three Heading styles, and Default Paragraph Font (**Figure 42**).

■ To include all built-in template styles on the Style menu, hold down ⎣Shift⎦ while clicking to display the menu (**Figure 45**).

■ The Style menu displays each style name using the formatting of that style (**Figure 42**).

■ You can distinguish between character styles and paragraph styles in the Style menu by the symbol to the right of the style name (**Figure 42**).

■ If you enter the name of a style that does not yet exist in the document in step 2 above, Word creates a new style for you, based on the selected paragraph. The formatting of the paragraph does not change, but the new style name appears on the Style menu.

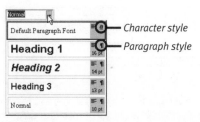

Figure 42 The Style menu on the Formatting toolbar.

Figure 43 Click the style name to select it...

Figure 44 ...then type in the name of the style that you want to apply.

Figure 45 You can hold down ⎣Shift⎦ while displaying the Style menu to see all available styles.

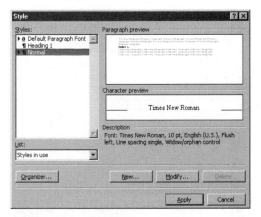

Figure 46 The Style dialog box.

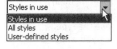

Figure 47 Use the List menu to determine which styles should appear in the Styles list.

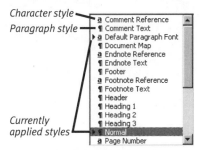

Character style
Paragraph style
Currently applied styles

Figure 48 Another example of the Styles in use list in the Style dialog box.

To apply a style with the Style dialog box

1. Choose Format > Style (**Figure 5**) to display the Style dialog box (**Figure 46**).

2. If necessary, use the List menu (**Figure 47**) to display a specific group of styles:

   ▲ **Styles in use** are the styles already applied within the document.

   ▲ **All styles** are the styles included within the template on which the document is based.

   ▲ **User-defined styles** are the styles that you add to the document.

3. Click on the name of the style that you want to apply to select it.

4. Click the Apply button.

✔ Tips

■ You can distinguish between character styles and paragraph styles in the Style dialog box by the symbol to the left of the style name (**Figure 48**).

■ Triangle markers appear to the left of the currently applied character and paragraph styles (**Figure 48**).

■ The Description area of the Style dialog box provides information about the formatting that the style includes (**Figure 46**).

To modify a style

1. Choose Format > Style (**Figure 5**) to display the Style dialog box (**Figure 46**).

2. If necessary, use the List menu (**Figure 47**) to display a specific group of styles.

3. Click the name of the style that you want to modify to select it.

4. Click the Modify button to display the Modify Style dialog box (**Figure 49**).

5. To change the style's name, enter a new name in the Name box.

6. To change the style that should be applied to the new paragraph created each time you press [Enter] with the current style applied, choose a style from the Style for following paragraph menu. (This step only applies if you are modifying a paragraph style.)

7. To change the style's formatting, choose an option from the Format menu in the dialog box (**Figure 50**). Each option displays the appropriate formatting dialog box.

8. Make changes as desired in the dialog box that appears and click OK.

9. Repeat steps 7 and 8 as necessary to make all desired formatting changes.

10. To add the revised style to the template on which the document is based, turn on the Add to template check box.

11. To instruct Word to automatically update the style's definition whenever you apply manual formatting to text with the style applied, turn on the Automatically update check box. (This step only applies if you are modifying a paragraph style.)

12. Click OK to save changes in the Modify Style dialog box.

13. Click the Close button to dismiss the Style dialog box.

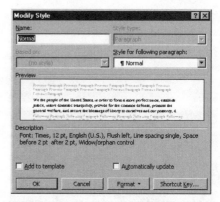

Figure 49 The Modify Style dialog box.

Figure 50
Use the Format menu in the Modify Style dialog box to choose the type of formatting you want to modify.

MODIFYING STYLES

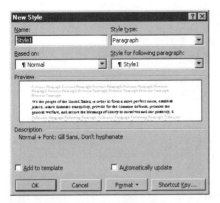

Figure 51 The New Style dialog box.

Figure 52 Use the Style type menu to specify the type of style you are creating.

To create a new style

1. Choose Format > Style (**Figure 5**) to display the Style dialog box (**Figure 46**).

2. Click the New button to display the New Style dialog box (**Figure 51**).

3. Enter a name for the style in the Name box.

4. Choose the type of style that you want to create from the Style type menu (**Figure 52**).

5. To base the style on an existing style, choose the style from the Based on menu. This menu lists all styles of the type you selected in step 4 that are included in the template on which the document is based.

6. To specify the style that should be applied to the new paragraph created each time you press (Enter) with the current style applied, choose a style from the Style for following paragraph menu. (This step only applies if you are creating a paragraph style.)

7. To specify the style's formatting, choose an option from the Format menu (**Figure 50**).

8. Make changes as desired in the dialog box that appears and click OK.

9. Repeat steps 7 and 8 as necessary to set all desired formatting options.

10. To add the new style to the template on which the document is based, turn on the Add to template check box.

11. To instruct Word to automatically update the style whenever you apply manual formatting to text with the style applied, turn on the Automatically update check box. (This step only applies if you are creating a paragraph style.)

12. Click OK to save changes in the New Style dialog box.

13. In the Style dialog box, click the Apply button to apply the new style to selected text; otherwise click the Close button to dismiss the Style dialog box.

To delete a style

1. Choose Format > Style (**Figure 5**) to display the Style dialog box (**Figure 46**).

2. If necessary, use the List menu (**Figure 47**) to display a specific group of styles.

3. Click to select the name of the style that you want to delete.

4. Click the Delete button.

5. Word asks you to confirm that you really do want to delete the style (**Figure 53**). Click Yes.

✔ Tip

■ When you delete a style, the default style (Normal for paragraph styles and Default Paragraph Font for character styles) is applied to any text to which the deleted style was applied.

To use the Style Gallery

1. Choose Format > Theme (**Figure 5**) to display the Theme dialog box.

2. Click the Style Gallery button.

3. In the Style Gallery dialog box that appears, click the name of a template in the Template list to select it. An example of the document with the template's styles applied appears in the Preview of area (**Figure 54**).

4. To apply the styles of a selected template to the current document, click OK.

   or

   To close the Style Gallery dialog box without changing styles, click Cancel.

✔ Tips

■ You can use the option buttons under the Template list to see other examples using the selected template (**Figures 55** and **56**).

■ I tell you about Themes in **Chapter 13**.

Figure 53 Word confirms that you really do want to delete the selected style.

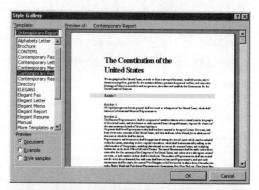

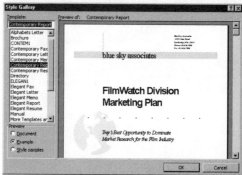

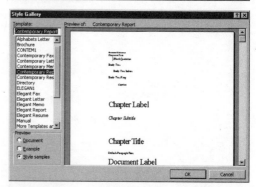

Figures 54, 55, & 56 The Style Gallery showing a template's styles applied to the active document (top), applied to a sample document (middle), and as samples (bottom).

Figure 57 The AutoFormat dialog box.

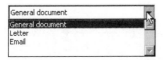

Figure 58 Use this menu to tell Word what kind of document it will format.

AutoFormat

Word's AutoFormat feature can automatically format a document either as you type or when the document is finished. Word formats documents by applying appropriate styles to text based on how it is used in the document—for example, as titles, lists, headings, or body text. Word can also format Internet addresses as hyperlinks and replace typed symbols (such as --) with actual symbols (such as —).

✔ Tip

■ I tell you more about Internet addresses and hyperlinks in **Chapter 13** and about symbols in **Chapter 7**.

To use AutoFormat on a completed document

1. Choose Format > AutoFormat (**Figure 5**) to display the AutoFormat dialog box (**Figure 57**).

2. To use AutoFormat without reviewing changes, select the AutoFormat now option button.

   or

   To review changes as you use AutoFormat, select the AutoFormat and review each change option button.

3. Select the appropriate type of document from the menu in the dialog box (**Figure 58**).

4. Click OK to begin the AutoFormat process.

   ▲ If you selected AutoFormat now in step 2, Word formats the document and displays it. The process is complete; the rest of the steps do not apply.

   ▲ If you selected AutoFormat and review each change in step 2, Word formats the document. Continue with step 5.

Continued on next page...

USING AUTOFORMAT

Continued from previous page.

5. A different AutoFormat dialog box appears (**Figure 59**). Click one of its four buttons to proceed:

▲ **Accept All** accepts all changes to the document. The AutoFormat process is complete; the rest of the steps do not apply.

▲ **Reject All** rejects all changes to the document. The AutoFormat process is reversed; the rest of the steps do not apply.

▲ **Review Changes** enables you to review the changes one by one. The Review AutoFormat Changes dialog box appears. Continue with step 6.

▲ **Style Gallery** displays the Style Gallery dialog box so you can select a different template's styles. I tell you how to use the Style Gallery earlier in this chapter. When you are finished using the Style Gallery, you will return to this dialog box; click one of the other buttons to continue.

6. In the Review AutoFormat Changes dialog box, click the second Find button to begin reviewing changes throughout the document (**Figure 60**):

▲ To accept a change, click the Find button again.

▲ To reject a change and move to the next change, click the Reject button.

7. Repeat step 6 to review every change.

8. Word tells you when you reach the end of the document (**Figure 61**). Click Cancel to dismiss the dialog box.

9. Click Cancel again to return to the Auto-Format Dialog box (**Figure 59**).

10. Click Accept All to accept all changes that you did not reject.

Figure 59 This AutoFormat dialog box appears when Word has finished the AutoFormat process and is waiting for you to review its changes.

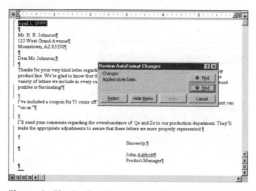

Figure 60 The Review AutoFormat Changes dialog box lets you accept or reject each change as it is highlighted in the document window.

Figure 61 Word tells you when you reach the end of the document.

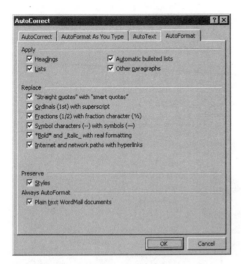

Figure 62 The AutoFormat tab of the AutoCorrect dialog box. These are the default settings.

To set AutoFormat options

1. Choose Format > AutoFormat (**Figure 5**) to display the AutoFormat dialog box (**Figure 57**).

2. Click the Options button. The AutoFormat tab of the AutoCorrect dialog box appears (**Figure 62**).

3. Set options as desired:

   ▲ **Headings** applies Heading styles to text that appears as a heading.

   ▲ **Lists** applies list and bullet styles to numbered, bulleted, and other lists.

   ▲ **Automatic bulleted lists** applies bulleted list formatting to paragraphs beginning with *, o, or - followed by a space or tab.

   ▲ **Other paragraphs** applies other styles such as Body Text, Inside Address, and Salutation.

   ▲ **"Straight quotes" with "smart quotes"** replaces plain quotes with curly quotes.

   ▲ **Ordinals (1st) with superscript** formats ordinals (1st) with superscript (1st).

   ▲ **Fractions (1/2) with fraction character ($^{1}/_{2}$)** replaces common fractions with fraction characters.

   ▲ **Symbol characters (- -) with symbols (—)** replaces single and double hyphens with en (–) or em (—) dashes.

   ▲ ***Bold* and _italic_ with real formatting** formats text between asterisks as bold and text between underscores as italic.

   ▲ **Internet paths with hyperlinks** formats URLs as clickable hyperlink fields.

   ▲ **Styles** prevents styles already applied in the document from being changed.

   ▲ **Plain text WordMail documents** always AutoFormats e-mail messages you open and edit with Word.

4. Click OK to save your settings.

✔ Tips

■ To convert other characters to corresponding symbols, such as (tm) to ™ or (c) to ©, use the AutoCorrect feature, which I explain in **Chapter 5**.

■ I tell you about hyperlinks and other Internet-related features in **Chapter 13**.

To set automatic formatting options

1. Choose Format > AutoFormat (**Figure 5**) to display the AutoFormat dialog box (**Figure 57**).

2. Click the Options button. The AutoFormat tab of the AutoCorrect dialog box appears (**Figure 62**).

3. Click the AutoFormat As You Type tab to display its options (**Figure 63**).

4. Set options as desired. Most of the options are the same as those in the AutoFormat tab, which I discuss on the previous page. Here are the others:

   ▲ **Borders** automatically applies paragraph border styles when you type three or more hyphens, underscores, or equal signs.

   ▲ **Tables** creates a table when you type a series of hyphens with plus signs to indicate column edges, such as:
   +----------+-----+.

   ▲ **Automatic numbered lists** applies numbered list formatting to paragraphs beginning with a number or letter followed by a space or tab.

   ▲ **Format beginning of list item like the one before it** repeats character formatting that you apply to the beginning of a list item. For example, if the first word of the previous list item was bold, the first word of the next list item is automatically formatted as bold.

   ▲ **Define styles based on your formatting** automatically creates or modifies styles based on manual formatting that you apply in the document.

5. Click OK to save your settings.

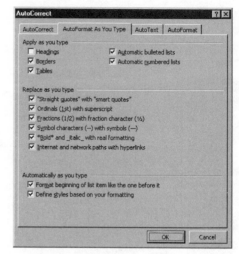

Figure 63 The AutoFormat As You Type tab of the AutoCorrect dialog box. These are the default settings.

✔ Tips

■ I tell you about borders, list formatting, and styles earlier in this chapter and about tables in **Chapter 10**.

■ Most AutoFormatting As You Type options are turned on by default. The only way to disable this feature is to turn off all options in the AutoFormat As You Type tab of the AutoCorrect dialog box (**Figure 63**).

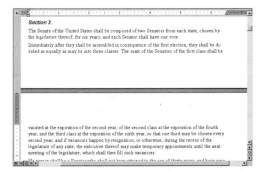

Figure 64 A page break in Print Layout view.

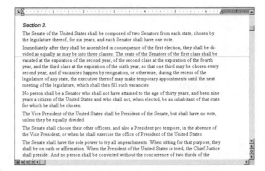

Figure 65 The same page break in Normal view.

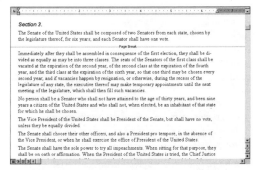

Figure 66 A manual page break adjusts all the subsequent automatic page breaks.

Page, Section, & Column Breaks

As you work with a document, Word automatically sets page breaks based on page size, margins, and contents. A *page break* marks the end of a page; anything after the page break will appear on the next page when the document is printed. This is easy to see in Print Layout view (**Figure 64**) and Print Preview. In Normal view, automatic page breaks appear as dotted lines across the document (**Figure 65**).

Although you cannot change an automatic page break directly, you can change it indirectly by inserting a manual page break before it (**Figure 66**). This forces the page to end where you specify and, in most cases, forces subsequent automatic page breaks in the document to change.

In addition to page breaks, Word also enables you to insert section and column breaks. A *section break* marks the end of a document section. Sections are commonly used to divide a document into logical parts, each of which can have its own settings in the Page Setup dialog box. A *column break* marks the end of a column of text. Column breaks are usually used in conjunction with multi-column text.

✔ Tips

- Automatic page breaks do not appear in Online Layout, Outline, or Master Document view.

- As discussed in **Chapter 3**, section breaks may be automatically inserted by Word in a document when you change settings in the Document dialog box.

- I tell you more about columns and multi-column text a little later in this chapter.

To insert a break

1. Position the insertion point where you want the break to occur (**Figure 67**).

2. Choose Insert > Break (**Figure 68**).

3. In the Break dialog box that appears (**Figure 69**), select the option button for the type of break that you want to insert. Your options are:

   ▲ **Page break** inserts a page break.

   ▲ **Column break** inserts a column break.

   ▲ **Text wrapping break** is used for formatting Web pages; I discuss it in **Chapter 13**.

   ▲ **Next page** inserts a section break that also acts as a page break.

   ▲ **Continuous** inserts a section break in the middle of a page.

   ▲ **Even page** inserts a section break that acts as a page break. The following page will always be an even-numbered page.

   ▲ **Odd page** inserts a section break that acts as a page break. The following page will always be an odd-numbered page.

4. Click OK to insert the break. **Figure 66** shows an inserted page break.

or

1. Position the insertion point where you want the break to occur (**Figure 67**).

2. Use one of the following shortcut keys:

   ▲ To insert a page break, press Ctrl Enter.

   ▲ To insert a column break, press Ctrl Shift Enter.

To remove a break

1. In Normal view, select the break by clicking in the selection bar to its left (**Figure 70**).

2. Press Backspace or Delete.

Section 3.

The Senate of the United States shall be composed of tw the legislature thereof, for six years; and each Senator sl

Immediately after they shall be assembled in consequen vided as equally as may be into three classes. The seats vacated at the expiration of the second year, of the secol year, and the third class at the expiration of the sixth yea second year; and if vacancies happen by resignation, or legislature of any state, the executive thereof may make meeting of the legislature, which shall then fill such vac

Figure 67 Position the insertion point where you want the break to occur.

Figure 68
The Insert menu.

Figure 69
The Break dialog box.

Figure 70 Click in the selection bar to the left of the break to select it.

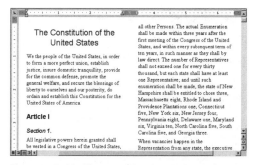

Figure 71 Multi-column text in Print Layout view.

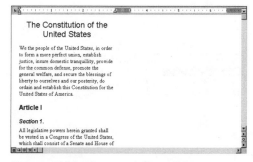

Figure 72 Multi-column text in Normal view.

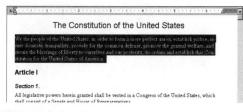

Figure 73 Select the text for which you want to set columns.

Figure 74
Choose the number of columns you want from the Columns menu on the Standard toolbar.

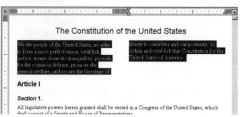

Figure 75 Word sets the columns for the selected text, inserting section breaks, if necessary.

Columns

Word enables you to format text with multiple columns, like those in a newspaper.

✔ Tips

- Although you can edit multi-column text in any view, you must be in Print Layout view (**Figure 71**) or Print Preview to see the columns side by side. In Normal view, the text appears in the same narrow column (**Figure 72**).

- Column formatting applies to sections of text. You can insert section breaks as discussed on the previous page to set up various multi-column sections.

To set the number of columns

1. Select the text for which you want to set the number of columns (**Figure 73**).

2. Click the Columns button ▦ on the Standard toolbar to display a menu of columns (**Figure 74**) and choose the number of columns you want.

3. If you are not in Print Layout view, word automatically switches to it to show the multiple-column text (**Figure 75**).

✔ Tips

- To set the number of columns for an entire single-section document, in step 1 above, position the insertion point anywhere in the document.

- To set the number of columns for one section of a multi-section document, in step 1 above, position the insertion point anywhere in the section.

- If necessary, Word inserts section breaks to mark the beginning and end of multi-column text.

To set column options

1. Position the insertion point in the section for which you want to change column options.

   or

   Select the sections for which you want to change column options.

2. Choose Format > Columns (**Figure 5**) to display the Columns dialog box (**Figure 76**).

3. To set the number of columns, click one of the icons in the Presets section or enter a value in the Number of columns box.

4. To set different column widths for each column, make sure the Equal column width check box is turned off, then enter values in the Width boxes for each column. You can also enter values in the Spacing boxes to specify the amount of space between columns.

5. To put a vertical line between columns, turn on the Line between check box.

6. To specify the part of the document that you want the changes to apply to, choose an option from the Apply to menu (**Figure 77**).

   or

   To insert a column break at the insertion point, choose This point forward from the Apply to menu (**Figure 77**), then turn on the Start new column check box.

7. When you are finished setting options, click OK to save them.

✔ Tip

■ You can see the effect of your changes in the Preview area as you change settings in the Columns dialog box.

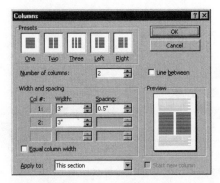

Figure 76 The Columns dialog box.

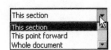

Figure 77 Use the Apply to menu to specify what part of the document the column settings should apply to.

Figure 78
The View menu.

Figure 79 The Header area of a document window.

Figure 80 The Footer area of a document window.

Headers & Footers

A *header* is a part of the document that appears at the top of every page. A *footer* is a part of the document that appears at the bottom of every page. Headers and footers are commonly used to place page numbers, revision dates, or other document information on document pages.

To display a header or footer

Choose Header and Footer from the View menu (**Figure 78**).

If necessary, Word switches to Print Layout view and displays the Header area of the current document section and the Header and Footer toolbar (**Figure 79**).

◆ To view the footer for the current section, click the Switch Between Header and Footer button 🖫 on the Header and Footer toolbar. The Footer area appears (**Figure 80**).

◆ To view the header or footer for the previous or next section of a multi-section document, click the Show Previous 🖫 or Show Next 🖫 button on the Header and Footer toolbar.

To hide a header or footer

Click the Close button in the Header and Footer toolbar.

or

Double-click anywhere in the document window other than in the Header or Footer area.

The document returns to the view you were in before you viewed the header or footer and the Header and Footer toolbar disappears.

To create a header or footer

1. Display the Header or Footer area (**Figure 79** or **80**) for the header or footer that you want to create.

2. Enter the header (**Figure 81**) or footer (**Figure 82**) information.

3. When you're finished, hide the header or footer area to continue working on the document.

✔ Tip

■ You can format the contents of a header or footer the same way that you format any other part of the document. You can find detailed formatting instructions in **Chapter 3** and earlier in this chapter.

To edit a header or footer

1. Display the header (**Figure 81**) or footer (**Figure 82**) area for the header or footer that you want to edit.

2. Edit the header or footer information.

3. When you're finished, hide the header or footer area to continue working on the document.

Header - Section 1 -
The Constitution of the United States

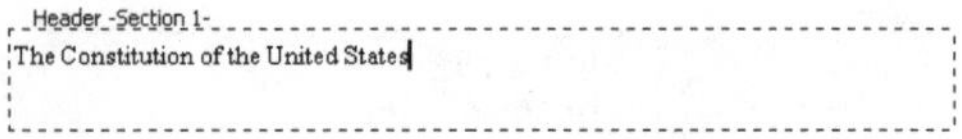

Figure 81 A simple header.

Footer - Section 1 -
Revised 3/19/1789

Figure 82 A simple footer.

CREATING & EDITING HEADERS & FOOTERS

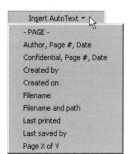

Figure 83
The Insert AutoText menu on the Header and Footer toolbar.

Figure 84 This footer example uses Word fields to insert the date (which will change each day the document is printed), page number (which will change for each page), and total number of pages (which will change if the document length changes).

Figure 85 The Page Number Format dialog box lets you set options for formatting page numbers.

To insert AutoText entries or Word fields in a header or footer

1. Position the insertion point in the Header or Footer area where you want the Auto-Text entry or field to appear.

2. To insert an AutoText entry, click the Insert AutoText button on the Header and Footer toolbar to display a menu of entries (**Figure 83**). Choose the one that you want to insert.

3. To insert a Word field, click the appropriate button on the Header and Footer toolbar (**Figure 84**) to insert the field:

   ▲ **Insert Page Number** ⊞ inserts the current page number.

   ▲ **Insert Number of Pages** ⊞ inserts the total number of pages in the document.

   ▲ **Insert Date** ⊞ inserts the current date.

   ▲ **Insert Time** ⊘ inserts the current time.

✔ Tips

- I tell you about AutoText entries and Word fields in **Chapter 7**.

- Word fields change as necessary to provide accurate, up-to-date information.

- To number pages, use the Insert Page Number button ⊞ on the Header and Footer toolbar to insert a page number in the header or footer. **Figure 84** shows an example. *This is the best way to number pages in a document.* Using the Page Numbers command on the Insert menu inserts page numbers in frames that can be difficult to work with. The Page Numbers command is not covered in this book.

- To format page numbers, click the Format Page Number button ⊞ on the Header and Footer toolbar. Then use the Page Number Format dialog box (**Figure 85**) to set formatting options and click OK.

USING FIELDS IN HEADERS & FOOTERS

To create a different first page or odd and even header and footer

1. Choose File > Page Setup (**Figure 86**) to display the Page Setup dialog box. If necessary, click the Layout tab.

   or

   Click the Page Setup button  on the Header and Footer toolbar.

   The Layout tab of the Page Setup dialog box appears (**Figure 87**).

2. To create a different header and footer on odd- and even-numbered pages of the document, turn on the Different odd and even check box.

3. To create a different header and footer on the first page of the document or document section, turn on the Different first page check box.

4. Click OK.

5. Follow the instructions on the previous pages to create headers and footers as desired. Use the Show Previous <img> and Show Next <img> buttons on the Header and Footer toolbar to display and edit each header and footer.

To remove a header or footer

1. Display the Header or Footer area for the header or footer that you want to remove.

2. Select its contents and press (Backspace) or (Delete). The header or footer is removed.

3. Hide the header or footer area to continue working on the document.

Figure 86
The File menu.

Figure 87 The Layout tab of the Page Setup dialog box.

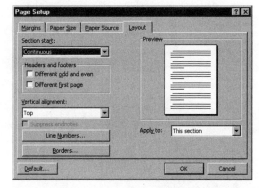

WRITING TOOLS 5

Word's Writing Tools

Word includes a number of features to help you be a better writer. Some of these features can help you find and fix errors in your documents, while other features can help you fine tune your documents for publication.

This chapter covers the following writing tools:

◆ The **spelling checker** compares words in your document to words in dictionary files to identify unknown words.

◆ The **grammar checker** checks sentences against a collection of grammar rules to identify questionable sentence construction.

◆ **AutoCorrect** automatically corrects common errors as you type.

◆ The **thesaurus** enables you to find synonyms or antonyms for words in your document.

◆ **Hyphenation** automatically hyphenates words based on hyphenation rules.

◆ **Word count** counts the words in a selection or the entire document.

◆ The **change-tracking** feature enables you to review and incorporate edits by other people who work on the document.

✔ Tip

■ No proofing tool is a substitute for carefully rereading a document to manually check it for errors. Use Word's spelling and grammar checkers to help you find and fix errors, but don't depend on them to find all spelling or grammar errors in your documents.

The Spelling & Grammar Checkers

Word's spelling and grammar checkers help you to identify potential spelling and grammar problems in your documents. They can be set to check text automatically as you type or when you have finished typing.

The spelling checker compares the words in a document to the words in its main spelling dictionary, which includes over 100,000 words. If it cannot find a match for a word, it then checks the active custom dictionaries—the dictionary files that you create. If Word still cannot find a match, it flags the word as unknown so you can act on it.

The grammar checker works in much the same way. It compares the structure of sentences in the document with predetermined rules for a specific writing style. When it finds a sentence or sentence fragment with a potential problem, it identifies it for you so you can act on it.

Both the spelling and grammar checkers are highly customizable so they work the way that you want them to.

✔ Tips

■ The spelling checker cannot identify a misspelled word if it correctly spells another word. For example, if you type *from* when you meant to type *form*, the spelling checker would not find the error. The grammar checker, on the other hand, might find this particular error, depending on its usage.

■ Do not add a word to a custom dictionary unless you know it is correctly spelled. Otherwise, the word will never be flagged as an error.

Figure 1
The Tools menu is where you'll find most of Word's writing tools.

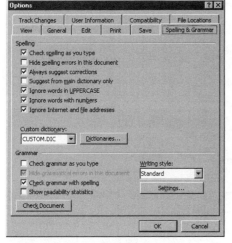

Figure 2 The default settings in the Spelling & Grammar tab of the Options dialog box.

To enable or disable automatic spelling and/or grammar checking

1. Choose Tools > Options (**Figure 1**).

2. In the Options dialog box that appears, click the Spelling & Grammar tab to display its options (**Figure 2**).

3. To enable automatic spelling checking, turn on the Check spelling as you type check box.

   or

   To disable automatic spelling checking, turn off the Check spelling as you type check box.

4. To enable automatic grammar checking, turn on the Check grammar as you type check box.

   or

   To disable automatic grammar checking, turn off the Check grammar as you type check box.

5. Click OK.

✔ Tips

- By default, Word is set up to automatically check spelling, but not grammar, as you type.

- I explain how to set other spelling and grammar preferences in **Chapter 14**.

To check spelling as you type

1. Make sure that the automatic spelling checking feature has been enabled.

2. As you enter text into the document, a red wavy underline appears beneath each unknown word (**Figure 3**).

3. Right-click on a flagged word. The spelling shortcut menu appears (**Figure 4**).

4. Choose the appropriate option:

   ▲ Suggested spellings appear at the top of the menu. Choosing one changes the word and removes the wavy underline.

   ▲ **Ignore All** tells Word to ignore all occurrences of the word in the document. Choosing this option removes the wavy underline from the word throughout the document.

   ▲ **Add** adds the word to the current custom dictionary. The wavy underline disappears and the word is never flagged again as unknown.

   ▲ **AutoCorrect** enables you to create an AutoCorrect entry for the word using one of the suggested spellings. Choose the appropriate word from the submenu (**Figure 5**). The word is replaced in the document and will be automatically replaced each time you type in the unknown word.

   ▲ **Language** enables you to change the language of the spelling dictionary.

   ▲ **Spelling** opens the Spelling dialog box (**Figure 6**), which offers more options.

✔ Tips

■ As shown in **Figure 7**, Word's spelling checker also identifies repeated words and offers appropriate options.

■ I tell you more about AutoCorrect and the Spelling dialog box later in this chapter.

The Constitution of the United

Figure 3 Two possible errors identified by the spelling checker.

Figure 4
A shortcut menu displays options to fix a possible spelling problem.

Figure 5
The AutoCorrect option displays a submenu with the suggested words. Choose one to create an AutoCorrect entry.

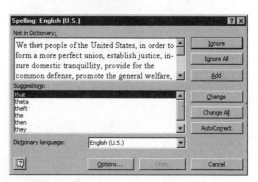

Figure 6 The Spelling dialog box offers additional options for dealing with possible spelling errors. This dialog box is very similar to the Spelling and Grammar dialog box shown in **Figure 13**.

Figure 7 The shortcut menu offers different options for repeated words.

The Constitution of the United States

We the people of the United States, in order to form a more perfect union, establish justice, insure domestic tranquillity, provide for the common defense, promote the general welfare, and secure the blessings of liberty to ~~ourselves and our posterity,~~ do ordain and establish this Constitution for the United States of America.

Article I

Section 1.

All legislative powers herein granted ~~shall~~ be vested in a Congress of the United States, which shall consist of a Senate and House of Representatives.

Figure 8 Two possible errors identified by the grammar checker.

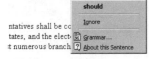

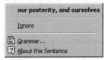

Figures 9 & 10 Using the grammar shortcut menu to correct possible grammar problems.

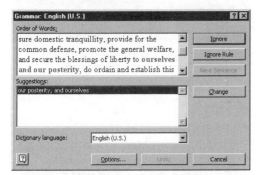

Figure 11 The Grammar dialog box offers additional options for working with possible grammar problems. This dialog box is very similar to the Spelling and Grammar dialog box shown in **Figure 14**.

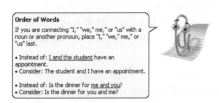

Figure 12 Word can display information about the grammar rule that caused the problem to be flagged.

To check grammar as you type

1. Make sure that the automatic grammar checking feature has been enabled.

2. As you enter text into the document, a green wavy underline appears beneath each questionable word, phrase, or sentence (**Figure 8**).

3. Right-click on a flagged problem. The grammar shortcut menu appears (**Figures 9** and **10**).

4. Choose the appropriate option:

   ▲ Suggested corrections appear at the top of the shortcut menu. Choosing one of these corrections changes the text and removes the wavy underline.

   ▲ **Ignore** tells Word to ignore the problem. Choosing this option removes the wavy underline.

   ▲ **Grammar** opens the Grammar dialog box (**Figure 11**), which offers additional options.

   ▲ **About this Sentence** displays information about the grammar rule that caused the sentence to be flagged (**Figure 12**).

✔ Tips

■ I tell you more about the Grammar dialog box later in this chapter.

■ Word's grammar checker doesn't always have a suggestion to fix a problem.

■ Don't choose a suggestion without examining it carefully. The suggestion Word offers may not be correct or, as shown in **Figure 10**, it may change the meaning of the sentence.

To check spelling and grammar at once

1. Choose Tools > Spelling and Grammar (**Figure 1**) or press F7.

   or

   Click the Spelling and Grammar button
   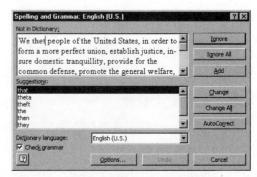 on the Standard toolbar.

   Word begins checking spelling and grammar. When it finds a possible error, it displays the Spelling and Grammar dialog box (**Figure 13** or **14**).

Figure 13 The Spelling and Grammar dialog box displaying options for a spelling problem.

2. For a spelling or grammar problem:

   ▲ To ignore the problem, click Ignore.

   ▲ To ignore all occurrences of the problem in the document, click Ignore All (spelling) or Ignore Rule (grammar).

   ▲ To use one of Word's suggestions, click the suggestion and then click Change.

   ▲ To change the problem manually, edit the text in the top part of the dialog box. Then click Change.

   For a spelling problem only:

   ▲ To add the word to the current custom dictionary, click Add.

   ▲ To change all occurrences of the word throughout the document to one of the suggestions, click the suggestion and then click Change All.

   ▲ To create an AutoCorrect entry for the word, select one of the suggestions and then click AutoCorrect.

   For a grammar problem only:

   ▲ To skip the current sentence, click Next Sentence.

3. Word continues checking spelling and grammar. It displays the Spelling and Grammar dialog box for each possible error. Repeat step 2 until the entire document has been checked.

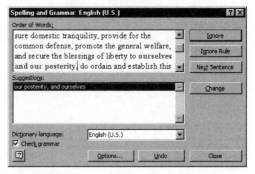

Figure 14 The Spelling and Grammar dialog box displaying options for a grammar problem.

✔ Tips

■ The Spelling and Grammar dialog box contains elements found in both the Spelling dialog box (**Figure 6**) and the Grammar dialog box (**Figure 11**).

■ If the Office Assistant is open, a balloon appears to explain each grammar problem Word finds (**Figure 12**). If the Office Assistant is not open, you can click the Help button in the Spelling and Grammar dialog box to display it and the additional information.

■ To disable grammar checking during a manual spelling check, turn off the Check grammar check box in the Spelling and Grammar dialog box (**Figure 13**).

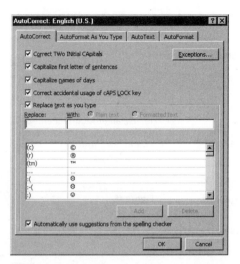

Figure 15 The AutoCorrect tab of the AutoCorrect dialog box.

AutoCorrect

Word's AutoCorrect feature can correct common errors as you make them. You set up AutoCorrect entries by entering the incorrect and correct text in the AutoCorrect dialog box. Then, each time you make an error for which an AutoCorrect entry exists, Word automatically replaces the error with the correction.

✔ Tips

- Word comes preconfigured with hundreds of AutoCorrect entries.

- AutoCorrect is enabled by default.

To set AutoCorrect options

1. Choose Tools > AutoCorrect (**Figure 1**).

2. The AutoCorrect dialog box appears. If necessary, click the AutoCorrect tab to display its options (**Figure 15**).

3. Set options as desired:

   ▲ **Correct TWo INitial CApitals** changes the second letter in a pair of capital letters to lowercase.

   ▲ **Capitalize first letter of sentences** capitalizes the first letter following the end of a sentence.

   ▲ **Capitalize names of days** capitalizes the names of the days of the week.

   ▲ **Correct accidental usage of cAPS LOCK key** corrects the capitalization of any word you type in Title Case with the Caps Lock key on.

   ▲ **Replace text as you type** enables the AutoCorrect feature for the AutoCorrect entries in the bottom of the dialog box.

   ▲ **Automatically use suggestions from the spelling checker** replaces unknown words with words from the spelling checker's dictionary.

4. Click OK to save your settings.

✔ Tip

- To disable AutoCorrect, turn off all check boxes in the AutoCorrect tab of the Auto-Correct dialog box.

AUTOCORRECT

To add an AutoCorrect entry

1. Choose Tools > AutoCorrect (**Figure 1**).
2. The AutoCorrect dialog box appears. If necessary, click the AutoCorrect tab to display its options (**Figure 15**).
3. Type the text that you want to automatically replace in the Replace box.
4. Type the text that you want to replace it with in the With box (**Figure 16**).
5. Click the Add button.
6. Click OK.

✔ Tip

- To add a formatted text entry, enter and format the replacement text in your document. Then select that text and follow the steps above. Make sure the Formatted text option button is selected before clicking the Add button in step 5.

To use AutoCorrect

Type the text that appears on the Replace side of the AutoCorrect entries list (**Figure 17**). When you press Spacebar, Enter, Shift Enter, or some punctuation, the text you typed changes to the corresponding text on the With side of the AutoCorrect entries list (**Figure 18**).

To delete an AutoCorrect entry

1. Choose Tools > AutoCorrect (**Figure 1**).
2. The AutoCorrect dialog box appears. If necessary, click the AutoCorrect tab to display its options (**Figure 15**).
3. Scroll through the list of AutoCorrect entries in the bottom half of the dialog box to find the entry that you want to delete and click it once to select it.
4. Click the Delete button.
5. Click OK to save your change and dismiss the AutoCorrect dialog box.

Replace:
With:
Plain text
Formatted text
mll
Maria L. Langer

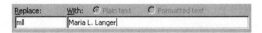

Figure 16 The two parts of an AutoCorrect entry.

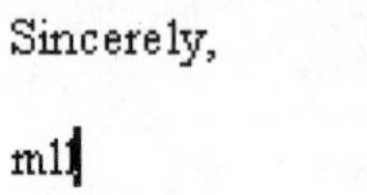

Sincerely,
mll

Figure 17
To use an AutoCorrect entry, type the text from the Replace part of the entry...

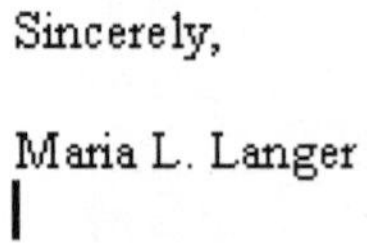

Sincerely,
Maria L. Langer

Figure 18
...and the With part of the entry appears automatically as you continue typing.

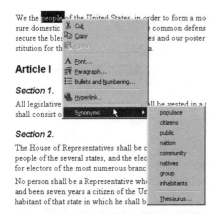

Figure 19 The shortcut menu for a word may include synonyms.

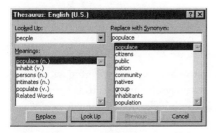

Figure 20
The Language submenu under the Tools menu.

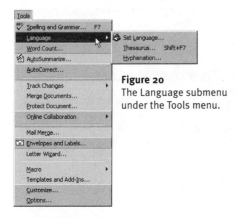

Figure 21 The Thesaurus dialog box.

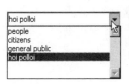

Figure 22
The Looked Up menu keeps track of all the words you've looked up.

The Thesaurus

Word's thesaurus enables you to find synonyms or antonyms for words in your document—right on your computer.

To find a synonym quickly

1. Right-click on the word for which you want to find a synonym.

2. A shortcut menu appears. If the Synonyms option is available, click it to display a sub-menu of synonyms for the word (**Figure 19**).

3. To replace the word with one of the synonyms, choose it from the submenu.

To use the Thesaurus dialog box

1. Select the word for which you want to find a synonym or antonym.

2. Choose Tools > Language > Thesaurus (**Figure 20**) or press (Shift)(F7) to display the Thesaurus dialog box (**Figure 21**).

3. Click to select a meaning in the Meanings list. A list of synonyms (or antonyms) appears on the right side of the dialog box.

4. To replace the selected word, click to select the synonym or antonym with which you want to replace it. Then click Replace. The dialog box disappears.

    or

    To look up a synonym or antonym, click it to select it and then click Look Up. Then repeat step 3.

✔ Tips

■ The Looked Up menu (**Figure 22**) keeps track of all the words you looked up while using the Thesaurus dialog box. Choose a word from the menu to look it up again.

■ To close the Thesaurus dialog box without replacing a word, click its Cancel or close button.

THE THESAURUS

Hyphenation

Word's hyphenation feature can hyphenate words so they fit better on a line. Word can hyphenate the words in your documents automatically as you type or manually when you have finished typing.

✔ Tips

- Hyphenation helps prevent ragged right margins in left aligned text and large gaps between words in full justified text. I tell you about alignment in **Chapter 3**.

- To prevent text from being hyphenated, select it and then turn on the Don't hyphenate option in the Line and Page Breaks tab of the Paragraph dialog box (**Figure 23**). I explain other options in the Paragraph dialog box in **Chapters 3** and **4**.

To set hyphenation options

1. Choose Tools > Language > Hyphenation (**Figure 20**) to display the Hyphenation dialog box (**Figure 24**).

2. Set options as desired:

   ▲ **Automatically hyphenate document** enables automatic hyphenation as you type.

   ▲ **Hyphenate words in CAPS** hyphenates words entered in all uppercase letters, such as acronyms.

   ▲ **Hyphenation zone** is the distance from the right indent within which you want to hyphenate the document. The lower the value you enter, the more words are hyphenated.

   ▲ **Limit consecutive hyphens to** is the maximum number of hyphens that can appear in a row.

3. Click OK.

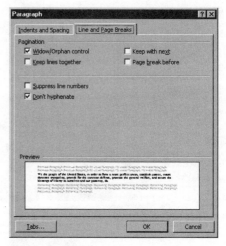

Figure 23 Use the Line and Page Breaks tab of the Paragraph dialog box to prevent hyphenation in selected paragraphs.

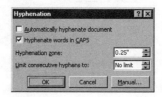

Figure 24 The default settings in the Hyphenation dialog box.

✔ Tips

- To remove hyphenation inserted with the automatic hyphenation feature, turn off the Automatically hyphenate document check box in the Hyphenation dialog box (**Figure 24**).

- Use the Limit consecutive hyphens to option to prevent excessive hyphenation in your document, thus enhancing a document's appearance.

HYPHENATION

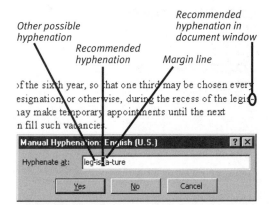

Other possible hyphenation

Recommended hyphenation

Recommended hyphenation in document window

Margin line

of the sixth year, so that one third may be chosen every esignation, or otherwise, during the recess of the legis- lay make temporary appointments until the next n fill such vacancies.

Figure 25 The Manual Hyphenation dialog box in action.

To manually hyphenate a document

1. Follow steps 1 and 2 on the previous page to open the Hyphenation dialog box (**Figure 24**) and set options. Be sure to leave the Automatically hyphenate document check box turned off.

2. Click the Manual button. Word begins searching for hyphenation candidates. When it finds one, it displays the Manual Hyphenation dialog box (**Figure 25**).

3. Do one of the following:

   ▲ To hyphenate the word at the recommended break, click Yes.

   ▲ To hyphenate the word at a different break, click the hyphen at the desired break and then click Yes. (The hyphen that you click must be to the left of the gray margin line.)

   ▲ To continue without hyphenating the word, click No.

4. Word continues looking for hyphenation candidates. It displays the Manual Hyphenation dialog box for each one. Repeat step 3 until the entire document has been hyphenated.

✔ Tips

■ To hyphenate only part of a document, select the part that you want to hyphenate before following the above steps.

■ You can also manually insert two types of special hyphens within words:

   ▲ Press (Ctrl)(-) to insert an *optional hyphen*, which only breaks the word when necessary. Use this to manually hyphenate a word without using the Manual Hyphenation dialog box.

   ▲ Press (Shift)(Ctrl)(-) to insert a *non-breaking hyphen*, which displays a hyphen but never breaks the word.

MANUALLY HYPHENATING

Word Count

The word count feature counts the pages, words, characters, paragraphs, and lines in a selection or the entire document.

✔ Tip

■ The word count feature is especially useful for writers who often have word count limitations or get paid by the word.

To count words

1. If necessary, select the text that you want to count.

2. Choose Tools > Word Count (**Figure 1**) to display the Word Count dialog box. After a moment, complete count figures appear (**Figure 26**).

3. To include footnotes and endnotes in the count, turn on the Include footnotes and endnotes check box.

4. When you are finished working with the count figures, click Close to dismiss the dialog box.

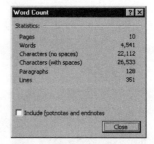

Figure 26 The Word Count dialog box.

Changed   Inserted   Deleted
lines   text   text

We the people of the United States of America, in order to form a more perfect union, establish justice, insure domestic tranquility, provide for the common defense, promote the general welfare, and secure the blessings of liberty to ourselves and our posterity,our posterity, and ourselves do ordain and establish this Constitution for the United States of America.

Figure 27 Revision marks show inserted and deleted text and mark every changed line.

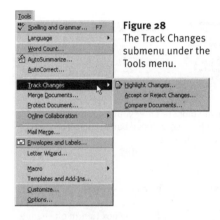

Figure 28
The Track Changes submenu under the Tools menu.

Figure 29 The Highlight Changes dialog box.

Change-Tracking

Word's change-tracking feature enables you to share a document with other contributors or editors. Although each editor can make changes to the document, the changes are not finalized. Instead, changes appear as *revision marks* (**Figure 27**) that indicate what text was added, removed, or modified and which editor made the change. At the end of the editing process, you can review each edit and accept or reject it to finalize the document.

✔ Tip

- The change-tracking feature is also known as the revision or reviewing feature.

To enable/disable change-tracking

1. Choose Tools > Track Changes > Highlight Changes (**Figure 28**).

2. The Highlight Changes dialog box appears (**Figure 29**).

   To enable change-tracking, turn on the Track changes while editing check box.

   or

   To disable change-tracking, turn off the Track changes while editing check box.

3. Set other options as desired:

   ▲ **Highlight changes on screen** displays document changes on screen using revision marks (**Figure 27**).

   ▲ **Highlight changes in printed document** displays revision marks when the document is printed.

4. Click OK.

To prevent someone from disabling change tracking

1. Choose Tools > Protect Document (**Figure 1**) to display the Protect Document dialog box (**Figure 30**).

2. Make sure the Tracked changes option is selected.

3. Enter a password in the Password box.

4. Click OK.

5. In the Confirm Password dialog box that appears (**Figure 31**), re-enter the password and click OK.

✔ Tip

- This feature is especially useful when circulating a document among several editors, especially if one or more of them may prefer not to use the change-tracking feature.

- Once a document is password protected for Tracked Changes, a password must be provided to disable the change-tracking feature. Choose Tools > Unprotect Document to display the Unprotect Document dialog box (**Figure 32**), enter the password in the Password box, and click OK.

- Do not lose or forget the password! Without the password, change-tracking cannot be disabled!

To track changes

Use standard editing techniques to modify the document. Your changes are indicated with colored revision marks (**Figure 27**).

Figure 30
The Protect Document dialog box offers a way to ensure that all changes are tracked.

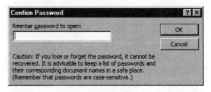

Figure 31 You must re-enter your password in the Confirm Password dialog box to complete the protection process.

Figure 32
Use the Unprotect Document dialog box to turn off change tracking protection.

Figure 33 The Accept or Reject Changes dialog box.

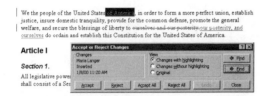

Figure 34 Word provides information about who made a change and when it was made and offers options for dealing with it.

To review tracked changes

1. If change-tracking is enabled, turn it off.

2. Choose Tools > Track Changes > Accept or Reject Changes (**Figure 28**) to display the Accept or Reject Changes dialog box (**Figure 33**).

3. Click the second Find button to highlight a change (**Figure 34**).

4. Act on the change using one of the following options:

   ▲ **Accept** incorporates the change into the document and moves on to the next change.

   ▲ **Reject** removes the change from the document and moves on to the next change.

   ▲ **Accept All** incorporates all changes into the document.

   ▲ **Reject All** removes all changes from the document.

   ▲ **Undo** reverses your action for the previous change. (This option is only available after you have acted on at least one change.)

   ▲ **Close** closes the Accept or Reject Changes dialog box without continuing.

   ▲ **Find** skips the selected change and moves on to another one.

5. Repeat step 4 until you have reviewed and acted on all changes.

6. Click Close in the Accept or Reject Changes dialog box.

Continued on next page...

REVIEWING TRACKED CHANGES

Continued from previous page.

✔ Tips

- You can select options in the View area of the Accept or Reject Changes dialog box (**Figure 33**) to see the document with changes highlighted, with changes not highlighted (as if all changes were accepted), and without changes (as if no changes were made).

- You can also review changes one-by-one. Right-click on a change to display a shortcut menu like the one in **Figure 35**. Select the appropriate option for dealing with the change.

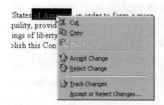

Figure 35 You can also act on individual changes with a shortcut menu.

PRINTING DOCUMENTS

Printing Documents

In most cases, when you're finished writing, formatting, and proofreading a document, you'll want to print it. This chapter tells you about the three parts to the printing process:

- **Page Setup** enables you to specify information about the paper size, print orientation, and paper source options.

- **Print Preview** enables you to view the document on screen before you print it. You can also use this view to set page breaks and margins to fine-tune printed appearance.

- **Print** enables you to specify the page range, number of copies, and other options for printing. It then sends the document to your printer.

✔ Tips

- Although it's a good idea to go through all three of the above parts of the printing process, you don't have to. You can just print. But as I explain throughout this chapter, each part of the printing process has its own purpose that may benefit a print job.

- When you save a document, Word saves most Page Setup and Print options with it.

- I provide specific information for printing mailing labels, form letters, and envelopes in **Chapters 11** and **12**.

Page Setup

The Page Setup dialog box (**Figures 1** and **2**) enables you to set a number of options to be used when printing your document. Here's a list of the most commonly offered options:

- **Paper Size** is the size of the paper. Options include standard US and European paper sizes, but you can also specify a custom paper size.

- **Orientation** is the direction of the page contents.

- **Paper Source** is the location of the paper to be used to print the first and subsequent pages of the document.

✔ Tips

- Some Page Setup options—such as paper size and orientation—affect a page's margins. If you plan to use non-standard Page Setup options, consider setting them *before* you create and format your document.

- I discuss options in the Margins and Layout tabs of the Page Setup dialog box in **Chapters 3** and **4**.

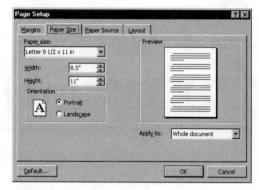

Figure 1 The Paper Size tab of the Page Setup dialog box enables you to set paper size and orientation.

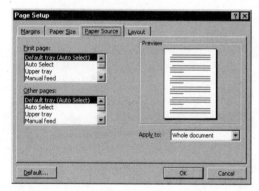

Figure 2 The Paper Source tab of the Page Setup dialog box.

Figure 3
The File menu offers all three commands you'll use for setting up, previewing, and printing a document.

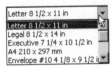

Figure 4
The Paper size menu.

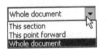

Figure 5
The Apply to menu.

Figure 6 When you set options in the Paper size and Orientation areas, the Preview area changes.

To set paper size and orientation

1. Choose File > Page Setup (**Figure 3**).

2. If necessary, click the Paper Size tab in the Page Setup dialog box that appears to display its options (**Figure 1**).

3. Choose a standard paper size from the Paper size menu (**Figure 4**).

   or

   To set a custom paper size, choose Custom from the Paper size menu and then enter paper dimensions in the Width and Height boxes.

4. Select one of the orientation options.

5. If necessary, choose an option from the Apply to menu (**Figure 5**).

6. Click OK.

✔ Tips

- The changes you make in the Paper Size tab of the Page Setup dialog box are reflected in the Preview illustration (**Figure 6**).

- If you choose an option other than Whole document from the Apply to menu in step 5, you may add section breaks to your document. I tell you about multisection documents in **Chapter 4**.

To set paper source options

1. Choose File > Page Setup (**Figure 3**).

2. If necessary, click the Paper Source tab in the Page Setup dialog box that appears to display its options (**Figure 2**).

3. Select a paper source location in the First page and Other pages lists.

4. Click OK.

Figure 7 When you click OK in this dialog box, you change the default Page Setup options for the current template—in this case, Normal.

✔ Tip

- Paper source options vary from one printer to another. If you don't know what options to select, use the Default Tray (AutoSelect) option.

To save Page Setup options as default settings

1. Set options as desired in any tab of the Page Setup dialog box.

2. Click the Default button.

3. A dialog box like the one in **Figure 7** appears. Click OK.

   From that point forward, all new documents created with the current template will have the settings specified in the Page Setup dialog box.

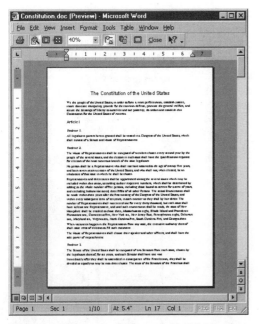

Figure 8 A single page of a document in Print Preview.

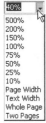

Figure 9
The Zoom menu on the Print Preview toolbar.

Print Preview

Word's Print Preview (**Figure 8**) displays one or more pages of a document exactly as they will appear when printed. It also enables you to make last-minute changes to margins and document contents before printing.

✔ Tip

- Print Preview can save a lot of time and paper—it's a lot quicker to look at a document on screen than wait for it to print, and it doesn't use a single sheet of paper!

To switch to Print Preview

Choose File > Print Preview (**Figure 3**).

or

Click the Print Preview button 🔍 on the Standard toolbar.

✔ Tip

- The Print Preview toolbar appears automatically at the top of the screen when you switch to Print Preview (**Figure 8**).

To zoom in or out

1. If necessary, click to select the Magnifier button 🔍 on the Print Preview toolbar.

2. Click on the page that you want to zoom. With each click, the view toggles between 100% and the current Zoom percentage on the Print Preview toolbar.

or

Choose an option from the Zoom menu on the Print Preview toolbar (**Figure 9**).

or

1. Click in the Zoom box on the Print Preview toolbar.

2. Enter a value.

3. Press (Enter).

To view multiple pages

Click the Multiple Pages button on the Print Preview toolbar to display a menu of page layouts and choose the one that you want (**Figure 10**).

The view and magnification change to display the pages as you specified (**Figure 11**).

✔ Tip

■ To return to a single-page view, click the One Page button 🔳 on the Print Preview toolbar.

To change margins

1. If necessary, click the Show Ruler button 🔳 on the Print Preview toolbar to display the ruler in the Print Preview window (**Figure 8**).

2. Position the mouse pointer on the ruler in the position corresponding to the margin you want to change. The mouse pointer turns into a two-headed arrow and a yellow box appears, identifying the margin (**Figure 12**).

3. Press the mouse button down and drag to change the margin. As you drag, a dotted line indicates the position of the margin. When you release the mouse button, the margin changes.

✔ Tips

■ A better way to change margins is with the Margins tab of the Page Setup dialog box (**Figure 13**), which I tell you about in **Chapter 3**.

■ You can also use the ruler to change indentation and set tabs for selected paragraphs. I explain how in **Chapter 3**.

Figure 10
Use the Multiple Pages button's menu to choose a layout for displaying multiple document pages in Print Preview.

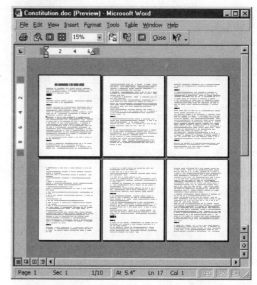

Figure 11 Six pages of a document in Print Preview.

Figure 12
The mouse pointer changes when you position it on a margin on the ruler.

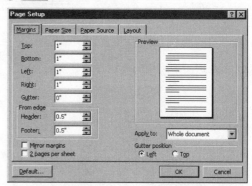

Figure 13 The Margins tab of the Page Setup dialog box offers an easier way to set margins.

Previous Page

Next Page

Figure 14 Use the Previous Page and Next Page buttons at the bottom of the vertical scroll bar to move from one page to another.

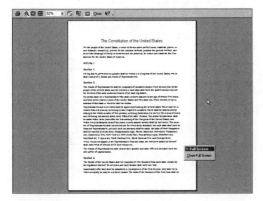

Figure 15 Full screen view in Print Preview.

To move from page to page

In Print Preview, click the Previous Page or Next Page button at the bottom of the vertical scroll bar (**Figure 14**).

To edit the document

1. If necessary, zoom in to get a better look at the text you want to edit.

2. Deselect the Magnifier button on the Print Preview toolbar.

3. Click in the document window to position the insertion point.

4. Edit the document as desired.

To reduce the number of pages

Click the Shrink to Fit button on the Print Preview toolbar.

Word squeezes the document onto one less page by making minor adjustments to font size and paragraph spacing. When it's finished, it displays the revised document.

✔ Tip

■ This feature is useful for squeezing a two-page letter onto one page when the second page only has a line or two.

To switch to a full-screen view

Click the Full Screen button on the Print Preview toolbar.

The screen redraws to remove the status bar (**Figure 15**). This enables you to get a slightly larger view of the document page(s).

✔ Tip

■ To return to a regular Print Preview view, click the Close Full Screen button on the Full Screen toolbar.

To leave Print Preview

Click the Close button on the Print Preview toolbar (**Figure 8**).

PREVIEWING PAGES

Printing

You use the Print dialog box (**Figure 16**) to set a number of options for the print job, including:

- **Name** is the name of the printer to which you want to print.

- **Page range** is the range of document pages you want to print.

- **Copies** is the number of copies of the document you want to print.

- **Zoom** is the number of pages to be printed per sheet of paper and the magnification to be used for printing.

After setting options, clicking the OK button sends the document to the printer.

✔ Tip

- These are just a few of the options offered in the Print dialog box. I tell you about others on the next few pages.

To set print options & print

1. Choose File > Print (**Figure 3**) or press Ctrl P to display the Print dialog box (**Figure 16**).

2. Choose a printer from the Name menu (**Figure 17**).

3. Select a page range option:

   ▲ **All** prints all pages.

   ▲ **Current page** prints the currently selected page or the page in which the insertion point is blinking.

   ▲ **Pages** enables you to enter one or more page ranges. Separate first and last page numbers with a hyphen; separate multiple page ranges with commas.

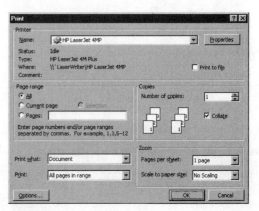

Figure 16 The Print dialog box.

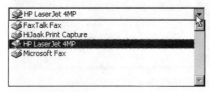

Figure 17 The Name menu lists all available printing devices.

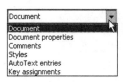

Figure 18 The Print what menu enables you to print more than just the document.

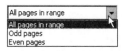

Figure 19 Use the Print menu to print only odd or even pages.

Figure 20 Use the Pages per sheet menu to print more than one page on each sheet of paper.

Figure 21 The Scale to paper size menu enables you to resize a document so it fits on any size paper.

4. Choose an option from the Print what menu (**Figure 18**):

   ▲ **Document** prints the Word document.

   ▲ **Document properties** prints information about the document.

   ▲ **Comments** prints comments inserted into the document. I tell you about comments in **Chapter 7**.

   ▲ **Styles** prints style information. I cover styles in **Chapter 4**.

   ▲ **AutoText entries** prints a list of AutoText entries. I explain AutoText entries in **Chapter 7**.

   ▲ **Key assignments** prints a list of shortcut keys available thoughout Word.

5. If desired, choose an option from the Print menu (**Figure 19**):

   ▲ **All pages in range** prints all pages in the range specified in step 3.

   ▲ **Odd pages** prints only the odd pages in the range specified in step 3.

   ▲ **Even pages** prints only the even pages in the range specified in step 3.

6. Enter the number of copies to print in the Copies box.

7. To print more than one page on each sheet of paper, choose an option from the Pages per sheet menu (**Figure 20**).

8. To scale the printout so it fits on a specific paper size, choose an option from the Scale to paper size menu (**Figure 21**).

9. Click OK to send the document to the printer.

Continued on next page...

PRINTING

Continued from previous page.

✔ Tips

■ Clicking the Print button 🖨 on the Standard or Print Preview toolbar sends the document directly to the printer without displaying the Print dialog box.

■ The options that appear on the Name menu vary depending on the printers set up for your computer. Your menu will probably not match the one in **Figure 17**.

■ Clicking the Properties button displays the Properties dialog box (**Figure 22**), which you can use to set printer-specific options.

■ If you enter a value greater than one in the Copies box in step 6, you can use the Collate check box to determine whether copies should be collated as they are printed.

■ To print the document as a file on disk, turn on the Print to file check box in the Print dialog box (**Figure 16**). When you click OK, you can use the Print to File dialog box that appears (**Figure 23**) to save the document as a .PRN file.

Figure 22 Use the Properties dialog box to set printer-specific options.

Figure 23 The Print to File dialog box enables you to save a document as a .PRN file.

INSERTING SPECIAL TEXT

Figure 1
The Insert menu.

Special Text

Word's Insert menu (**Figure 1**) includes a number of commands that you can use to insert special text into your documents:

◆ **AutoText** enables you to create and insert AutoText entries, which are commonly used text snippets, such as your name or the closing of a letter.

◆ **Field** enables you to insert Word fields, which are pieces of information that change as necessary, such as the date, file size, or page number.

◆ **Symbol** enables you to insert symbols and special characters such as bullets, smiley faces, and the copyright symbol (©).

◆ **Comment** enables you to insert notes to annotate a document. These notes do not print unless you want them to.

◆ **Footnote** enables you to insert footnotes or endnotes, which are annotations that appear (and print) beneath text, at the bottom of the page, at the end of the section, or at the end of the document.

✔ Tip

■ I tell you about other Insert menu options in **Chapters 4** and **8**.

AutoText & AutoComplete

Word's *AutoText* feature makes it quick and easy to insert text snippets that you use often in your documents. First, create the AutoText entry that you want to use. Then use one of two methods to insert it:

- Begin to type the entry or entry name. When an AutoComplete tip appears (**Figure 7**), press [Enter] to enter the rest of the entry. This feature is known as *Auto-Complete*.

- Use options on the AutoText submenu under the Insert menu (**Figure 3**) to insert the entry.

✔ Tip

- Word comes preconfigured with dozens of AutoText entries.

To create an AutoText entry

1. Select the text that you want to use as an AutoText entry (**Figure 2**).

2. Choose Insert > AutoText > New (**Figure 3**).

3. The Create AutoText dialog box appears (**Figure 4**). It displays a default name for the entry. If desired, change the name.

4. Click OK.

or

1. Choose Insert > AutoText > AutoText (**Figure 3**) to display the AutoText tab of the AutoCorrect dialog box (**Figure 5**).

2. Enter the text that you want to use as an AutoText entry in the Enter AutoText entries here box.

3. Click Add. The entry appears in the list.

4. Repeat steps 2 and 3, if desired, to add additional entries.

5. When you are finished, click OK.

Figure 2 Select the text that you want to use as an AutoText entry.

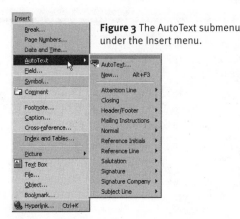

Figure 3 The AutoText submenu under the Insert menu.

Figure 4
The Create AutoText dialog box.

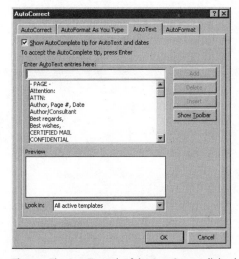

Figure 5 The AutoText tab of the AutoCorrect dialog box.

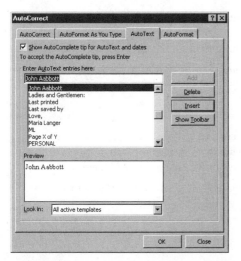

Figure 6 Selecting an AutoText entry.

To delete an AutoText entry

1. Choose Insert > AutoText > AutoText (**Figure 3**) to display the AutoText tab of the AutoCorrect dialog box (**Figure 5**).

2. In the list of AutoText entries, click to select the entry that you want to delete (**Figure 6**). You can confirm that you have selected the correct entry by checking its contents in the Preview area.

3. Click Delete. The entry is removed from the list.

4. Repeat steps 2 and 3, if desired, to delete other entries.

5. When you are finished, click OK.

To enable/disable AutoComplete

1. Choose Insert > AutoText > AutoText (**Figure 3**) to display the AutoText tab of the AutoCorrect dialog box (**Figure 5**).

2. To enable the AutoComplete feature, turn on the Show AutoComplete tip for Auto-Text and dates check box.

   or

   To disable the AutoComplete feature, turn off the Show AutoComplete tip for Auto-Text and dates check box.

3. Click OK.

✔ Tip

- The AutoComplete feature is turned on by default.

AUTOTEXT ENTRIES & AUTOCOMPLETE

To insert an AutoText entry with AutoComplete

1. Type text into your document.

2. When you type the first few characters of an AutoText entry, a yellow AutoComplete tip box appears (**Figure 7**).

3. To enter the text displayed in the Auto-Complete tip, press (Enter). The text you were typing is completed with the text from the AutoText entry (**Figure 8**).

   or

   To ignore the AutoComplete tip, keep typing.

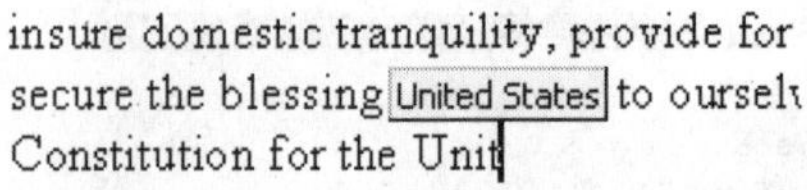

To insert an AutoText entry with the AutoText submenu

1. Position the insertion point where you want the AutoText entry to appear.

2. Use your mouse to display the AutoText submenu under the Insert menu (**Figure 3**).

3. Select the submenu option that contains the entry that you want (**Figure 9**) and select the entry. It is inserted into the document.

insure domestic tranquility, provide for secure the blessing United States to ourseh Constitution for the Unit

Figure 7 When you begin to type text for which there is an AutoText entry, an AutoComplete tip box appears.

insure domestic tranquility, provide for secure the blessings of liberty to ourseh Constitution for the United States

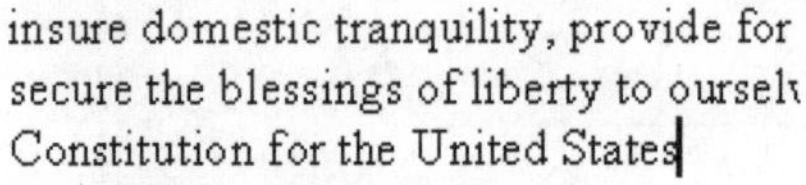

Figure 8 Press (Enter) to complete the text you are typing with the AutoText entry.

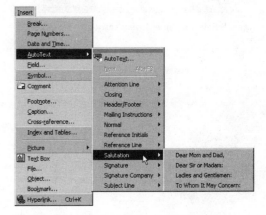

Figure 9 Each submenu on the AutoText submenu contains one or more AutoText entries.

To: John Aabbott

From: Maria Langer

Date: |

Figure 10
Position the insertion point where you want the field to appear.

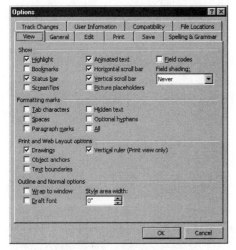

Figure 11 The Field dialog box.

To: John Aabbott

From: Maria Langer

Date: 1/9/00|

Figure 12
In this example, the Date field was inserted.

Date: {DATE * MERGEFORMAT }

Figure 13 Here's the same field with the field codes displayed rather than the field contents.

Figure 14 The View tab of the Options dialog box determines which document elements appear.

Word Fields

Word fields are special codes that, when inserted in a document, display specific information. But unlike typed text, Word fields can change when necessary so the information they display is always up-to-date.

For example, the PrintDate field displays the date the document was last printed. If you print it again on a later date, the contents of the PrintDate field will change to reflect the new date.

✔ Tip

■ Word fields is an extremely powerful feature of Word. A thorough discussion would go far beyond the scope of this book. Instead, the following pages will provide the basic information you need to get started using Word fields.

To insert a field

1. Position the insertion point where you want the field information to appear (**Figure 10**).

2. Choose Insert > Field (**Figure 1**) to display the Field dialog box (**Figure 11**).

3. In the Categories list, click to select the category for the field you want to insert.

4. In the Field names list, click to select the name of the field you want to insert.

5. Click OK. The field is inserted in the document (**Figure 12**).

✔ Tip

■ If field codes display instead of field contents (**Figure 13**), choose Tools > Options, click the View tab in the Options dialog box (**Figure 14**), and turn off the Field codes check box.

To select a field

Use your mouse pointer to drag over the field.

or

Double-click the field.

When the field is completely highlighted (**Figure 15**), it is properly selected.

✔ Tip

■ Once you have selected a field, you can format it using formatting techniques discussed in **Chapter 3** or delete it by pressing Backspace or Delete.

To update a field

1. Right-click on the field to display its shortcut menu (**Figure 16**).

2. Choose Update Field.

or

1. Select the field.

2. Press F9.

If necessary, the contents of the field changes.

✔ Tip

■ To ensure that all fields are automatically updated before the document is printed, choose Tools > Options, click the Print tab in the Options dialog box (**Figure 17**), and turn on the Update fields check box.

Figure 15 A selected field.

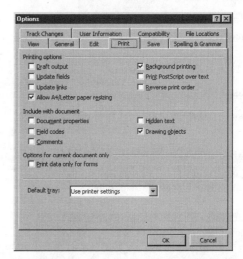

Figure 16 A field's shortcut menu includes the Update Field command.

Figure 17 To assure that all fields are updated before a document is printed, turn on the Update fields check box in the Print tab of the Options dialog box.

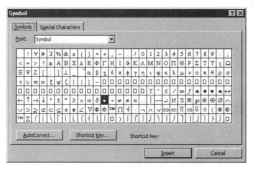

Figure 18 The Symbols tab of the Symbol dialog box.

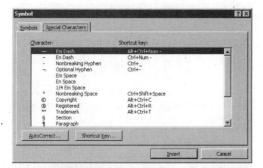

Figure 19 The Special Characters tab of the Symbol dialog box.

Symbols & Special Characters

Symbols are characters that don't appear on the keyboard. They include special characters within a font, such as ®, ©, ™, or é, and characters that appear only in special "dingbats" fonts, such as ■, ▲, ➡, and ♣.

Word's Symbol dialog box (**Figures 18** and **19**), makes it easy to insert all kinds of symbols and special characters in your documents.

✔ Tips

- You don't need to use the Symbol dialog box to insert symbols or special characters in your documents. You just need to know the keystrokes and, if necessary, the font to apply. The Symbol dialog box takes all the guesswork out of inserting these characters.

- A *dingbats font* is a typeface that displays graphic characters rather than text characters. Monotype Sorts, Webdings, Wingdings, and Zapf Dingbats are four examples.

- The Symbols tab of the Symbol dialog box (**Figure 18**) enables you to insert symbols that use a variety of text, symbol, and dingbats fonts.

- The Special Characters tab of the Symbol dialog box (**Figure 19**) enables you to insert special characters that use the current font.

To insert a symbol or special character

1. Position the insertion point where you want the character to appear (**Figure 20**).

2. Choose Insert > Symbol (**Figure 1**).

3. If necessary, click the Symbols tab in the Symbol dialog box that appears to display its options (**Figure 18**).

4. Choose the font that you want to use to display the character from the Font menu (**Figure 21**). The characters displayed in the Symbol dialog box change accordingly.

5. If applicable, choose the font subset that you want to use from the Subset menu (**Figure 22**). This menu only appears for certain fonts and the subsets listed vary depending on the font selected.

6. Click the character that you want to insert to select it (**Figure 23**).

7. Click Insert. The character that you clicked appears at the insertion point (**Figure 24**).

8. Repeat steps 4 though 6, if desired, to insert additional characters.

9. When you are finished inserting characters, click the Close button.

✔ Tip

■ When inserting a symbol or special character in the normal (current) font, you may prefer to use the Special Characters tab of the Symbol dialog box (**Figure 19**). The list of special characters includes the shortcut key you can use to type the character without using the Symbol dialog box.

This document 1999 by Peachpit Press
All rights reserved.

Figure 20 Position the insertion point where you want the symbol or special character to appear.

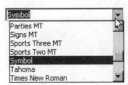

Figure 21
The Font menu in the Symbol dialog box.

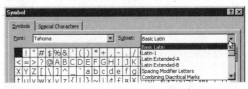

Figure 22 Some fonts, such as Tahoma, offer a variety of font subsets, each with its own collection of special characters.

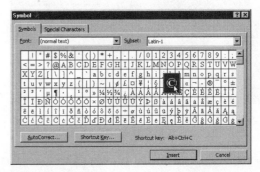

Figure 23 Click the character you want to insert to select it.

This document ©1999 by Peachpit Press
All rights reserved.

Figure 24 The character you selected appears at the insertion point.

We the people of the United Sta
insure domestic tranquility, pro

Figure 25 Start by selecting the text for which you want to enter a comment.

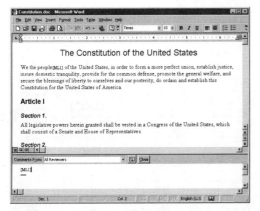

Figure 26 Word prepares to accept your comment.

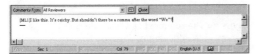

Figure 27 Enter your comment in the bottom pane of the window.

Comments

Comments are annotations that you and other document reviewers can add to a document. These notes can be viewed on screen but don't print unless you want them to.

To insert a comment

1. Select the text for which you want to insert a comment (**Figure 25**).

2. Choose Insert > Comment (**Figure 1**).

   A few things happen: A comment marker (your initials and a number within brackets) is inserted after the selected text, the window splits, and the insertion point moves to the bottom pane of the window beside your initials there (**Figure 26**).

3. Type in your comment. It can be as long or short as you like (**Figure 27**).

✔ Tips

- Word gets your initials from the User Information tab of the Options dialog box. I tell you more about that in **Chapter 14**.

- The initials, number, and brackets that appear in the document window (**Figure 26**) do not print.

To close the comment pane

Click the Close button at the top of the comment pane (**Figure 27**).

The pane closes and the initials disappear.

To view comments

Choose View > Comments (**Figure 28**). The window splits again. The bottom pane scrolls, enabling you to see all comments entered for the document (**Figure 29**).

✔ Tips

■ To view only those comments made by a specific person, choose the person's name from the Comments From menu (**Figure 30**) at the top of the comments pane.

■ If Word's screen tips feature is enabled, text for which a comment exists appears highlighted in yellow. Simply point to the text to view the comment in a screen tip (**Figure 31**). To enable screen tips, choose Tools > Options, click the View tab, and turn on the Screen Tips check box (**Figure 14**).

To delete a comment

1. If necessary, display the comments pane (**Figure 29**).

2. In the document window, select the comment marker for the comment that you want to remove.

3. Press Backspace or Delete. The marker is removed from the document and the comment is removed from the comment pane.

To print comments

1. Follow the instructions in **Chapter 6** to prepare the document for printing and open the Print dialog box.

2. Choose Comments from the Print what menu (**Figure 32**).

3. Click Print.

Figure 28
The View menu.

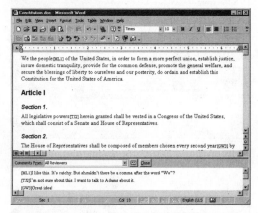

Figure 29 The comments pane displays all comments entered in the document.

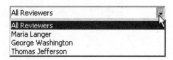

Figure 30 Use this menu to see comments from a specific person.

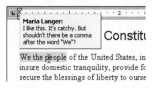

Figure 31 With screen tips enabled, you can simply point to text to see its comment.

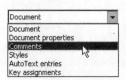

Figure 32
Use the Print what menu in the Print dialog box to print a document's comments.

VIEWING, DELETING, & PRINTING COMMENTS

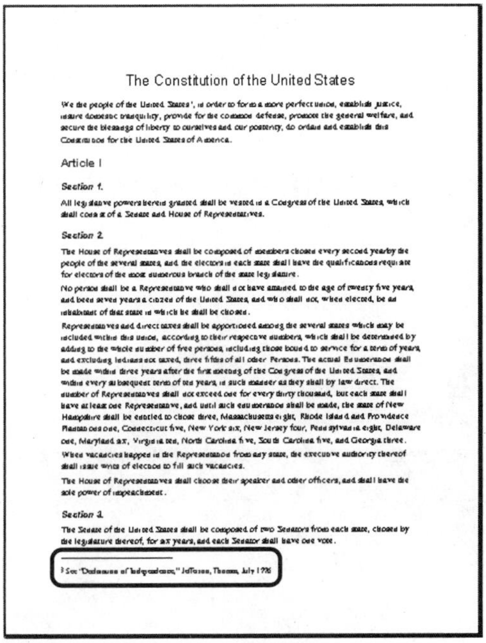

The Constitution of the United States

We the people of the United States[1], in order to form a more perfect union, establish justice, insure domestic tranquility, provide for the common defense, promote the general welfare, and secure the blessings of liberty to ourselves and our posterity, do ordain and establish this Constitution for the United States of America.

Article I

Section 1.

All legislative powers herein granted shall be vested in a Congress of the United States, which shall consist of a Senate and House of Representatives.

Section 2.

The House of Representatives shall be composed of members chosen every second year by the people of the several states, and the electors in each state shall have the qualifications requisite for electors of the most numerous branch of the state legislature.

No person shall be a Representative who shall not have attained to the age of twenty five years, and been seven years a citizen of the United States, and who shall not, when elected, be an inhabitant of that state in which he shall be chosen.

Representatives and direct taxes shall be apportioned among the several states which may be included within this union, according to their respective numbers, which shall be determined by adding to the whole number of free persons, including those bound to service for a term of years, and excluding Indians not taxed, three fifths of all other Persons. The actual Enumeration shall be made within three years after the first meeting of the Congress of the United States, and within every subsequent term of ten years, in such manner as they shall by law direct. The number of Representatives shall not exceed one for every thirty thousand, but each state shall have at least one Representative, and until such enumeration shall be made, the state of New Hampshire shall be entitled to chose three, Massachusetts eight, Rhode Island and Providence Plantations one, Connecticut five, New York six, New Jersey four, Pennsylvania eight, Delaware one, Maryland six, Virginia ten, North Carolina five, South Carolina five, and Georgia three.

When vacancies happen in the Representation from any state, the executive authority thereof shall issue writs of election to fill such vacancies.

The House of Representatives shall choose their speaker and other officers, and shall have the sole power of impeachment.

Section 3.

The Senate of the United States shall be composed of two Senators from each state, chosen by the legislature thereof, for six years, and each Senator shall have one vote.

[1] See "Declaration of Independence," Jefferson, Thomas, July 1776

Figure 33 A page with a footnote. Word automatically inserts the footnote separator line, too.

Footnotes & Endnotes

Footnotes and endnotes are annotations for specific document text. You insert a marker—usually a number or symbol—right after the text, tell Word where you want the note to go, and enter the note. When you view the document in Page Layout view or Print Preview or print the document, the note appears where you specified.

The difference between a footnote and an endnote is its position in the document:

- **Footnotes** appear either after the last line of text on the page on which the annotated text appears or at the bottom of the page on which the annotated text appears (**Figure 33**).
- **Endnotes** appear either at the end of the section in which the annotated text appears or at the end of the document.

✓ Tips

- Footnotes and endnotes are commonly used to show the source of a piece of information or provide additional information that may not be of interest to every reader.
- I tell you about multiple-section documents in **Chapter 4**.
- Word automatically renumbers footnotes or endnotes when necessary when you insert or delete a note.
- If you're old enough to remember preparing high school or college term papers on a *typewriter*, you'll recognize this feature as another example of how easy kids have it today. (Gee, I sound like my grandmother.)

To insert a footnote or endnote

1. Position the insertion point immediately after the text that you want to annotate (**Figure 34**).

2. Choose Insert > Footnote (**Figure 1**) to display the Footnote and Endnote dialog box (**Figure 35**).

3. In the Insert part of the dialog box, select the option button for the type of note you want to insert.

4. In the Numbering part of the dialog box, select the type of mark you want to insert.

5. If you select the Custom mark option in step 4, enter the character for the mark in the edit box beside it.

6. Click OK. Word inserts a marker at the insertion point, then one of two things happens:

   ▲ If you are in Normal view, the window splits to display a footnote or endnote pane with the insertion point blinking beside the marker there (**Figure 36**).

   ▲ If you are in Print Layout view, the view shifts to the location of the footnote or endnote where a separator line is inserted. The insertion point is blinking beside the marker there (**Figure 37**).

7. Enter the footnote or endnote text (**Figure 38**).

✔ Tips

■ In step 5, You can click the Symbol button to display the Symbol dialog box (**Figure 18**), click a symbol to select it, and click OK to insert it in the box. I tell you about the Symbol dialog box earlier in this chapter.

■ In Normal view, to close the footnote pane, click the Close button at the top of the pane.

Figure 34 Position the insertion point immediately after the text that you want to annotate.

Figure 35
The Footnote and Endnote dialog box.

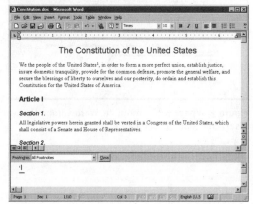

Figure 36 Entering a footnote in Normal view.

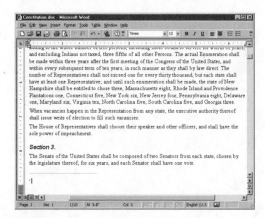

Figure 37 Entering a footnote in Print Layout view.

[1] See "Declaration of Independence," Jefferson, Thomas, July 1776.

Figure 38 Enter footnote text right after the marker.

Figure 39
The All Footnotes tab of the Note Options dialog box.

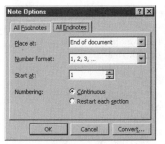

Figure 40
The All Endnotes tab of the Note Options dialog box.

Figures 41 & 42 The Place at menu for footnotes (left) and endnotes (right).

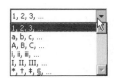

Figure 43
The Number format menu.

Figure 44 When you make changes in the Note Options dialog box, the Cancel button turns into a Close button so you can close the dialog box without inserting a footnote or endnote.

To set options for footnotes or endnotes

1. Choose Insert > Footnote (**Figure 1**).

2. Click the Options button in the Footnote and Endnote dialog box (**Figure 35**).

3. In the Note Options dialog box that appears, click the All Footnotes tab to display footnote options (**Figure 39**) or the All Endnotes tab to display endnote options (**Figure 40**).

4. Set options as desired:

   ▲ Use the Place at menu (**Figures 41** and **42**) to set the note position.

   ▲ Use the Number format menu (**Figure 43**) to specify the note numbering scheme.

   ▲ Enter a value in the Start at box to specify the start number.

   ▲ Select one of the Numbering options to specify whether numbering should be continuous throughout the document, restarted in each section, or, in the case of footnotes, restarted on each page.

5. Click OK to save your settings and dismiss the Note Options dialog box.

6. To insert a new footnote or endnote at the insertion point, follow steps 3 through 7 on the previous page.

   or

   To save your settings without inserting a new footnote or endnote, click the Close button in the Footnote and Endnote dialog box (**Figure 44**).

✔ Tip

■ The last three options in the Note Options dialog box apply only if you selected Auto-Number in the Footnote and Endnote dialog box (**Figure 36**).

SETTING FOOTNOTE & ENDNOTE OPTIONS

To convert notes

1. Choose Insert > Footnote (**Figure 1**) to display the Footnote and Endnote dialog box (**Figure 35**).

2. Click Options to display the Note Options dialog box (**Figures 39** and **40**).

3. Click the Convert button to display the Convert Notes dialog box (**Figure 45**).

4. Select the option button for the type of conversion that you want to do.

5. Click OK to make the conversion and dismiss the Convert Notes dialog box.

6. Click OK to dismiss the Note Options dialog box.

7. Click Close to dismiss the Footnote and Endnote dialog box.

✔ Tip

- The options available in the Convert Notes dialog box (**Figure 45**) vary depending on the type(s) of notes in the document.

To delete a note

1. In the document window (not the note area or pane), select the note marker (**Figure 46**).

2. Press ⌊Backspace⌋ or ⌊Delete⌋. The note marker and corresponding note are removed from the document. If the note was numbered using the AutoNumber option, all notes after it are properly renumbered.

✔ Tip

- If you have trouble selecting the tiny note marker in the document, use the Zoom menu on the Standard toolbar (**Figure 47**) to increase the window's magnification so you can see it better. I tell you more about zooming a window's view in **Chapter 1**.

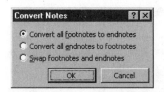

Figure 45 The Convert Notes dialog box for a document that contains both footnotes and endnotes.

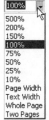

Figure 46 To delete a footnote or endnote, begin by selecting the note marker.

Figure 47
You can use the Zoom menu on the Standard toolbar to increase the window's magnification so you can see tiny note markers.

INSERTING OBJECTS

Figure 1
The Insert menu.

Objects & Multimedia Elements

Word's Insert menu (**Figure 1**) offers a number of commands for inserting various objects and multimedia elements into documents:

◆ **File** enables you to insert another file.

◆ **Object** enables you to insert an OLE object, which is created with an OLE-aware application. An OLE object can be edited from within Word, even if it was created with another application.

◆ **Picture** enables you to insert a variety of graphic objects, including clip art, graphic files, AutoShapes, WordArt, scanned or digital photographs, and charts.

✔ Tip

■ I tell you about other Insert menu options in **Chapters 4** and **7**.

OBJECTS & MULTIMEDIA ELEMENTS

Files

You can use the File command under the Insert menu to insert one file (the *source file*) within another file (the *destination file*). The source file then becomes part of the destination file.

✔ Tips

- The source file can be in any format that Word recognizes.

- Copy and paste and drag and drop are two other methods for inserting the contents of one file into another. I explain these techniques in **Chapter 2**.

- A file can be inserted with or without a *link*. If the source file is linked, when you update the link, the destination file is updated with fresh information from the source. This means that changes in the source file are reflected in the destination file.

To insert a file

1. Position the insertion point where you want the source file to be inserted (**Figure 2**).

2. Choose Insert > File (**Figure 1**).

3. Use the Insert File dialog box that appears (**Figure 3**) to locate and select the file that you want to insert.

4. Click the Insert button.

   The file is inserted (**Figure 4**).

✔ Tip

- You can use the Files of type menu (**Figure 5**) to view only specific types of files in the Insert File dialog box (**Figure 3**).

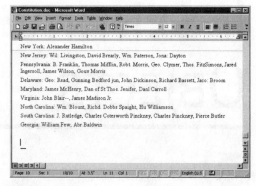

Figure 2 Position the insertion point where you want to insert the file.

Figure 3 Use the Insert File dialog box to select the file you want to insert.

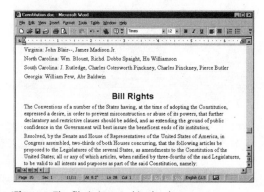

Figure 4 The file is inserted in the document.

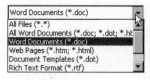

Figure 5 You can use the Files of type menu to list only certain file types in the Insert File dialog box.

Figure 6 Clicking the arrow on the Insert button enables you to insert a file as a link.

Bill Rights

Figure 7 The shortcut menu for a linked file enables you to update the link, which is a Word field.

Figure 8 Word displays an error message when you attempt to update a link and Word can't find the source file.

To insert a file as a link

1. Follow steps 1 through 3 on the previous page.

2. Choose Insert as Link from the Insert button's menu (**Figure 6**).

   The file is inserted as a link to the original file on disk.

✔ Tips

- Any changes you make in the destination file to the contents of a linked file are lost when the link is updated.

- Technically speaking, a linked file is inserted as a field. I tell you about fields in **Chapter 7**.

To update a link

1. Right-click on the linked file to display its shortcut menu (**Figure 7**).

2. Choose Update Field.

   The link's contents are updated to reflect the current contents of the source file.

✔ Tip

- If Word cannot find the source file when you attempt to update a link, it replaces the contents of the source file with an error message (**Figure 8**). There are three ways to fix this problem:

   ▲ Undo the update.

   ▲ Remove the link and reinsert it.

   ▲ Choose Edit > Links to fix the link with the Links dialog box.

To remove an inserted file

1. Select the contents of the inserted file.

2. Press Backspace or Delete.

Objects

An *object* is all or part of a file created with an OLE-aware application. *OLE* or *Object Linking and Embedding* is a Microsoft technology that enables you to insert a file as an object within a document (**Figure 9**)—even if the file was created with a different application. Double-clicking the inserted object launches the application that created it so you can modify its contents.

Word's Object command enables you to insert OLE objects in two different ways:

◆ **Create and insert a new OLE object.** This method launches a specific OLE-aware application so you can create an object. When you are finished, you quit the application to insert the new object in your document.

◆ **Insert an existing OLE object.** This method displays a standard Open dialog box that you can use to locate, select, and insert an existing file as an object.

✔ Tips

■ All Microsoft applications are OLE-aware. Many software applications created by other developers are also OLE-aware; check the documentation that came with a specific software package for details.

■ Microsoft Word comes with a number of OLE-aware applications that can be used to insert objects. The full Microsoft Office package includes even more of these applications.

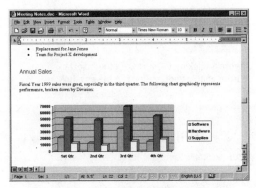

Figure 9 A Microsoft Graph 2000 chart inserted as an OLE object in a Microsoft Word 2000 document.

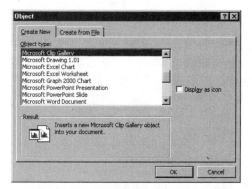

Figure 10 Use the Create New tab of the Object dialog box to insert a brand new OLE object.

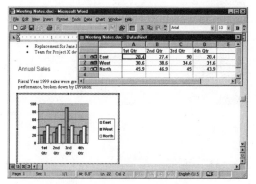

Figure 11 The default Microsoft Graph 2000 datasheet window and chart. Notice how Word's menu bar and toolbars have changed to include options for Microsoft Graph.

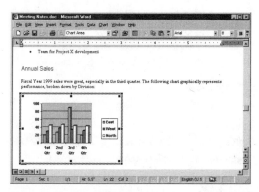

Figure 12 The default Microsoft Graph 2000 chart inserted into a Word document.

To insert a new OLE object

1. Position the insertion point where you want the object to appear.

2. Choose Insert > Object (**Figure 1**) to display the Object dialog box.

3. If necessary, click the Create New tab to display its options (**Figure 10**).

4. Click to select the type of object that you want to insert.

5. Click OK.

6. Word launches the application that you selected. It may take a moment for it to appear. **Figure 11** shows Microsoft Graph 2000's datasheet window overlapping the Word window.

7. Use the application to create the object that you want.

8. When you are finished creating the object, exit the application by closing its application window.

   The object is inserted in the document (**Figure 12**).

✔ Tips

- If Microsoft Excel is installed on your computer, you can click the Insert Microsoft Excel Worksheet button 🔲 on the Standard toolbar to create and insert a new Excel worksheet object.

- For more information about using one of the OLE-aware applications that come with Word or Office, use the application's Help menu or Office Assistant.

INSERTING OLE OBJECTS

To insert an existing OLE object

1. Position the insertion point where you want the object to appear.

2. Choose Insert > Object (**Figure 1**) to display the Object dialog box.

3. Click the Create from File tab to display its options (**Figure 13**).

4. Click the Browse button.

5. Use the Browse dialog box that appears (**Figure 14**) to locate and select the file that you want to insert.

6. Click Insert to return to the Object dialog box. The file's name appears in the File name box (**Figure 15**).

7. Click OK. The file is inserted as an object in the document (**Figure 16**).

✔ Tip

■ To insert a file as an object, the program that created the file must be installed on your computer or accessible via network.

To customize an inserted object

Follow the instructions in the previous two sections to insert a new or existing OLE object. In the Object dialog box, (**Figure 10** or **13**), turn on check boxes as desired:

◆ **Display as icon** displays an icon that represents the object rather than the object itself (**Figure 17**). Double-clicking the icon, opens the file.

◆ **Link to File** creates a link to the object's file. This is similar to inserting a link, which I tell you about earlier in this chapter. This option is only available when inserting an existing file as an object.

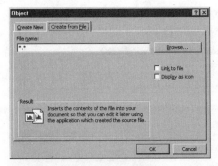

Figure 13 Use the Create from File tab of the Object dialog box to insert an existing file.

Figure 14 Use the Browse dialog box to select a file.

Figure 15 The file's name appears in the File name box.

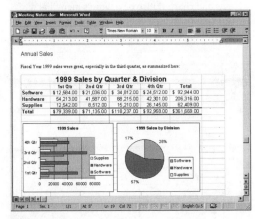

Figure 16 The file is inserted as an OLE object.

"Sales for 1999.xls" **Figure 17** A Microsoft Excel worksheet file inserted as an icon.

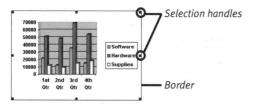

Figure 18 A selected object has a border with selection or resizing handles around it.

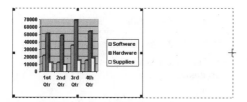

Figure 19 Drag a selection handle away from the object to make the object larger.

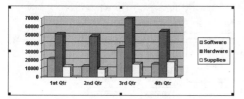

Figure 20 When you release the mouse button, the object resizes.

To resize an inserted object

1. Click the object once to select it. A border and selection handles appear around it (**Figure 18**).

2. Position the mouse pointer on a selection handle, press the mouse button down, and drag as follows:

   ▲ Drag away from the object to make it bigger (**Figure 19**).

   ▲ Drag toward the object to make it smaller.

   When you release the mouse button, the object resizes (**Figure 20**).

✔ Tip

■ Not all objects can be resized this way without distortion. If you resize an object and don't like the way it looks, use the Undo command. Then try resizing it in the program that created it as discussed below.

To edit an object's contents

1. Double-click the object to open the program that created it.

2. Make changes as desired using the options offered by the program.

3. Choose the program's Exit command. Be sure to save your changes.

   The modifications you made are reflected in the inserted object.

To remove an object

1. Click the object once to select it. A border and selection handles appear around it (**Figures 18**).

2. Press Backspace.

✔ Tip

■ If you remove an object that exists in another file, the object is deleted from the Word document, but not from disk.

Pictures

Pictures are graphic objects. Word's Picture submenu (**Figure 21**) enables you to insert a variety of picture types:

◆ **Clip Art** inserts clip art, pictures, sounds, and videos from the Microsoft Clip Gallery.

◆ **From File** inserts an existing picture file.

◆ **AutoShapes** displays the AutoShapes and Drawing toolbars, which you can use to draw shapes and lines.

◆ **WordArt** inserts stylized text.

◆ **From Scanner or Camera** inserts images directly from a scanner or digital camera connected to your computer.

◆ **Chart** inserts Microsoft Graph 2000 charts.

✔ Tips

■ Word inserts pictures two different ways, depending on the command you use:

▲ The Clip Art, From File, and Chart commands insert *inline* pictures. Inline pictures act just like characters on a line of text—but they're usually much bigger!

▲ The AutoShapes and Word Art commands insert pictures in the *drawing layer*. Pictures in the drawing layer can be dragged anywhere within the document window and manipulated with Drawing toolbar options. I tell you about the Drawing toolbar later in this chapter.

■ In this chapter, I explain how to use each of the Picture submenu's options except From Scanner or Camera. If you have a scanner or camera, you can explore this option on your own.

Figure 21 The Picture submenu under the Insert menu.

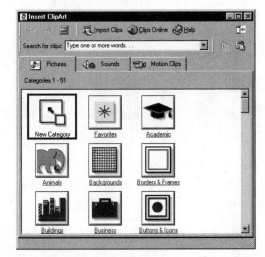

Figure 22 The Pictures tab of the Insert ClipArt window displaying categories of clip art.

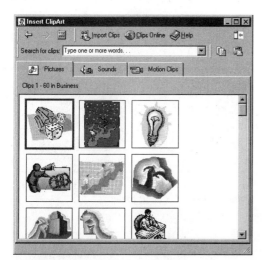

Figure 23 The pictures within the Business category of clip art.

Figure 24
When you select a picture, a menu of buttons appears.

Figure 25 Clip Art inserted in a document.

To insert clip art

1. Position the insertion point where you want the clip art to appear.

2. Choose Insert > Picture > Clip Art (**Figure 21**) to display the Insert ClipArt window.

3. Click a tab for a specific type of clip (**Figure 22**).

4. Click a category name or icon to display the clips within that category (**Figure 23**).

5. Click the clip that you want to insert. The clip becomes selected and a menu of buttons appears (**Figure 24**).

6. Click the Insert button.

7. Click the Insert ClipArt window's close button to dismiss it.

   The clip art is inserted in the document at the insertion point (**Figure 25**).

✔ Tips

- Only the Pictures tab includes content—clips that you can insert into a document. You can add content by clicking the Import Clips button.

- If you used a Typical installation to install Word or Microsoft Office, Clip Art may not have been installed. If a dialog box offers to install it, do so to access this useful feature.

To insert a picture from a file

1. Position the insertion point where you want the picture to appear.

2. Choose Insert > Picture > From File (**Figure 21**) to display the Insert Picture dialog box (**Figure 26**).

3. Locate and select the file that you want to insert.

4. Click the Insert button.

   The file is inserted in the document (**Figure 27**).

✔ Tips

- To create a link between the file on disk and the Word document, choose Insert and Link from the Insert button's menu (**Figure 28**) in step 4. I tell you more about links earlier in this chapter.

- A preview area on the right side of the Insert Picture dialog box helps identify pictures with cryptic names (**Figure 26**).

- Word comes with a variety of clip art files you can insert into documents using this feature. But you can also use this feature to insert your own graphic files.

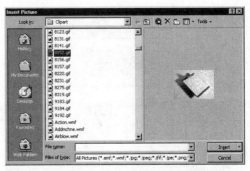

Figure 26 The Insert Picture dialog box displaying the contents of Word's Clipart folder.

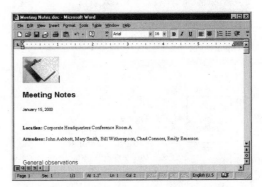

Figure 27 A picture file inserted in a document.

Figure 28 To create a link to the picture file you are inserting, choose Insert and Link from the Insert button's menu.

AutoShapes toolbar   *Drawing toolbar*

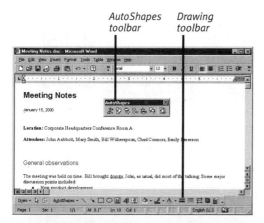

Figure 29 When you choose the AutoShapes command, the AutoShapes and Drawing toolbars appear.

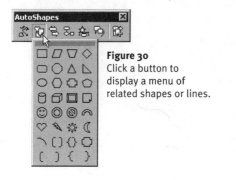

Figure 30
Click a button to display a menu of related shapes or lines.

Figure 31
Position the crosshairs pointer were you want to begin the shape.

Figure 32
Press the mouse button down and drag. The shape begins to emerge.

Figure 33
When you release the mouse button, the shape appears as a selected picture in the document.

To insert an AutoShape

1. Choose Insert > Picture > AutoShapes (**Figure 21**). The AutoShapes toolbar appears as a floating toolbar in the document window while the Drawing toolbar appears docked at the bottom of the document window (**Figure 29**).

2. Click a button on the AutoShapes toolbar to display a menu of related shapes (**Figure 30**) or lines and choose the shape or line that you want to draw.

3. Move the mouse pointer, which becomes a crosshairs pointer (**Figure 31**), into the document window where you want to begin to draw the shape or line.

4. Press the mouse button down and drag. As you drag, the shape (**Figure 32**) or line appears.

5. Release the mouse button to complete the shape (**Figure 33**) or line.

✔ Tips

■ The shape or line pop-up menu that appears when you click an AutoShapes toolbar button (**Figure 30**) can be dragged off the toolbar to create a separate toolbar (**Figure 34**).

■ You can also access a menu of shapes or lines from the AutoShapes button's menu on the Drawing toolbar (**Figure 35**).

Figure 34 Drag a menu off the toolbar to create a floating toolbar.

Figure 35 The AutoShapes button on the Drawing toolbar offers another way to choose a shape.

INSERTING AUTOSHAPES

To change an AutoShape

1. Click the shape or line to select it. Selection handles appear around it (**Figure 33**).

2. Choose a new shape from the Change AutoShape submenu on the Drawing toolbar's Draw menu (**Figure 36**).

To format a shape or line

1. Click the shape or line to select it. Selection handles appear around it (**Figure 33**).

2. Use buttons and menus on the Drawing toolbar (**Figure 29**) to change the appearance of the selected shape or line.

or

1. Double-click the shape to open the Format AutoShape dialog box (**Figure 37**).

2. Use options under the appropriate tabs in the dialog box to change the appearance of the shape.

3. Click OK.

✔ Tips

- The Drawing toolbar offers many options for formatting the shapes and lines you draw—far too many to cover in detail in this book. Explore them on your own. Remember, the Undo command is always available to reverse an undesired action.

- To learn what a button on the Drawing toolbar does, point to it to view its tool tip.

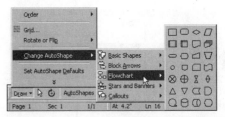

Figure 36 You can use the Draw menu on the Drawing toolbar to change a selected AutoShape.

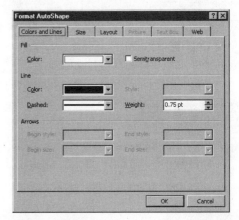

Figure 37 You can use the Format AutoShape dialog box to change the appearance of an AutoShape shape or line.

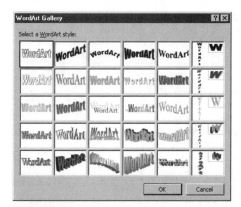

Figure 38 Use the WordArt Gallery dialog box to select a WordArt style.

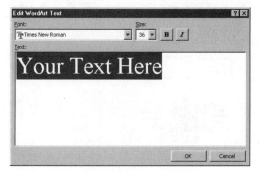

Figure 39 Enter the text you want to display as WordArt in the Edit WordArt Text dialog box.

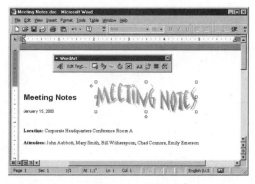

Figure 40 A document with selected WordArt and the WordArt toolbar displayed.

To insert WordArt

1. Choose Insert > Picture > WordArt (**Figure 21**).

2. In the WordArt Gallery dialog box that appears (**Figure 38**), click to select a WordArt style.

3. Click OK.

4. In the Edit WordArt Text dialog box that appears next (**Figure 39**), change the sample text to the text that you want to display. You can also select a different font and font size and turn on bold and/or italic formatting.

5. Click OK. The WordArt image is inserted in your document and the WordArt toolbar appears (**Figure 40**).

To modify a WordArt image

1. Click the image once to select it. Selection handles appear around it (**Figure 40**).

2. Use buttons on the WordArt toolbar to change the appearance of the image.

or

1. Double-click the WordArt image to open the Edit WordArt Text dialog box (**Figure 39**).

2. Change the text as desired.

3. Click OK to apply your changes.

✔ Tip

- To learn what a button on the WordArt toolbar does, point to it to view its tool tip.

To insert a chart

1. Position the insertion point where you want the chart to appear.

2. Choose Insert > Picture > Chart (**Figure 21**). Word launches Microsoft Graph 2000 and displays its window on top of the Word document window (**Figure 11**).

3. Edit the contents of the Datasheet window to reflect the data that you want to chart. The chart is updated automatically (**Figure 41**).

4. Use menu commands and toolbar buttons to format the chart as desired.

5. Click anywhere in the Word document window (other than on the chart) to exit Microsoft Graph 2000. The chart is inserted into the document (**Figure 42**).

✔ Tip

■ The Chart command inserts a Microsoft Graph 2000 chart object, which you can edit by double-clicking. I discuss inserting objects earlier in this chapter.

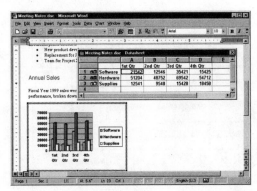

Figure 41 As you make changes in the datasheet, the chart changes automatically.

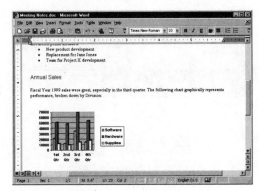

Figure 42 The finished chart is inserted into the document.

Figure 43 Drag a selection handle toward the picture to make it smaller.

Figure 44 When you release the mouse button, the picture resizes.

Figure 45 You can drag a drawing layer picture anywhere in the document.

Figure 46 When you release the mouse button, the picture moves.

To select a picture

Click the picture once. One of two things happens:

◆ On an inline picture, a black selection box and selection handles appear around it (**Figure 18**).

◆ On a drawing layer picture, white selection handles appear around it (**Figures 33** and **40**).

To resize a picture

1. Select the picture you want to resize.

2. Position the mouse pointer on a selection handle, press the mouse button down, and drag as follows:

▲ Drag away from the object to make it bigger.

▲ Drag toward the center of the object to make it smaller (**Figure 43**).

When you release the mouse button, the picture resizes (**Figure 44**).

✔ Tip

■ To resize the picture proportionally, hold down (Shift) while dragging a corner handle.

To move a drawing layer picture

1. Select the picture you want to move.

2. Position the mouse pointer in the middle of the picture, press the mouse button down, and drag to a new position (**Figure 45**).

3. When you release the mouse button, the picture moves (**Figure 46**).

To remove a picture

1. Select the picture you want to remove.

2. Press (Backspace). The picture disappears.

RESIZING, MOVING, & REMOVING PICTURES

Outlines

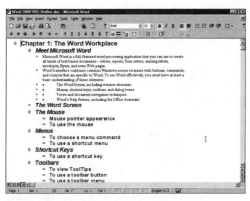

Figure 1 Part of an outline in Outline view.

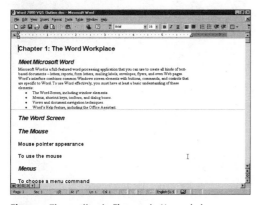

Figure 2 The outline in **Figure 1** in Normal view.

✔ Tips

- Word's outline feature automatically applies the Heading and Normal styles as you work. You can redefine these styles to meet your needs; I tell you how in **Chapter 4**.

Outlines

As any writer knows, an outline is a great tool for organizing ideas. By grouping topics and subtopics under main headings, you can set up the logical flow of a lengthy or complex document. A well-prepared outline is like a document "skeleton"—a solid framework on which the document can be built.

An outline has two types of components (**Figure 1**):

- **Headings** are topic names. Various levels of headings (1 through 9) are arranged in a hierarchy to organize and develop relationships among them.

- **Body text** provides information about each heading.

Word's Outline view makes it easy to build and refine outlines. You start by adding headings that you can set to any level of importance. Then add body text. You can use drag-and-drop editing to rearrange headings and body text at any time. You can also switch to Normal view (**Figure 2**) or another view to continue working with your document.

- You can distinguish headings from body text in Outline view by their symbols. As shown in **Figure 1**, hollow dashes or plus signs appear beside headings while small hollow boxes appear beside body text.

Building an Outline

Building an outline is easy. Just create a new document, switch to Outline view, and start adding headings and body text.

✔ Tip

- You can turn an existing document into an outline by simply switching to Outline view and adding headings.

To create an outline

1. Create a new blank document.

2. Choose View > Outline (**Figure 3**).

   or

   Click the Outline View button at the bottom of the document window (**Figure 4**).

   The document switches to Outline view and the Outlining toolbar appears (**Figure 5**).

✔ Tips

- The Outlining toolbar (**Figure 6**) appears automatically any time you switch to Outline view. If it does not appear, you can display it by choosing View > Toolbars > Outline. I tell you more about displaying and hiding toolbars in **Chapter 1**.

- The Outlining toolbar (**Figure 6**) includes buttons for working with a master document feature, which enables you to include multiple documents in one Word document. This advanced feature is beyond the scope of this book.

Figure 3
One way to switch to Outline view is to choose Outline from the View menu.

Outline View button

Figure 4 Another way to switch to Outline view is to click the Outline View button at the bottom of the window.

Figure 5 The document window in Outline view.

Outline modification buttons   *Outline display buttons*   *Master Document buttons*

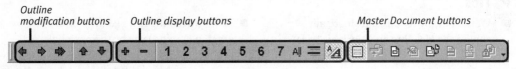

Figure 6 The Outlining toolbar.

> ▫ Introduction to Word 2000|
> ▫

Figure 7 Enter the text that you want to use as a heading.

> ▫ Introduction to Word 2000
> ▫ |

Figure 8 When you press [Enter], Word creates a new paragraph at the same heading level.

> ▫ Introduction to Word 2000
> ▫ **The Word Workplace**
> ▫ |

Figure 9 To create a new heading on the same level, simply type it in.

> ▫ Introduction to Word 2000
> ⊹ **The Word Workplace**
>   ▫ *Meet Microsoft Word*
>   ▫ /

Figure 10 To create a heading at a lower level, click the Demote button before typing it in. When you press [Enter], Word creates a new paragraph at the same (lower) heading level.

> ▫ Introduction to Word 2000
> ⊹ **The Word Workplace**
>   ▫ *Meet Microsoft Word*
> ▫ **New and Improved Features in Word 2000**
> ▫ |

Figure 11 To create a heading at a higher level, click the Promote button while the insertion point is in the heading. When you press [Enter], Word creates a new paragraph at the same (higher) heading level.

To add headings

1. Type the text that you want to use as a heading (**Figure 7**).

2. Press [Enter]. A new paragraph at the same heading level appears (**Figure 8**).

3. To add a heading at the same level, repeat steps 1 and 2 (**Figure 9**).

   or

   To add a heading at the next lower level, press [Tab] or click the Demote button ⇨ on the Outlining toolbar. Then repeat steps 1 and 2 (**Figure 10**).

   or

   To add a heading at the next higher level, press [Shift][Tab] or click the Promote button ⇦ on the Outlining toolbar. Then repeat steps 1 and 2 (**Figure 11**).

✔ Tips

- By default, the first heading you create is Heading 1—the top level.

- When you create a lower level heading beneath a heading, the marker to the left of the heading changes to a hollow plus sign to indicate that the heading has subheadings (**Figure 10**).

- Don't worry about entering a heading at the wrong level. You can promote or demote a heading at any time—I tell you how next.

To promote or demote a heading

1. Click anywhere in the heading to position the insertion point within it (**Figure 12**).

2. To promote the heading, press Shift Tab or click the Promote button ⬅ on the Outlining toolbar. The heading shifts to the left and changes into the next higher level heading.

   or

   To demote the heading, press Tab or click the Demote button ➡ on the Outlining toolbar. The heading shifts to the right and changes into the next lower level heading (**Figure 13**).

✔ Tips

- You cannot promote a Heading 1 level heading. Heading 1 is the highest level.

- You cannot demote a Heading 9 level heading. Heading 9 is the lowest level.

- To promote or demote multiple headings at the same time, select the headings, then follow step 2 above.

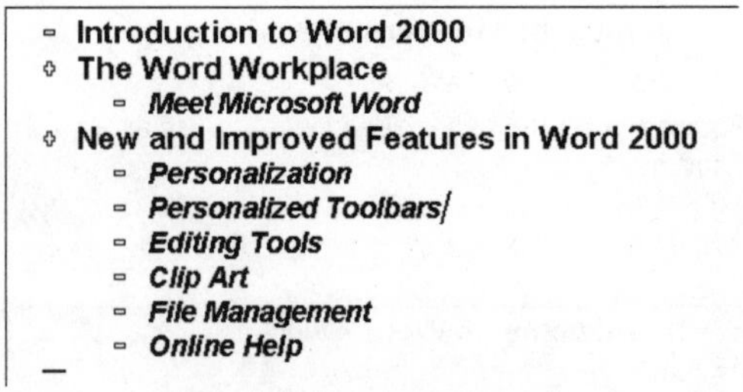

- Introduction to Word 2000
- ✧ **The Word Workplace**
  - *Meet Microsoft Word*
- ✧ **New and Improved Features in Word 2000**
  - *Personalization*
  - *Personalized Toolbars/*
  - *Editing Tools*
  - *Clip Art*
  - *File Management*
  - *Online Help*

Figure 12 Position the insertion point in the heading that you want to promote or demote.

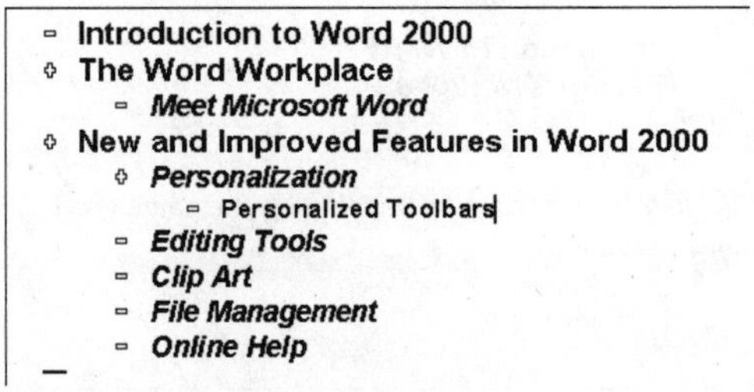

- Introduction to Word 2000
- ✧ **The Word Workplace**
  - *Meet Microsoft Word*
- ✧ **New and Improved Features in Word 2000**
  - ✧ *Personalization*
    - Personalized Toolbars|
  - *Editing Tools*
  - *Clip Art*
  - *File Management*
  - *Online Help*

Figure 13 Clicking the Demote button shifts the heading to the right and changes it to the next lower heading level.

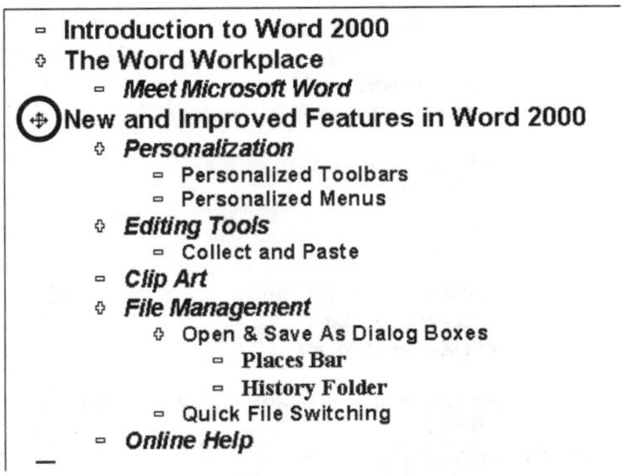

- Introduction to Word 2000
- The Word Workplace
  - *Meet Microsoft Word*
- (⊕) New and Improved Features in Word 2000
  - *Personalization*
    - Personalized Toolbars
    - Personalized Menus
  - *Editing Tools*
    - Collect and Paste
  - *Clip Art*
  - *File Management*
    - Open & Save As Dialog Boxes
      - **Places Bar**
      - History Folder
    - Quick File Switching
  - *Online Help*

Figure 14 Position the mouse pointer over a heading marker; it turns into a four-headed arrow.

- Introduction to Word 2000
- The Word Workplace
  - *Meet Microsoft Word*
- New and Improved Features in Word 2000
  - *Personalization*
    - Personalized Toolbars
    - Personalized Menus
  - *Editing Tools*
    - Collect and Paste
  - *Clip Art*
  - *File Management*
    - Open & Save As Dialog Boxes
      - Places Bar
      - History Folder
    - Quick File Switching
  - *Online Help*

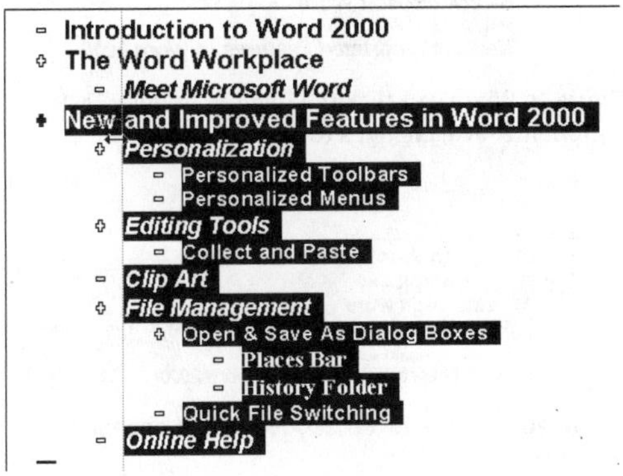

Figure 15 When you drag the heading marker, a line indicates the heading's level when you release the mouse button.

- Introduction to Word 2000
- The Word Workplace
  - *Meet Microsoft Word*
  - *New and Improved Features in Word 2000*
    - Personalization
      - Personalized Toolbars
      - Personalized Menus
    - Editing Tools
      - Collect and Paste
    - Clip Art
    - File Management
      - Open & Save As Dialog Boxes
        - *Places Bar*
        - *History Folder*
      - Quick File Switching
    - Online Help

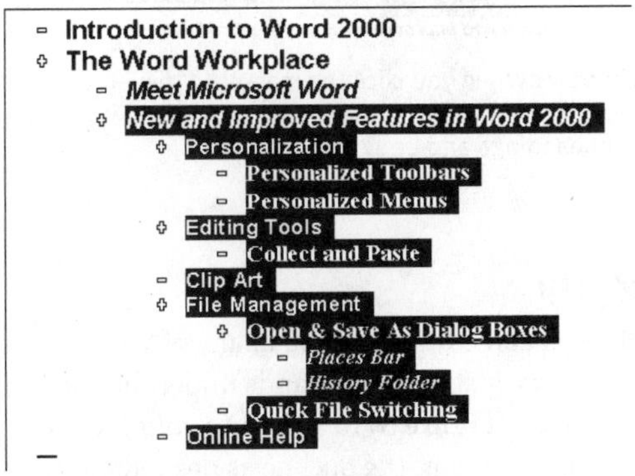

Figure 16 Release the mouse button to change the level of the heading and all of its subheadings.

To promote or demote a heading with its subheadings

1. Position the mouse pointer over the hollow plus sign to the left of the heading. The mouse pointer turns into a four-headed arrow (**Figure 14**).

2. To promote the headings, press the mouse button down and drag to the left.

   or

   To demote the headings, press the mouse button down and drag to the right (**Figure 15**).

   The heading and its subheadings are selected. As you drag, a line indicates the level to which the heading will be moved when you release the mouse button. You can see all this in **Figure 15**.

3. Release the mouse button to change the level of the heading and its subheadings (**Figure 16**).

✔ Tips

- You can also use this method to promote or demote a heading with no subheadings. Simply drag the hollow dash as instructed in step 2 to change its level.

- Another way to promote or demote a heading with its subheadings is with the Promote or Demote button on the Outlining toolbar. Just click the hollow plus sign marker (**Figure 14**) to select the heading and its subheadings. Then click the Promote or Demote button to change the selected headings' levels.

PROMOTING & DEMOTING HEADINGS

To add body text

1. Position the insertion point at the end of the heading after which you want to add body text (**Figure 17**).

2. Press ⎡Enter⎤ to create a new line with the same heading level (**Figure 18**).

3. Click the Demote to Body Text button ⇨ on the Outlining toolbar. The marker to the left of the insertion point changes into a small hollow square to indicate that the paragraph is body text (**Figure 19**).

4. Type the text that you want to use as body text (**Figure 20**).

✔ Tips

- Word automatically applies the Normal style to body text. You can modify the style to meet your needs; I tell you how in **Chapter 4**.

- Each time you press ⎡Enter⎤ while typing body text, Word creates a new paragraph of body text.

- You can convert body text to a heading by clicking the Promote ⬅ or Demote ➡ button on the Outlining toolbar.

To remove outline components

1. To remove a single heading or paragraph of body text, click the hollow dash or small square marker to the left of the heading or body text. This selects the entire paragraph of the heading or body text.

    or

    To remove a heading with its subheadings and body text, click the hollow plus sign marker to the left of the heading. This selects the heading and all of its subheadings and body text (**Figure 21**).

2. Press ⎡Backspace⎤. The selection is removed.

- Introduction to Word 2000
- ◇ **The Word Workplace**
    - *Meet Microsoft Word*|
    - ◇ *New and Improved Features in Word 2000*

Figure 17 Position the insertion point.

- Introduction to Word 2000
- ◇ **The Word Workplace**
    - *Meet Microsoft Word*
    - |
    - ◇ *New and Improved Features in Word 2000*

Figure 18 Press ⎡Enter⎤.

- Introduction to Word 2000
- ◇ **The Word Workplace**
    - ◇ *Meet Microsoft Word*
    - |
    - ◇ *New and Improved Features in Word 2000*

Figure 19 When you click the Demote to Body Text button, the level changes to body text.

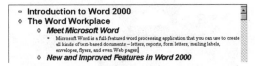

Figure 20 Type the text that you want to appear as body text.

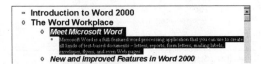

Figure 21 When you click the marker to the left of a heading, Word selects the heading and all of its subheadings and body text.

✔ Tip

- You can edit an outline in any of Word's views. Just use commands under the View menu (**Figure 3**) to switch to your favorite view and edit the outline as desired.

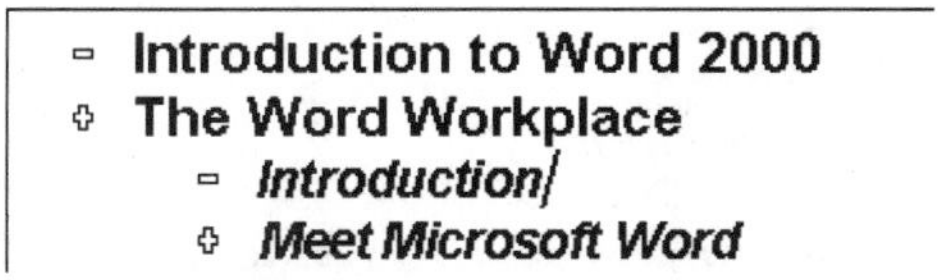

- Introduction to Word 2000
- The Word Workplace
  - *Introduction|*
  - *Meet Microsoft Word*

Figure 22 Click to position the insertion point.

- Introduction to Word 2000
  - **Introduction**
- The Word Workplace
  - *Meet Microsoft Word*

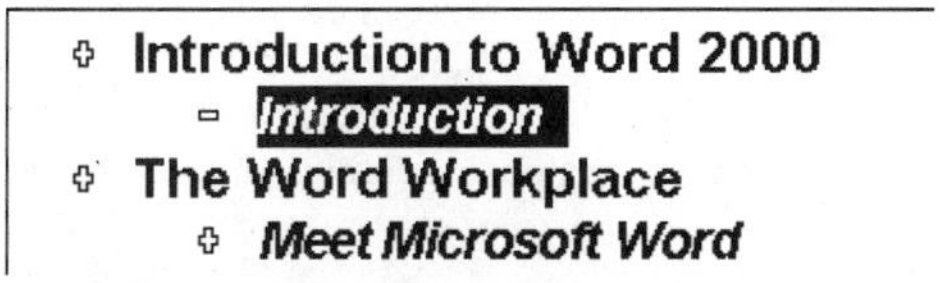

Figure 23 When you click the Move Up button, the heading moves up.

Rearranging Outline Components

Word's outline feature offers two methods to rearrange outline components:

- ◆ You can click the Move Up 🔼 or Move Down 🔽 button to move selected outline components up or down.

- ◆ You can drag heading or body text markers to move selected outline components up or down.

✔ Tips

- ■ Rearranging outline components using these methods changes the order in which they appear but not their level of importance.

- ■ Either of these methods can be used to move a single heading or paragraph of body text, multiple headings, or a heading with all of its subheadings and body text.

To move headings and/or body text with toolbar buttons

1. To move a single heading or paragraph of body text, click to position the insertion point within it (**Figure 22**).

   or

   To move a heading with its subheadings and body text, click the hollow plus sign marker to the left of the heading to select the heading, its subheadings, and its body text (**Figure 21**).

2. To move the heading up, click the Move Up 🔼 button on the Outlining toolbar. The heading moves one paragraph up (**Figure 23**).

   or

   To move the heading down, click the Move Down 🔽 button on the Outlining toolbar. The heading moves one paragraph down.

To move headings and/or body text by dragging

1. To move a single heading or paragraph of body text, position the mouse pointer over the hollow dash or small square marker to its left.

   or

   To move a heading with its subheadings and body text, position the mouse pointer on the plus sign marker to its left (**Figure 24**).

   The mouse pointer turns into a four-headed arrow (**Figure 24**).

2. To move the component(s) up, press the mouse button down and drag up (**Figure 25**).

   or

   To move the component(s) down, press the mouse button down and drag down.

   The components are selected. As you drag, a line indicates the location to which they will be moved when you release the mouse button. You can see all this in **Figure 25**.

3. Release the mouse button to move the component(s) (**Figure 26**).

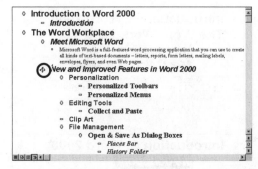

Figure 24 Position the mouse pointer over the heading marker.

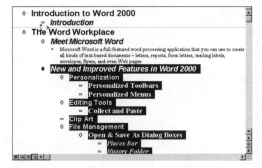

Figure 25 As you drag, a line indicates the new position when you release the mouse button.

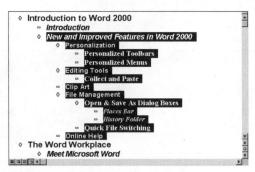

Figure 26 When you release the mouse button, the headings move.

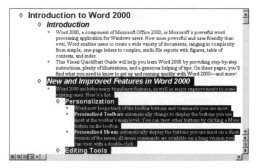

Figure 27 Click a heading's marker to select its contents.

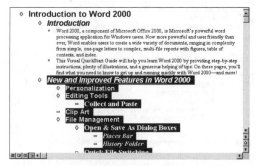

Figure 28 When you click the Collapse button, the lowest displayed level—in this example, the body text—is hidden.

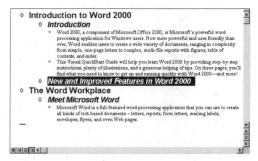

Figure 29 You can click the Collapse button repeatedly to hide multiple levels.

Viewing Outlines

Buttons on the Outlining toolbar (**Figure 6**) enable you to change your view of an outline:

◆ Collapse headings to hide subheadings and body text.

◆ Expand headings to show subheadings and body text.

◆ Show only specific heading levels.

◆ Show all heading levels.

◆ Show only the first line of text in each paragraph.

◆ Show all lines of text in each paragraph.

◆ Show or hide formatting.

✔ Tip

■ These viewing options do not change the document's content—just your view of it.

To collapse a heading

1. Click the marker to the left of the heading that you want to collapse to select the heading, its subheadings, and its body text (**Figure 27**).

2. Click the Collapse button ■ on the Outlining toolbar. The heading collapses to hide the lowest displayed level (**Figure 28**).

3. Repeat step 2 until only the levels you want to see are displayed (**Figure 29**).

or

Double-click the marker to the left of the heading that you want to collapse. The heading collapses to its level (**Figure 29**).

✔ Tip

■ When you collapse a heading with subheadings or body text, a gray line appears beneath it to indicate hidden items (**Figures 28** and **29**).

To expand a heading

1. Click the marker to the left of the heading that you want to expand to select the heading and all of its subheadings and body text (**Figure 29**).

2. Click the Expand button ⊞ on the Outlining toolbar. The heading expands to display the highest hidden level (**Figure 28**).

3. Repeat step 2 as desired to display all of the levels you want to see (**Figure 27**).

or

Double-click the marker to the left of the heading that you want to expand. The heading expands to show all levels (**Figure 27**).

To view only certain heading levels

Click the numbered button **1** **2** **3** **4** **5** **6** **7** on the Outlining toolbar that corresponds to the lowest level of heading that you want to display.

The outline collapses or expands to show just that level (**Figures 30** and **31**).

To view all heading levels

Click the Show All Headings button **All** on the Outlining toolbar.

The outline expands to show all headings and body text (**Figure 32**).

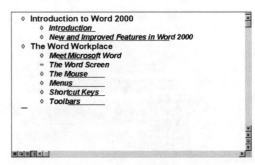

Figure 30 In this example, the Show Heading 2 button was clicked to display heading levels 1 and 2.

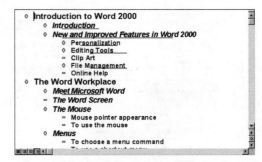

Figure 31 In this example, the Show Heading 3 button was clicked to display heading levels 1, 2, and 3.

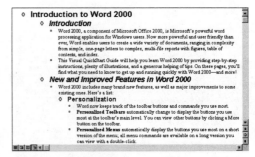

Figure 32 Clicking the Show All Headings button displays all levels of headings and the body text.

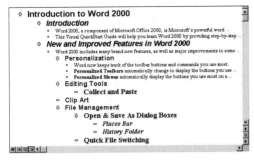

Figure 33 Turning on the Show First Line Only button displays only the first line of each heading or paragraph of body text.

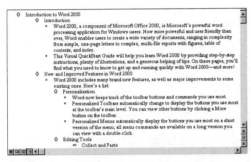

Figure 34 Turning off the Show Formatting button displays all text in the default paragraph font for the Normal style—in this case, 10-point Times New Roman.

To display only the first line of every paragraph

Click the Show First Line Only button ▤ on the Outlining toolbar to turn it off.

The outline view changes to display only the first line of each heading and paragraph of body text (**Figure 33**).

✔ Tip

■ The Show First Line Only button works like a toggle switch which is turned off by default.

To display all lines of every paragraph

Click the Show First Line Only button ▤ on the Outlining toolbar to turn it on.

The outline view changes to display all lines of each heading and paragraph of body text (**Figure 32**).

To hide formatting

Click the Show Formatting button ᴬ𝐀 on the Outlining toolbar to turn it off.

The outline view changes to display all headings and body text in the default paragraph font for the Normal style (**Figure 34**).

✔ Tip

■ The Show Formatting button works like a toggle switch which is turned on or selected by default.

To show formatting

Click the Show Formatting button ᴬ𝐀 on the Outlining toolbar to turn it on.

The outline view changes to display all headings and body text with the Heading and Normal styles applied to them (**Figure 32**).

Working with an Outline in another View

You can switch to Normal (**Figure 35**), Print Layout (**Figure 36**), or Web Layout (**Figure 37**) view while working with an outline. There's nothing special about an outline except the additional outlining features available in Outline view. It's the same document when you switch to another view.

✔ Tips

- You can switch between any of Word's views at any time.

- I explain how to switch from one view to another in **Chapter 1**.

- Once the structure of a lengthy or complex document has been established in Outline view, you may find it easier to complete the document in Normal or Print Layout view.

- In Normal, Page Layout, and Online Layout views, you can apply the Heading and Normal styles using the Style menu on the Formatting toolbar. I tell you more about styles in **Chapter 4**.

- You can use Word's Document Map feature to quickly navigate throughout a document that uses heading styles—like any document created with Word's outlining feature. **Figure 37** shows Web layout view with the Document Map displayed. I explain how to display and use the Document Map in **Chapter 1**.

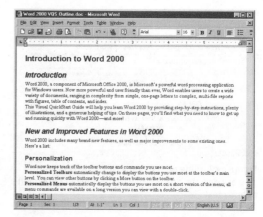

Figure 35 An outline in Normal view,...

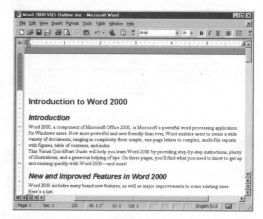

Figure 36 ...Print Layout view,...

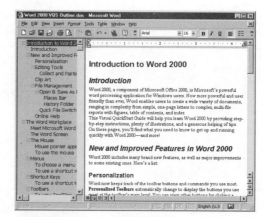

Figure 37 ...and Web Layout view with the Document Map displayed.

Figure 38
The Insert menu.

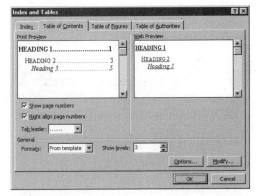

Figure 39 The Table of Contents tab of the Index and Tables dialog box.

Figure 40
The Formats menu determines the overall appearance of the table of contents.

Figure 41
The Tab leader menu enables you to select the character to appear between the entry and its page reference.

Creating a Table of Contents

One of the benefits of using Word's outline feature is that headings are easily gathered together to create a table of contents.

✔ Tip

■ Although there are other ways to generate a table of contents in Word, basing a table of contents on an outline is the easiest way.

To create a table of contents based on an outline

1. Position the insertion point where you want the table of contents to appear.

2. Choose Insert > Index and Tables (**Figure 38**).

3. In the Index and Tables dialog box that appears, click the Table of Contents tab to display its options (**Figure 39**).

4. Choose an option from the Formats menu (**Figure 40**). A sample of the printed format appears in the Print Preview area.

5. Set other options in the dialog box:

   ▲ **Show page numbers** tells Word to include page references for each table of contents entry.

   ▲ **Right align page numbers** aligns page numbers along the right side of the page.

   ▲ **Tab leader** (**Figure 41**) enables you to select the characters that should appear between the table of contents entry and its page number.

   ▲ **Show levels** enables you to specify the number of heading levels that should be included in the table of contents.

6. Click OK.

   Word generates the table of contents and inserts it as a field (**Figure 42**).

Continued on next page...

CREATING A TABLE OF CONTENTS

Continued from previous page.

✔ Tips

- The Web Preview area of the Index and Tables dialog box (**Figure 39**) shows what the table of contents would look like if the document was saved as a Web page. I explain how to create and work with Web pages in **Chapter 13**.

- Once a table of contents has been created, it can be updated like any other Word field; right-click on it to display a shortcut menu (**Figure 43**) and choose Update Field. I tell you more about Word fields in **Chapter 7**.

- To remove a table of contents, simply select it and press ⌷Backspace⌷.

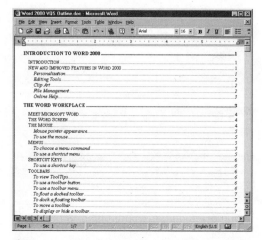

Figure 42 A table of contents for three heading levels, generated using the Formal format.

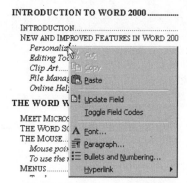

Figure 43 Use the table of contents' shortcut menu to update the table of contents entries and page references when necessary.

TABLES

10

Item Name	Description	Item Number	Price
Envelopes, #10	#10 envelopes, 20 lb. White, all-purpose. 500 per box.	ENV10	$15.99/box
Envelopes, #9	#9 envelopes, 20 lb. White, all-purpose. 500 per box.	ENV09	$12.99/box
Permanent Marker, Blue	Mark of Zorro brand permanent marker. 0.5 mm felt tip. Airtight cap. Blue.	MRK01	$2.99 each
Permanent Marker, Red	Mark of Zorro brand permanent marker. 0.5 mm felt tip. Airtight cap. Red.	MRK03	$2.99 each
Laser Paper, White	White, 20 lb. Paper, designed for use in laser printers. 8-1/2 x 11 inches. 500 sheets per ream.	PAP05	5.99/ream
Inkjet Paper, White	White, 20 lb. Paper, designed for use in inkjet printers. 8-1/2 x 11 inches. 500 sheets per ream.	PAP11	7.99/ream
Copier Paper, White	White, 20 lb. Paper, designed for use in copy machines. 8-1/2 x 11 inches. 500 sheets per ream.	PAP01	4.99/ream
Shipping Boxes, 9 x 12	9 x 12 inches, corrugated cardboard shipping boxes. White. 10 boxes per package.	BOX05	10.99/pkg

Figure 1 A four-column, nine-row table with borders. Each box is an individual cell.

Tables

Word's table feature enables you to create tables of information.

A table consists of table *cells* arranged in *columns* and *rows* (**Figure 1**). You enter information into each cell, which is like a tiny document of its own. You can put multiple paragraphs of text into a cell and format characters or paragraphs as discussed in **Chapters 3** and **4**.

Table structure and format are extremely flexible and can be modified to meet your needs. A cell can expand vertically to accommodate long blocks of text or graphics; you can also resize it manually as desired. You can format cells, merge cells, and split cells. These capabilities make the table feature a good choice for organizing a wide variety of data.

✔ Tip

- You can also use tab stops and tab characters to create simple tables without cells. I explain how to do this in **Chapter 3**. This method, however, is not nearly as flexible as using cell tables.

Creating a Table

Word offers three ways to create a table:

◆ Use the Insert Table command (**Figure 2**) or toolbar button  to create a table at the insertion point.

◆ Use the Draw Table command (**Figure 2**) to draw a table anywhere on a page.

◆ Use the Convert Text to Table command to convert existing text to a table.

Figure 2 Use commands near the top of the Table menu to create a table from scratch.

To insert a table

1. Position the insertion point where you want the table to appear.

2. Choose Table > Insert > Table (**Figure 2**) to display the Insert Table dialog box (**Figure 3**).

3. Enter the number of columns and rows for the table in the Number of columns and Number of rows boxes.

4. Select an AutoFit behavior option:

   ▲ **Fixed column width** enables you to specify the width for each column.

   ▲ **AutoFit to contents** automatically changes column width to best fit the column's contents.

   ▲ **AutoFit to window** automatically changes column width to best fit the table in the document window.

5. Click OK.

or

1. Position the insertion point where you want the table to appear.

2. Click the Insert Table button 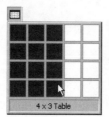 on the Standard toolbar to display a menu of columns and rows.

3. Select the number of columns and rows you want in the table (**Figure 4**).

The table appears, with the insertion point in the top left cell (**Figure 5**).

Figure 3 The Insert Table dialog box.

Figure 4
The Insert Table button's menu.

Figure 5 An empty three-column, four-row table.

✔ Tips

■ You can click the AutoFormat button in the Insert Table dialog box (**Figure 3**) to format the table as you create it. I tell you about AutoFormatting tables later in this chapter.

■ To use the current settings in the Insert Table dialog box (**Figure 3**) as the default settings for every new table you create, turn on the Use as default for new tables check box.

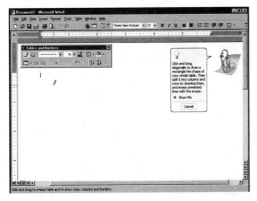

Figure 6 The Tables and Borders toolbar appears when you draw a table.

Figure 7 Drag diagonally to draw a box the size and shape of the table you want.

Figure 8 The outside border for a single-cell table appears.

Figure 9 Draw vertical lines for column boundaries...

Figure 10 ...and horizontal lines for row boundaries.

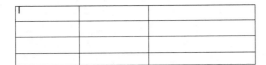

Figure 11 A drawn table.

To draw a table

1. Choose Table > Draw Table (**Figure 2**). If you are not in Print Layout mode, Word automatically switches to it and the Tables and Borders toolbar appears (**Figure 6**).

2. If necessary, click the Draw Table button to select it.

3. Position the Draw Table tool where you want the upper-left corner of the table.

4. Press the mouse button down and drag diagonally to draw a box the size and shape of the table you want (**Figure 7**). When you release the mouse button, the outside border of the table appears (**Figure 8**).

5. Drag the Draw Table tool from the top border of the table to the bottom to draw each column boundary (**Figure 9**).

6. Drag the Draw Table tool from the left border of the table to the right to draw each row boundary (**Figure 10**).

When you're finished, the table might look something like the one in **Figure 11**.

✔ Tips

- The first time you draw a table, the Office Assistant appears and provides instructions (**Figure 6**).

- To remove a cell boundary, click the Eraser button on the Tables and Borders toolbar and then drag the eraser tool over the boundary you want to remove (**Figure 12**). When you release the mouse button, the boundary disappears.

- I explain how to change column widths and row heights later in this chapter.

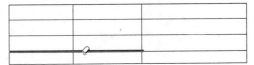

Figure 12 Use the eraser tool to erase a boundary.

To convert text to a table

1. Select the text that you want to convert to a table (**Figure 13**).

2. Choose Table > Convert > Text to Table (**Figure 14**) to display the Convert Text to Table dialog box (**Figure 15**).

3. Confirm that the correct separator is selected in the Separate text at area and that the correct values appear in the Number of columns and Number of rows boxes. Make any required changes.

4. Select an AutoFit behavior option.

5. Click OK.

   The text turns into a table (**Figure 16**).

✔ Tips

- This method works best with tab- or comma-separated text.

- In most instances, Word will correctly "guess" the settings for the Convert Text to Table dialog box (**Figure 15**) and no changes will be required in step 3 above.

- I explain the AutoFit behavior options earlier in this section.

Figure 13 Select the text that you want to convert to a table. In this example, tab-separated text is selected.

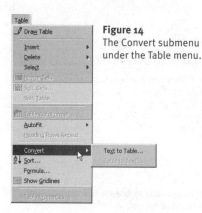

Figure 14 The Convert submenu under the Table menu.

Figure 15 The Convert Text to Table dialog box looks a lot like the Insert Table dialog box.

Substance	Date Tested	Tested By	Results
MSG	5/18/00	Maria Langer	42.5158
Magnesium	6/4/00	John Aabbott	51.2
Sulfur	6/15/00	Mary Johannesburg	142.365
Aspirin	8/12/00	Tim Jones	1.1

Figure 16 The text in Figure 13 converted to a table.

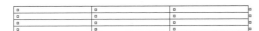

Figure 17 Table elements include column, row, and cell boundaries, end-of-cell markers, and, in this example, borders.

Figure 18 When a table has no borders, gridlines can identify the boundaries.

Figure 19
The Table menu.

Anatomy of a Table

A table includes a variety of different elements (**Figure 17**):

- ◆ **Column boundaries** appear on either side of a column.

- ◆ **Row boundaries** appear on the top and bottom of a row.

- ◆ **Cell boundaries** are the portions of column and row boundaries that appear around an individual cell.

- ◆ **End-of-cell markers** appear within each table cell. They indicate the end of the cell's contents—just like the end-of document marker marks the end of a Word document.

- ◆ **Borders** are lines that can appear on any column, row, or cell boundary. These lines print when the table is printed.

- ◆ **Gridlines** (**Figure 18**) are lines that appear on any column, row, or cell boundary. Unlike borders, however, gridlines don't print.

✔ Tips

- ■ To see the end-of-cell marker, display formatting marks by turning on the Show/ Hide ¶ button ¶ on the Standard toolbar. I tell you more about formatting marks and the Show/Hide ¶ button in **Chapter 1**.

- ■ By default, Word creates tables with borders on all column and row boundaries. You can change or remove them using techniques discussed in **Chapter 4**.

- ■ You can only see gridlines on boundaries that do not have borders (**Figure 18**). In addition, the Gridlines option on the Table menu (**Figure 19**) must be turned on for gridlines to appear.

Selecting Table Cells

In many cases, to format the contents of table cells or restructure a table, you must begin by selecting the cells you want to change. Selecting table cells is very similar to selecting other document text, but there are some tricks to make it easier.

To select a cell

1. Position the mouse pointer in the far left side of the cell so it points to the right (**Figure 20**). This is the cell's selection bar.

2. Click once. The cell becomes selected (**Figure 21**).

or

1. Position the mouse pointer at the beginning of a cell's contents. The mouse pointer must appear as an I-beam pointer (**Figure 22**).

2. Press the mouse button down and drag through the contents of the cell. When you release the mouse button, the cell is selected (**Figure 23**).

or

1. Click to position the blinking insertion point in the cell (**Figure 24**).

2. Choose Table > Select > Cell (**Figure 25**). The cell is selected (**Figure 23**).

To select a row

1. Position the mouse pointer in the selection bar of any cell in the row (**Figure 20**).

2. Double-click. The entire row becomes selected (**Figure 26**).

or

1. Click to position the blinking insertion point in any cell in the row (**Figure 24**) or select any cell in the row (**Figure 23**).

2. Choose Table > Select > Row (**Figure 25**). The entire row is selected (**Figure 27**).

Figure 20 Position the mouse pointer in the cell's selection bar.

Figure 21 Click once to select the cell.

Item Name	Description	Item Number	Price
Envelopes, #10	#10 envelopes, 20 lb. White, all-purpose. 500 per box.	ENV10	$15.99/box
Envelopes, #9	#9 envelopes, 20 lb. White, all-purpose. 500 per box.	ENV09	$12.99/box
Permanent Marker, Blue	Mark of Zorro brand permanent marker. 0.5 mm felt tip. Airtight cap. Blue.	MRK01	$2.99 each
Permanent Marker, Red	Mark of Zorro brand permanent marker. 0.5 mm felt tip. Airtight cap. Red.	MRK03	$2.99 each
Laser Paper, White	White, 20 lb. Paper, designed for use in laser printers. 8-1/2 x 11 inches. 500 sheets per ream.	PAP05	5.99/ream
Inkjet Paper, White	White, 20 lb. Paper, designed for use in inkjet printers. 8-1/2 x 11 inches. 500 sheets per ream.	PAP11	7.99/ream
Copier Paper, White	White, 20 lb. Paper, designed for use in copy machines. 8-1/2 x 11 inches. 500 sheets per ream.	PAP01	4.99/ream
Shipping Boxes, 9 x 12	9 x 12 inches, corrugated cardboard shipping boxes. White. 10 boxes per package.	BOX05	10.99/pkg

Figure 22 Position the I-beam pointer at the beginning of the cell's contents.

Item Name	Description	Item Number	Price
Envelopes, #10	#10 envelopes, 20 lb. White, all-purpose. 500 per box.	ENV10	$15.99/box
Envelopes, #9	#9 envelopes, 20 lb. White, all-purpose. 500 per box.	ENV09	$12.99/box
Permanent Marker, Blue	Mark of Zorro brand permanent marker. 0.5 mm felt tip. Airtight cap. Blue.	MRK01	$2.99 each
Permanent Marker, Red	Mark of Zorro brand permanent marker. 0.5 mm felt tip. Airtight cap. Red.	MRK03	$2.99 each
Laser Paper, White	White, 20 lb. Paper, designed for use in laser printers. 8-1/2 x 11 inches. 500 sheets per ream.	PAP05	5.99/ream
Inkjet Paper, White	White, 20 lb. Paper, designed for use in inkjet printers. 8-1/2 x 11 inches. 500 sheets per ream.	PAP11	7.99/ream
Copier Paper, White	White, 20 lb. Paper, designed for use in copy machines. 8-1/2 x 11 inches. 500 sheets per ream.	PAP01	4.99/ream
Shipping Boxes, 9 x 12	9 x 12 inches, corrugated cardboard shipping boxes. White. 10 boxes per package.	BOX05	10.99/pkg

Figure 23 Drag through the cell's contents to select it.

Item Name	Description	Item Number	Price
Envelopes, #10	#10 envelopes, 20 lb. White, all-purpose. 500 per box.	ENV10	$15.99/box
Envelopes, #9	#9 envelopes, 20 lb. White, all-purpose. 500 per box.	ENV09	$12.99/box
Permanent Marker, Blue	Mark of Zorro brand permanent marker. 0.5 mm felt tip. Airtight cap. Blue.	MRK01	$2.99 each
Permanent Marker, Red	Mark of Zorro brand permanent marker. 0.5 mm felt tip. Airtight cap. Red.	MRK03	$2.99 each
Laser Paper, White	White, 20 lb. Paper, designed for use in laser printers. 8-1/2 x 11 inches. 500 sheets per ream.	PAP05	5.99/ream
Inkjet Paper, White	White, 20 lb. Paper, designed for use in inkjet printers. 8-1/2 x 11 inches. 500 sheets per ream.	PAP11	7.99/ream
Copier Paper, White	White, 20 lb. Paper, designed for use in copy machines. 8-1/2 x 11 inches. 500 sheets per ream.	PAP01	4.99/ream
Shipping Boxes, 9 x 12	9 x 12 inches, corrugated cardboard shipping boxes. White. 10 boxes per package.	BOX05	10.99/pkg

Figure 24 Position the insertion point in the cell.

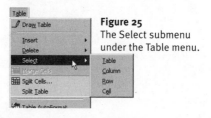

Figure 25 The Select submenu under the Table menu.

Figure 26 Double-click to select an entire row.

Item Name	Description	Item Number	Price
Envelopes, #10	#10 envelopes, 20 lb. White, all-purpose. 500 per box.	ENV10	$15.99/box
Envelopes, #9	#9 envelopes, 20 lb. White, all-purpose. 500 per box.	ENV09	$12.99/box
Permanent Marker, Blue	Mark of Zorro brand permanent marker. 0.5 mm felt tip. Airtight cap. Blue.	MRK01	$2.99 each
Permanent Marker, Red	Mark of Zorro brand permanent marker. 0.5 mm felt tip. Airtight cap. Red.	MRK03	$2.99 each
Laser Paper, White	White, 20 lb. Paper, designed for use in laser printers. 8-1/2 x 11 inches. 500 sheets per ream.	PAP05	5.99/ream
Inkjet Paper, White	White, 20 lb. Paper, designed for use in inkjet printers. 8-1/2 x 11 inches. 500 sheets per ream.	PAP11	7.99/ream
Copier Paper, White	White, 20 lb. Paper, designed for use in copy machines. 8-1/2 x 11 inches. 500 sheets per ream.	PAP01	4.99/ream
Shipping Boxes, 9 x 12	9 x 12 inches, corrugated cardboard shipping boxes. White. 10 boxes per package.	BOX05	10.99/pkg

Figure 27 When you use the Select Row command, the entire row is selected.

Figure 28 Position the mouse pointer on the top of the boundary of the column.

Figure 29 Click once to select the column.

Item Name	Description	Item Number	Price
Envelopes, #10	#10 envelopes, 20 lb. White, all-purpose. 500 per box.	ENV10	$15.99/box
Envelopes, #9	#9 envelopes, 20 lb. White, all-purpose. 500 per box.	ENV09	$12.99/box
Permanent Marker, Blue	Mark of Zorro brand permanent marker. 0.5 mm felt tip. Airtight cap. Blue.	MRK01	$2.99 each
Permanent Marker, Red	Mark of Zorro brand permanent marker. 0.5 mm felt tip. Airtight cap. Red.	MRK03	$2.99 each
Laser Paper, White	White, 20 lb. Paper, designed for use in laser printers. 8-1/2 x 11 inches. 500 sheets per ream.	PAP05	5.99/ream
Inkjet Paper, White	White, 20 lb. Paper, designed for use in inkjet printers. 8-1/2 x 11 inches. 500 sheets per ream.	PAP11	7.99/ream
Copier Paper, White	White, 20 lb. Paper, designed for use in copy machines. 8-1/2 x 11 inches. 500 sheets per ream.	PAP01	4.99/ream
Shipping Boxes, 9 x 12	9 x 12 inches, corrugated cardboard shipping boxes. White. 10 boxes per package.	BOX05	10.99/pkg

Figure 30 When you use the Select Column command, the entire column is selected.

Item Name	Description	Item Number	Price
Envelopes, #10	#10 envelopes, 20 lb. White, all-purpose. 500 per box.	ENV10	$15.99/box
Envelopes, #9	#9 envelopes, 20 lb. White, all-purpose. 500 per box.	ENV09	$12.99/box
Permanent Marker, Blue	Mark of Zorro brand permanent marker. 0.5 mm felt tip. Airtight cap. Blue.	MRK01	$2.99 each
Permanent Marker, Red	Mark of Zorro brand permanent marker. 0.5 mm felt tip. Airtight cap. Red.	MRK03	$2.99 each
Laser Paper, White	White, 20 lb. Paper, designed for use in laser printers. 8-1/2 x 11 inches. 500 sheets per ream.	PAP05	5.99/ream
Inkjet Paper, White	White, 20 lb. Paper, designed for use in inkjet printers. 8-1/2 x 11 inches. 500 sheets per ream.	PAP11	7.99/ream
Copier Paper, White	White, 20 lb. Paper, designed for use in copy machines. 8-1/2 x 11 inches. 500 sheets per ream.	PAP01	4.99/ream
Shipping Boxes, 9 x 12	9 x 12 inches, corrugated cardboard shipping boxes. White. 10 boxes per package.	BOX05	10.99/pkg

Figure 31 A selected table.

To select a column

1. Position the mouse pointer over the top boundary of the column that you want to select. It turns into an arrow pointing down (**Figure 28**).

2. Click once. The column is selected (**Figure 29**).

or

Hold down (Alt) while clicking anywhere in the column that you want to select.

or

1. Click to position the blinking insertion point in any cell in the column (**Figure 24**) or select any cell in the column (**Figure 23**).

2. Choose Table > Select > Column (**Figure 25**). The entire column is selected (**Figure 30**).

To select the entire table

Hold down (Alt) while double-clicking anywhere in the table. The table is selected (**Figure 31**).

or

1. Click to position the blinking insertion point in any cell in the table (**Figure 24**) or select any cell in the table (**Figure 23**).

2. Choose Table > Select > Table (**Figure 25**). The entire table is selected (**Figure 31**).

Entering & Formatting Table Information

You enter text and other information into a table the same way you enter it into any document: type, paste, or drag it in. Then format it as desired using techniques in **Chapters 3** and **4**.

✔ Tips

- Think of each cell as a tiny document window. The cell boundaries are like document margins. You can enter as much information as you like and apply character and paragraph formatting.

- As you enter information into a cell, it expands vertically to accommodate its contents (**Figure 36**).

- I tell you about copying and moving text with the Cut, Copy, and Paste commands and drag-and-drop text editing in **Chapter 2**.

To enter text into a cell

1. Position the insertion point in the cell (**Figure 32**).

2. Type the text that you want to appear in the cell (**Figure 33**).

   or

   Use the Paste command to paste a previously copied or cut selection into the cell.

   or

1. Select text in another part of the document (**Figure 34**) or another document.

2. Drag the selection into the cell in which you want it to appear (**Figure 35**). When you release the mouse button, the text appears in the cell (**Figure 36**).

✔ Tip

- To enter a tab character in a cell, press `Control` `Tab`.

Figure 32 Position the insertion point in the cell in which you want to enter text.

Envelopes, #10

Figure 33 Type to enter the text.

Here are some of the products we offer:

Envelopes, #10

Our #10 envelopes are the finest available. Made of 20 lb. Paper with a brightness of 39, they are perfect for any mailing use—including important letters that deserve the best.

Figure 34 Select the text that you want to move into a cell.

Here are some of the products we offer:

Envelopes, #10

Our #10 envelopes are the finest available. Made of 20 lb. Paper with a brightness of 39, they are perfect for any mailing use—including important letters that deserve the best.

Figure 35 Drag the selection into the cell.

Here are some of the products we offer:

Envelopes, #10 | Our #10 envelopes are the finest available. Made of 20 lb. Paper with a brightness of 39, they are perfect for any mailing use—including important letters that deserve the best.

Figure 36 When you release the mouse button, the selection moves into the cell.

Figure 37
You can use the Insert menu to insert special text or objects into a table.

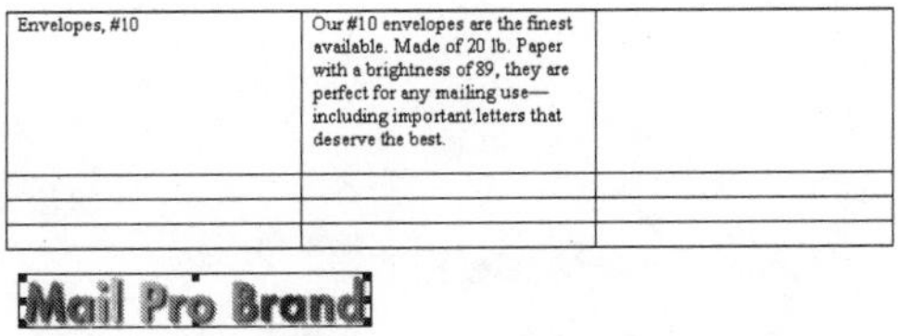

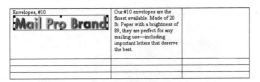

Figure 38 Select the object that you want to move into a cell.

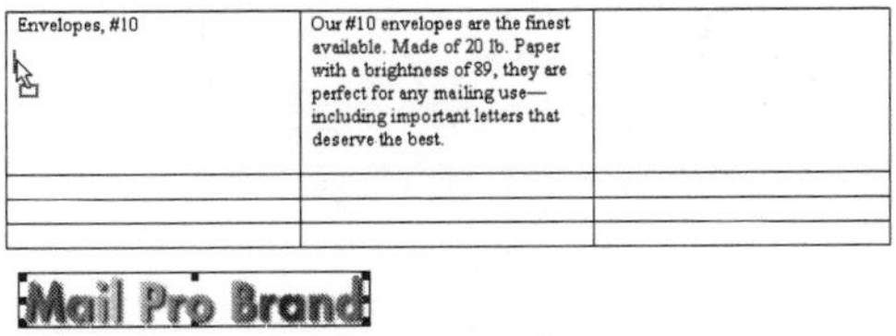

Figure 39 Drag the object into the cell.

Figure 40 When you release the mouse button, the object moves.

To enter special text or objects into a cell

1. Position the insertion point in the cell.

2. Choose the appropriate command from the Insert menu (**Figure 37**) to insert special text or objects.

   or

   Use the Paste command to paste a previously copied or cut selection into the cell.

or

1. Select special text or objects in another part of the document (**Figure 38**) or another document.

2. Drag the selection into the cell in which you want it to appear. When you release the mouse button (**Figure 39**), it appears in the cell (**Figure 40**).

✔ Tips

■ Special text, which I discuss in **Chapter 7**, can include Word fields, footnotes, endnotes, symbols, and comments.

■ I tell you about options under the Insert menu in **Chapters 7** and **8**.

To advance from one cell to another

To advance to the next cell in the table, press Tab.

or

To advance to the previous cell in the table, press Shift Tab.

✔ Tip

■ If you use either of these techniques to advance to a cell that is not empty, the cell's contents become selected. Otherwise, the insertion point appears in the cell.

ENTERING OTHER INFO INTO TABLE CELLS

To format characters or paragraphs in a cell

1. Select the characters that you want to format.

2. Apply font formatting and/or paragraph formatting as discussed in **Chapters 3** and **4**.

✔ Tips

- Almost every kind of font or paragraph formatting can be applied to the contents of individual cells.

- I tell you more about formatting tables when I discuss the Table AutoFormat feature later in this chapter.

To set table alignment & text wrapping

1. Select the entire table (**Figure 41**).

2. Choose Table > Table Properties (**Figure 19**).

3. If necessary, click the Table tab in the Table Properties dialog box that appears to display its options (**Figure 42**).

4. Select one of the Alignment options to specify whether the table should be left aligned, centered, or right aligned on the page. If you select Left, you can enter an indentation value in the Indent from left box.

5. Choose a Text wrapping option to specify whether text outside the table will wrap around the table.

6. Click OK.

Figure 43 shows an example of a centered table without any text wrapping.

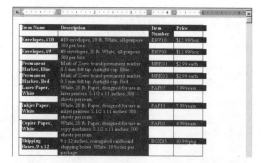

Figure 41 Select the table that you want to align.

Figure 42 The Table tab of the Table Properties dialog box.

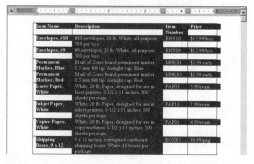

Figure 43 Here's an example of the table in **Figure 41** centered between the left and right document margins.

Item Name	Description	Item Number	Price
Envelopes, #10	#10 envelopes, 20 lb. White, all-purpose. 500 per box.	ENV10	$15.99/box
Envelopes, #9	#9 envelopes, 20 lb. White, all-purpose. 500 per box.	ENV09	$12.99/box
Permanent Marker, Blue	Mark of Zorro brand permanent marker. 0.5 mm felt tip. Airtight cap. Blue.	MRK01	$2.99 each
Permanent Marker, Red	Mark of Zorro brand permanent marker. 0.5 mm felt tip. Airtight cap. Red.	MRK03	$2.99 each
Laser Paper, White	White, 20 lb. Paper, designed for use in laser printers. 8-1/2 x 11 inches. 500 sheets per ream.	PAP05	5.99/ream
Inkjet Paper, White	White, 20 lb. Paper, designed for use in inkjet printers. 8-1/2 x 11 inches. 500 sheets per ream.	PAP11	7.99/ream
Copier Paper, White	White, 20 lb. Paper, designed for use in copy machines. 8-1/2 x 11 inches. 500 sheets per ream.	PAP01	4.99/ream
Shipping Boxes, 9 x 12	9 x 12 inches, corrugated cardboard shipping boxes. White. 10 boxes per package.	BOX05	10.99/pkg

Figure 44 Select the cells you want to align.

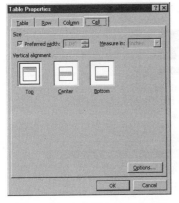

Figure 45 The Cell tab of the Table Properties dialog box.

Item Name	Description	Item Number	Price
Envelopes, #10	#10 envelopes, 20 lb. White, all-purpose. 500 per box.	ENV10	$15.99/box
Envelopes, #9	#9 envelopes, 20 lb. White, all-purpose. 500 per box.	ENV09	$12.99/box
Permanent Marker, Blue	Mark of Zorro brand permanent marker. 0.5 mm felt tip. Airtight cap. Blue.	MRK01	$2.99 each
Permanent Marker, Red	Mark of Zorro brand permanent marker. 0.5 mm felt tip. Airtight cap. Red.	MRK03	$2.99 each
Laser Paper, White	White, 20 lb. Paper, designed for use in laser printers. 8-1/2 x 11 inches. 500 sheets per ream.	PAP05	5.99/ream
Inkjet Paper, White	White, 20 lb. Paper, designed for use in inkjet printers. 8-1/2 x 11 inches. 500 sheets per ream.	PAP11	7.99/ream
Copier Paper, White	White, 20 lb. Paper, designed for use in copy machines. 8-1/2 x 11 inches. 500 sheets per ream.	PAP01	4.99/ream
Shipping Boxes, 9 x 12	9 x 12 inches, corrugated cardboard shipping boxes. White. 10 boxes per package.	BOX05	10.99/pkg

Figure 46 In this example, the selected cells are bottom aligned.

✔ Tips

- A quicker way to set alignment for a selected table is to click the Align Left ▤, Center ▤, or Align Right ▤ button on the Formatting toolbar.

- You will only notice a change in a table's alignment if the table is narrower than the printable area between the document's left and right margins.

- The Table tab of the Table Properties dialog box (**Figure 42**) also enables you to change the width of the table. I tell you how to change column and table widths later in this chapter.

To set vertical alignment for cell contents

1. Select the cells for which you want to set vertical alignment options (**Figure 44**).

2. Choose Table > Properties (**Figure 19**).

3. If necessary, click the Cell tab in the Table Properties dialog box that appears to display its options (**Figure 45**).

4. Select one of the Vertical alignment options to specify whether cell contents should be top, center, or bottom aligned.

5. Click OK.

Figure 46 shows an example of selected cells bottom aligned.

✔ Tip

- The Cell tab of the Table Properties dialog box (**Figure 45**) also enables you to change the width of the selected cell(s). I tell you how to change column and table widths later in this chapter.

Inserting & Deleting Cells

You can insert or remove columns, rows, or individual cells at any time to change the structure of a table.

To insert a column

1. Select the column beside where you want to insert a column (**Figure 47**).

2. Choose an option from the Insert submenu on the Table menu (**Figure 48**):

   ▲ **Columns to the Left** inserts a column to the left of the selection (**Figure 49**).

   ▲ **Columns to the Right** inserts a column to the right of the selection.

✔ Tip

■ To insert multiple columns, in step 1, select the same number of columns that you want to insert or repeat step 2 until the number of desired columns have been inserted.

To insert a row

1. Select the row above or below where you want to insert a row (**Figure 50**).

2. Choose an option from the Insert submenu on the Table menu (**Figure 48**):

   ▲ **Rows Above** inserts a row above the selection (**Figure 51**).

   ▲ **Rows Below** inserts a row below the selection.

✔ Tips

■ To insert a row at the bottom of the table, position the insertion point in the last cell of the table and press (Tab). An empty row is inserted (**Figure 52**).

■ To insert multiple rows, in step 1, select the same number of rows that you want to insert or repeat step 2 until the number of desired rows have been inserted.

Substance	Date Tested	Tested By	Results	
MSG	5/18/00	Maria Langer	42.5158	
Magnesium	6/4/00	John Abbott	51.2	
Sulfur	6/15/00	Mary Johannesburg	142.365	
Aspirin	8/12/00	Tim Jones	1.1	

Figure 47 Select a column beside where you want to insert a column.

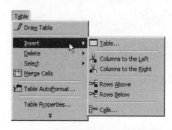

Figure 48 The Insert submenu under the Table menu.

Substance		Date Tested	Tested By	Results	
MSG		5/18/00	Maria Langer	42.5158	
Magnesium		6/4/00	John Abbott	51.2	
Sulfur		6/15/00	Mary Johannesburg	142.365	
Aspirin		8/12/00	Tim Jones	1.1	

Figure 49 Choosing Columns to the Left inserts a column to the left of the selected column.

Substance	Date Tested	Tested By	Results	
MSG	5/18/00	Maria Langer	42.5158	
Magnesium	6/4/00	John Abbott	51.2	
Sulfur	6/15/00	Mary Johannesburg	142.365	
Aspirin	8/12/00	Tim Jones	1.1	

Figure 50 Select the row above or below where you want to insert a row.

Substance	Date Tested	Tested By	Results	
MSG	5/18/00	Maria Langer	42.5158	
Magnesium	6/4/00	John Abbott	51.2	
Sulfur	6/15/00	Mary Johannesburg	142.365	
Aspirin	8/12/00	Tim Jones	1.1	

Figure 51 Choosing Rows Above inserts a row above the selected row.

Substance	Date Tested	Tested By	Results	
MSG	5/18/00	Maria Langer	42.5158	
Magnesium	6/4/00	John Abbott	51.2	
Sulfur	6/15/00	Mary Johannesburg	142.365	
Aspirin	8/12/00	Tim Jones	1.1	

Figure 52 Pressing (Tab) while the insertion point is in the last cell of the table creates a new row at the bottom of the table.

Substance¤	Date·Tested¤	Tested·By¤	Results¤	¤
MSG¤	5/18/00¤	Maria·Langer¤	42.51.58¤	¤
Magnesium¤	6/4/00¤	John·A·abbott¤	51.2¤	¤
Sulfur¤	6/15/00¤	Mary·Johannesburg¤	142.365¤	¤
Aspirin¤	8/12/00¤	Tim·Jones¤	1.1¤	¤

Figure 53 Select the cell at the location where you want to insert a cell.

Figure 54
The Insert Cells dialog box enables you to insert cells, rows, or columns.

Substance¤	Date·Tested¤	Tested·By¤	Results¤		
MSG¤	5/18/00¤	Maria·Langer¤	¤	42.51.58¤	¤
Magnesium¤	6/4/00¤	John·A·abbott¤	51.2¤		
Sulfur¤	6/15/00¤	Mary·Johannesburg¤	142.365¤		
Aspirin¤	8/12/00¤	Tim·Jones¤	1.1¤		

Figure 55 When you insert a cell, you can shift cells to the right...

Substance¤	Date·Tested¤	Tested·By¤	Results¤	¤
MSG¤	5/18/00¤	Maria·Langer¤	¤	¤
Magnesium¤	6/4/00¤	John·A·abbott¤	42.51.58¤	¤
Sulfur¤	6/15/00¤	Mary·Johannesburg¤	51.2¤	¤
Aspirin¤	8/12/00¤	Tim·Jones¤	142.365¤	¤
¤	¤	¤	1.1¤	¤

Figure 56 ...or you can shift cells down.

To insert a cell

1. Select a cell at the location where you want to insert a cell (**Figure 53**).

2. Choose Table > Insert > Cells (**Figure 48**).

3. In the Insert Cells dialog box that appears, (**Figure 54**), select an option:

   ▲ **Shift cells right** inserts a cell in the same row and moves the cells to its right to the right (**Figure 55**).

   ▲ **Shift cells down** inserts a cell in the same column and moves the cells below it down (**Figure 56**).

   ▲ **Insert entire row** inserts a row above the selected cell.

   ▲ **Insert entire column** inserts a column to the left of the selected cell.

4. Click OK.

✔ Tips

- To insert multiple cells, in step 1, select the same number of cells that you want to insert or repeat step 2 until the number of desired cells have been inserted.

- You can also use the Insert Cells dialog box (**Figure 54**) to insert columns or rows.

INSERTING CELLS

179

To delete a column, row, or cell

1. Select the column (**Figure 57**), row (**Figure 58**), or cell (**Figure 59**) that you want to remove.

2. Choose Columns, Rows, or Cells from the Delete submenu under the Table menu (**Figure 60**).

   or

   Press ⟨Backspace⟩.

3. If you delete a column, it disappears and the columns to its right shift to the left (**Figure 61**).

   or

   If you delete a row, it disappears and the rows below it shift up (**Figure 62**).

   or

   If you delete a cell, choose an option in the Delete Cells dialog box that appears (**Figure 63**):

   ▲ **Shift cells left** deletes the cell and moves the cells to its right to the left (**Figure 64**).

   ▲ **Shift cells up** deletes the cell and moves the cells below it up (**Figure 65**).

   ▲ **Delete entire row** deletes the row.

   ▲ **Delete entire column** deletes the column.

   Then click OK.

✔ Tips

- The contents of a column, row, or cell is deleted with it.

- You can select multiple contiguous columns, rows, or cells in step 1 above to delete them all at once.

Substance	Date Tested	Tested By	Results	
MSG	5/18/00	Maria Langer	42.5158	
Magnesium	6/4/00	John Aabbott	51.2	
Sulfur	6/15/00	Mary Johannesburg	142.365	
Aspirin	8/12/00	Tim Jones	1.1	

Substance	Date Tested	Tested By	Results	
MSG	5/18/00	Maria Langer	42.5158	
Magnesium	6/4/00	John Aabbott	51.2	
Sulfur	6/15/00	Mary Johannesburg	142.365	
Aspirin	8/12/00	Tim Jones	1.1	

Substance	Date Tested	Tested By	Results	
MSG	5/18/00	Maria Langer	42.5158	
Magnesium	6/4/00	John Aabbott	51.2	
Sulfur	6/15/00	Mary Johannesburg	142.365	
Aspirin	8/12/00	Tim Jones	1.1	

Figures 57, 58, & 59 Begin by selecting the column (top), row (middle), or cell (bottom) that you want to delete.

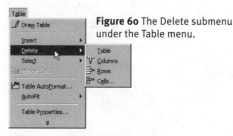

Figure 60 The Delete submenu under the Table menu.

Substance	Date Tested	Results	
MSG	5/18/00	42.5158	
Magnesium	6/4/00	51.2	
Sulfur	6/15/00	142.365	
Aspirin	8/12/00	1.1	

Substance	Date Tested	Tested By	Results	
MSG	5/18/00	Maria Langer	42.5158	
Sulfur	6/15/00	Mary Johannesburg	142.365	
Aspirin	8/12/00	Tim Jones	1.1	

Figures 61 & 62 When you delete a column (top) or a row (bottom), it simply disappears.

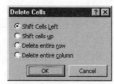

Figure 63 When you delete a cell, the Delete Cells dialog box appears.

Substance	Date Tested	Tested By	Results	
MSG	5/18/00	Maria Langer		
Magnesium	6/4/00	John Aabbott	51.2	
Sulfur	6/15/00	Mary Johannesburg	142.365	
Aspirin	8/12/00	Tim Jones	1.1	

Substance	Date Tested	Tested By	Results	
MSG	5/18/00	Maria Langer	51.2	
Magnesium	6/4/00	John Aabbott	142.365	
Sulfur	6/15/00	Mary Johannesburg	1.1	
Aspirin	8/12/00	Tim Jones		

Figures 64 & 65 You can shift cells to the left (top) or up (bottom) when you delete a cell.

Item Name	Description	Item Number	Price
Envelopes, #10	#10 envelopes, 20 lb. White, all-purpose. 500 per box.	ENV10	$15.99/box
Envelopes, #9	#9 envelopes, 20 lb. White, all-purpose. 500 per box.	ENV09	$12.99/box

Figure 66 Select the cells you want to merge.

Item Name	Description	Item Number	Price
Envelopes, #10 #10 lb. White, all-purpose. 500 per box.		ENV10	$15.99/box
Envelopes, #9	#9 envelopes, 20 lb. White, all-purpose. 500 per box.	ENV09	$12.99/box

Figure 67 The cells are merged into one cell.

Item Name	Description	Item Number	Price
Envelopes, #10	#10 envelopes, 20 lb. White, all-purpose. 500 per box.	ENV10	$15.99/box
Envelopes, #9	#9 envelopes, 20 lb. White, all-purpose. 500 per box.	ENV09	$12.99/box

Figure 68 Select the cell you want to split.

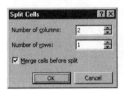

Figure 69
Use the Split Cells dialog box to specify how many columns and rows you want after the split.

Item Name	Description	Item Number	Price
Envelopes, #10	#10 envelopes, 20 lb. White, all-purpose. 500 per box.	ENV10	$15.99/box
Envelopes, #9	#9 envelopes, 20 lb. White, all-purpose. 500 per box.	ENV09	$12.99/box

Figure 70 The cell selected in **Figure 68** after being split into one column and two rows.

Item Name	Description	Item Number	Price
Envelopes, #10	#10 envelopes, 20 lb. White, all-purpose. 500 per box.	ENV10	$15.99/box
Envelopes, #9	#9 envelopes, 20 lb. White, all-purpose. 500 per box.	ENV09	$12.99/box
Permanent Marker, Blue	Mark of Zorro brand permanent marker. 0.5 mm felt tip. Airtight cap. Blue.	MRK01	$2.99 each
Permanent Marker, Red	Mark of Zorro brand permanent marker. 0.5 mm felt tip. Airtight cap. Red.	MRK03	$2.99 each

Figure 71 Position the insertion point where you want the split to occur.

Item Name	Description	Item Number	Price
Envelopes, #10	#10 envelopes, 20 lb. White, all-purpose. 500 per box.	ENV10	$15.99/box
Envelopes, #9	#9 envelopes, 20 lb. White, all-purpose. 500 per box.	ENV09	$12.99/box
Permanent Marker, Blue	Mark of Zorro brand permanent marker. 0.5 mm felt tip. Airtight cap. Blue.	MRK01	$2.99 each
Permanent Marker, Red	Mark of Zorro brand permanent marker. 0.5 mm felt tip. Airtight cap. Red.	MRK03	$2.99 each

Figure 72 The table is split at the insertion point.

Merging & Splitting Cells

You can modify the structure of a table by merging and splitting cells or the entire table:

◆ **Merging cells** turns multiple cells into one cell that spans multiple columns or rows.

◆ **Splitting a cell** turns a single cell into multiple cells in the same column or row.

◆ **Splitting a table** turns a single table into two tables.

To merge cells

1. Select the cells that you want to merge (**Figure 66**).

2. Choose Table > Merge Cells (**Figure 19**). The cells become a single cell (**Figure 67**).

✔ Tip

■ When you merge cells containing text, each cell's contents appear in a separate paragraph of the merged cell (**Figure 67**).

To split cells

1. Select the cell(s) that you want to split (**Figure 68**).

2. Choose Table > Split Cells (**Figure 19**) to display the Split Cells dialog box (**Figure 69**).

3. Enter the number of columns and rows for the cell split in the Number of columns and Number of rows text boxes.

4. Click OK. The cell splits as specified (**Figure 70**).

To split a table

1. Position the insertion point anywhere in the row below where you want the split to occur (**Figure 71**).

2. Choose Table > Split Table (**Figure 19**). The table splits (**Figure 72**).

Resizing Columns & Rows

Word offers three ways to change the width of columns or height of rows:

◆ Drag to change column widths and row heights.

◆ Use dialog boxes to change column widths and row heights.

◆ Use menu commands to equalize or AutoFit columns and rows.

To change a column's width by dragging

1. Position the mouse pointer on the boundary between the column that you want to change and the one to its right. The mouse pointer turns into a double-line with arrows (**Figure 73**).

2. Press the mouse button down and drag:

   ▲ Drag to the right to make the column wider (**Figure 74**).

   ▲ Drag to the left to make the column narrower.

   As you drag, a dotted line indicating the new boundary moves with the mouse pointer (**Figure 74**).

3. Release the mouse button. The column boundary moves to the new position, resizing both columns (**Figure 75**).

✔ Tips

■ To resize a column without changing the width of other columns, in step 1, position the mouse pointer on the Move Table Column area for the column's right boundary (**Figure 76**). Because this method changes only one column's width, it also changes the width of the table.

■ If a cell is selected when you drag to resize a column, only the selected cell's width changes.

Item Name	Description	Item Number	Price
Envelopes, #10	#10 envelopes, 20 lb. White, all-purpose. 500 per box.	ENV10	$15.99/box
Envelopes, #9	#9 envelopes, 20 lb. White, all-purpose. 500 per box.	ENV09	$12.99/box
Permanent Marker, Blue	Mark of Zorro brand permanent marker. 0.5 mm felt tip. Airtight cap. Blue.	MRK01	$2.99 each

Figure 73 Position the mouse pointer on the right boundary of the column you want to resize.

Item Name	Description	Item Number	Price
Envelopes, #10	#10 envelopes, 20 lb. White, all-purpose. 500 per box.	ENV10	$15.99/box
Envelopes, #9	#9 envelopes, 20 lb. White, all-purpose. 500 per box.	ENV09	$12.99/box
Permanent Marker, Blue	Mark of Zorro brand permanent marker. 0.5 mm felt tip. Airtight cap. Blue.	MRK01	$2.99 each

Figure 74 Drag the column boundary.

Item Name	Description	Item Number	Price
Envelopes, #10	#10 envelopes, 20 lb. White, all-purpose. 500 per box.	ENV10	$15.99/box
Envelopes, #9	#9 envelopes, 20 lb. White, all-purpose. 500 per box.	ENV09	$12.99/box
Permanent Marker, Blue	Mark of Zorro brand permanent marker. 0.5 mm felt tip. Airtight cap. Blue.	MRK01	$2.99 each

Figure 75 When you release the mouse button, the column resizes.

Item Name	Description	Item Number	Price
Envelopes, #10	#10 envelopes, 20 lb. White, all-purpose. 500 per box.	ENV10	$15.99/box
Envelopes, #9	#9 envelopes, 20 lb. White, all-purpose. 500 per box.	ENV09	$12.99/box

Figure 76 You can also resize a column by dragging the Move Table Column area for the column's right boundary.

Item Name	Description	Item Number	Price
Envelopes, #10	#10 envelopes, 20 lb. White, all-purpose. 500 per box.	ENV10	$15.99/box
Envelopes, #9	#9 envelopes, 20 lb. White, all-purpose. 500 per box.	ENV09	$12.99/box

Figure 77 Position the mouse pointer on the bottom boundary of the row you want to resize.

Item Name	Description	Item Number	Price
Envelopes, #10	#10 envelopes, 20 lb. White, all-purpose. 500 per box	ENV10	$15.99/box
Envelopes, #9	#9 envelopes, 20 lb. White, all-purpose. 500 per box.	ENV09	$12.99/box

Figure 78 Drag the row boundary.

Item Name	Description	Item Number	Price
Envelopes, #10	#10 envelopes, 20 lb. White, all-purpose. 500 per box.	ENV10	$15.99/box
Envelopes, #9	#9 envelopes, 20 lb. White, all-purpose. 500 per box.	ENV09	$12.99/box

Figure 79 When you release the mouse button, the row resizes.

	Item Name	Description	Item Number	Price
	Envelopes, #10	#10 envelopes, 20 lb. White, all-purpose. 500 per box	ENV10	$15.99/box
Adjust Table Row	Envelopes, #9	#9 envelopes, 20 lb. White, all-purpose. 500 per box.	ENV09	$12.99/box

Figure 80 You can also resize a column by dragging the Adjust Table Row area for the row's bottom boundary.

To change a row's height by dragging

1. If necessary, switch to Print Layout view.

2. Position the mouse pointer on the boundary between the row that you want to change and the one below it. The mouse pointer turns into a double-line with arrows (**Figure 77**).

3. Press the mouse button down and drag:

   ▲ Drag up to make the row shorter.

   ▲ Drag down to make the row taller (**Figure 78**).

   As you drag, a dotted line indicating the new boundary moves with the mouse pointer (**Figure 78**).

4. Release the mouse button. The row boundary moves to the new position. The rows beneath it shift accordingly (**Figure 79**).

✔ Tips

■ Another way to resize a row by dragging is to position the mouse pointer on the Adjust Table Row area of the row's bottom boundary (**Figure 80**). Then follow steps 3 and 4 above.

■ Changing a row's height changes the total height of the table.

■ You can't make a row's height shorter than the height of the text or other contents within the row.

To set row height & column width

1. Select a cell in the column or row for which you want to set height and/or width.

2. Choose Table > Table Properties (**Figure 19**) to display the Table Properties dialog box.

3. To set row height for the cell, click the Row tab to display its options (**Figure 81**). If necessary, turn on the Specify height check box. Then choose an option from the Row height is menu (**Figure 82**) and enter a value in the Specify height text box.

4. To set column width for the cell, click the Column tab to display its options (**Figure 83**). Then enter a value in the Preferred width text box.

5. Click OK.

✔ Tip

■ You can click the Previous Row and Next Row buttons in the Row tab (**Figure 81**) and the Previous Column and Next Column buttons in the Column tab (**Figure 83**) of the Table Properties dialog box to cycle through and set values for all the rows and columns in the table.

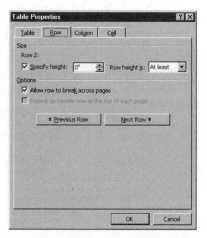

Figure 81 The Row tab of the Table Properties dialog box.

Figure 82 Use the Row height is menu to specify whether the measurement you enter is a minimum or exact value for the row height.

Figure 83 The Column tab of the Table Properties dialog box.

Figure 84 Select the columns or rows you want to equalize. In this example, an entire table is selected.

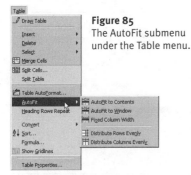

Figure 85
The AutoFit submenu under the Table menu.

Item Name	Description	Item Number	Price
Envelopes, #10	#10 envelopes, 20 lb. White, all-purpose. 500 per box.	ENV10	$15.99/box
Envelopes, #9	#9 envelopes, 20 lb. White, all-purpose. 500 per box.	ENV09	$12.99/box
Permanent Marker, Blue	Mark of Zorro brand permanent marker. 0.5 mm felt tip. Airtight cap. Blue.	MRK01	$2.99 each
Permanent Marker, Red	Mark of Zorro brand permanent marker. 0.5 mm felt tip. Airtight cap. Red.	MRK03	$2.99 each
Laser Paper, White	White, 20 lb. Paper, designed for use in laser printers. 8-1/2 x 11 inches. 500 sheets per ream.	PAP05	5.99/ream
Inkjet Paper, White	White, 20 lb. Paper, designed for use in inkjet printers. 8-1/2 x 11 inches. 500 sheets per ream.	PAP11	7.99/ream

Figure 86 The table in **Figure 84** after using the Distribute Columns Evenly command.

Item Name	Description	Item Number	Price
Envelopes, #10	#10 envelopes, 20 lb. White, all-purpose. 500 per box.	ENV10	$15.99/box
Envelopes, #9	#9 envelopes, 20 lb. White, all-purpose. 500 per box.	ENV09	$12.99/box
Permanent Marker, Blue	Mark of Zorro brand permanent marker. 0.5 mm felt tip. Airtight cap. Blue.	MRK01	$2.99 each
Permanent Marker, Red	Mark of Zorro brand permanent marker. 0.5 mm felt tip. Airtight cap. Red.	MRK03	$2.99 each
Laser Paper, White	White, 20 lb. Paper, designed for use in laser printers. 8-1/2 x 11 inches. 500 sheets per ream.	PAP05	5.99/ream
Inkjet Paper, White	White, 20 lb. Paper, designed for use in inkjet printers. 8-1/2 x 11 inches. 500 sheets per ream.	PAP11	7.99/ream

Figure 87 The table in **Figure 84** after using the Distribute Rows Evenly command.

To equalize the width of columns

1. Select the columns for which you want to equalize width (**Figure 84**).

2. Choose Table > AutoFit > Distribute Columns Evenly (**Figure 85**). The column widths change to evenly distribute space within the same area (**Figure 86**).

To equalize the height of rows

1. Select the rows for which you want to equalize height (**Figure 84**).

2. Choose Table > AutoFit > Distribute Rows Evenly (**Figure 85**). The row heights change so that all selected rows are the same height (**Figure 87**).

✔ Tip

■ Using the Distribute Rows Evenly command (**Figure 85**) usually increases the height of the table, since all selected rows become the same height as the tallest row.

To automatically size columns

1. Select the columns you want to size automatically.

2. Choose an AutoFit option from the AutoFit submenu under the Table menu (**Figure 85**):

▲ **AutoFit to Contents** resizes the columns based on their contents.

▲ **AutoFit to Window** resizes the columns to fill the window's width.

To remove automatic sizing

1. Select the columns that are set to automatically size based on contents or window width.

2. Choose Table > AutoFit > Fixed Column Width (**Figure 85**).

The columns will no longer resize automatically.

Table Headings

A table heading consists of one or more rows that appear at the top of the table. If page breaks occur within a table, the table heading appears at the top of each page of the table (**Figure 88**).

✔ Tips

- You can only see repeating heading row(s) in Print Layout view or Print Preview.

- Word only repeats heading row(s) when an automatic page break splits a table. If a table is split by a manual page break, the headings do not repeat. I tell you about Page Breaks in **Chapter 4**.

- Setting a row as a table heading does not change its appearance.

To set a table heading

1. Select the row(s) that you want to use as a table heading (**Figure 89**). Your selection must include the first row of the table.

2. Choose Table > Heading Rows Repeat (**Figure 19**).

   A check mark appears to the left of the command (**Figure 90**) and the selected rows are set as headings.

To remove a table heading

1. Select the row(s) that comprise the heading (**Figure 89**).

2. Choose Table > Heading Rows Repeat (**Figure 90**).

   The headings setting is removed from the selected rows.

✔ Tip

- Removing the heading feature from selected row(s) does not delete the row(s) from the table.

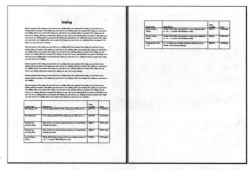

Figure 88 If a page break splits a table into multiple pages, the headings appear at the top of each page of the table.

Figure 89 Select the row(s) that you want to use as a heading.

Figure 90
Choose Heading Rows Repeat from the Table menu a second time to remove the heading feature from selected row(s).

Figure 91 Select the table you want to format.

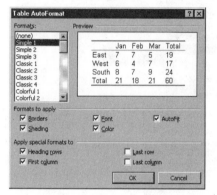

Figure 92 The Table AutoFormat dialog box.

Figure 93 The table from **Figure 91** with the List 7 format applied.

Table AutoFormat

Word's Table AutoFormat feature offers a quick and easy way to combine many formatting options for an entire table.

To use Table AutoFormat

1. Select the table that you want to format (**Figure 91**).

2. Choose Table > Table AutoFormat (**Figure 90**) to display the Table AutoFormat dialog box (**Figure 92**).

3. Click to select one of the formats in the scrolling list.

4. Toggle check boxes in the Formats to apply area to specify which part(s) of the Auto-Format should be applied to the selection.

5. Toggle check boxes in the Apply special formats to area to specify which part(s) of the table should get the special formatting.

6. When you're finished setting options, click OK. The formatting for the AutoFormat is applied to the table (**Figure 93**).

✔ Tips

- Each time you make a change in the Table AutoFormat dialog box (**Figure 92**), the Preview area changes to show the effect of your changes.

- If you don't like the formatting applied by the Table AutoFormat feature, use the Undo command to reverse it. Then try again or format the table manually.

To remove AutoFormatting

Follow steps 1 and 2 above, but select (none) in the scrolling list (**Figure 92**) in step 3, then click OK.

Removing a Table

You can remove a table two ways:

- Delete the table, thus removing it and its contents from the document.

- Convert the table to text, thus removing the structure of the table from the document but not the table's contents.

To delete a table

1. Select the table that you want to delete.

   or

   Position the insertion point anywhere in the table you want to delete.

2. Choose Table > Delete > Table (**Figure 60**).

   or

   Press (Backspace).

   The table and all of its data are removed from the document.

✔ Tip

- If a table is part of a large block of selected text, pressing (Backspace) deletes the entire selection, including the table.

To convert a table to text

1. Select the table that you want to convert to text (**Figure 94**).

2. Choose Table > Convert > Table to Text (**Figure 95**).

3. In the Convert Table to Text dialog box that appears (**Figure 96**), select the option for the character that you want to use to separate the contents of table cells when the cell boundaries are removed.

4. Click OK.

   The table is converted to text (**Figure 97**).

Figure 94 Select the table that you want to convert to plain text.

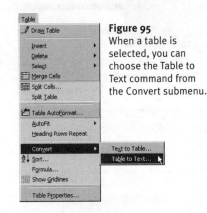

Figure 95 When a table is selected, you can choose the Table to Text command from the Convert submenu.

Figure 96 The Convert Table to Text dialog box.

Substance → Date Tested → Tested By → Results¶
MSG → 5/18/00 → Maria Langer → 42.5158¶
Magnesium → 6/4/00 → John Aabbott → 51.2¶
Sulfur → 6/15/00 → Mary Johannesburg → 142.365¶
Aspirin → 8/12/00 → Tim Jones → 1.1¶

Figure 97 The table from Figure 94 converted to tab-separated text. In this example, formatting marks are displayed so you can see the tab and return characters.

ENVELOPES & LABELS

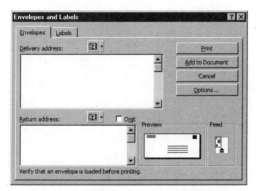

Figure 1 The Envelopes tab of the Envelopes and Labels dialog box.

Figure 2
Choosing Envelopes
and Labels from the
Tools menu.

Envelopes & Labels

Word's envelopes and labels feature can create and print addressed envelopes and mailing labels based on document contents or the information that you enter in the Envelopes and Labels dialog box (**Figure 1**). This feature makes it easy to print professional-looking envelopes and labels for all of your mailing needs.

✔ Tips

- Word supports all standard envelope and label sizes and formats. Settings can also be changed for printing on nonstandard envelopes or labels.

- You can use the mail merge feature to create envelopes and labels based on mail merge information. I tell you how in **Chapter 12**.

To open the Envelopes and Labels dialog box

1. Choose Tools > Envelopes and Labels (**Figure 2**).

2. In the Envelopes and Labels dialog box that appears (**Figure 1**), click the Envelopes or Labels tab to display appropriate options.

✔ Tip

- You cannot choose the Envelopes and Labels command from the Tools menu unless a document window is open.

Creating an Envelope

To create an envelope with Word, you must provide several pieces of information:

◆ **Addresses** include the delivery address and, if desired, a return address.

◆ **Envelope options** include the size of the envelope, bar code preferences, and the fonts and position for the addresses. Word supports all standard envelope sizes and enables you to set a custom size if necessary. Word can automatically set the address positions, so you don't have to worry about figuring them out for yourself.

◆ **Printing options** include the envelope feed method and rotation. Word can accommodate virtually any printer's envelope feed method.

✔ Tip

■ Word can save many of the envelope options in the template on which the active document was based. For example, if you create an envelope while a document based on the Normal template is active, Word saves envelope and printing settings to that template. The next time you create an envelope for a document based on Normal, these options are already set.

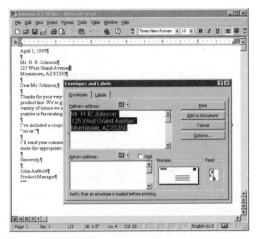

Figure 3 When you create an envelope for a letter, Word is usually "smart" enough to fill in the Delivery address for you.

To set envelope addresses

1. Open the Envelopes and Labels dialog box.

2. If necessary, click the Envelopes tab to display its options (**Figure 1**).

3. Enter the name and address of the person to whom the envelope should be addressed in the Delivery address box.

4. If desired, enter a return address in the Return address box.

   or

   To print an envelope without a return address, turn on the Omit check box. This omits the return address from the envelope, even if one appears in the Return address box.

✔ Tips

■ If you are creating an envelope for a letter in the active document window, the Delivery address may already be filled in based on the inside address of the letter (**Figure 3**). You can "help" Word enter the correct address in this box by selecting the recipient's address before opening the Envelopes and Labels dialog box.

■ If you entered your address in the User Information tab of the Options dialog box or have already created an envelope with a return address, the Return address box may already be filled in for you. I discuss User Information preferences in **Chapter 14**.

■ If you use Microsoft Exchange, you can click the Address button 📇 ▾ in the Envelopes and Labels dialog box to select and insert an address from your database. Using Microsoft Exchange to maintain an address book is beyond the scope of this book. If this feature is available to you, you can explore it on your own.

To set envelope options

1. Click the envelope in the Preview area of the Envelopes and Labels dialog box (**Figure 1**).

   or

   Click the Options button in the Envelopes and Labels dialog box (**Figure 1**), then click the Envelope Options tab in the Envelope Options dialog box.

   The Envelope Options tab of the Envelope Options dialog box appears (**Figure 4**).

2. Choose an envelope size from the Envelope size menu (**Figure 5**).

3. To include a barcode on the envelope, turn on the Delivery point barcode check box. You can then also turn on the FIM-A courtesy reply mail check box if desired.

4. To change the font formatting of the delivery or return address, click the Font button in the Delivery address or Return address area. Use the dialog box that appears (**Figure 6**) to set font formatting options, then click OK.

5. To adjust the printing position of the delivery or return address, enter values in the appropriate From left and From top boxes.

6. Click OK to save your settings and return to the Envelopes and Labels dialog box.

✔ Tips

- If you choose Custom size from the Envelope size menu, the Envelope Size dialog box appears (**Figure 7**). Enter measurements for your custom envelope size and click OK.

- The Preview area changes to show the effect of the changes you make in the dialog box.

- I tell you more about font formatting options in **Chapter 3**.

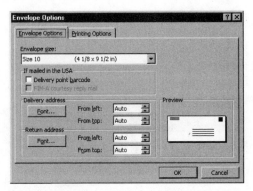

Figure 4 The Envelope Options tab of the Envelope Options dialog box.

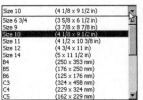

Figure 5 The Envelope size menu includes all standard envelope sizes.

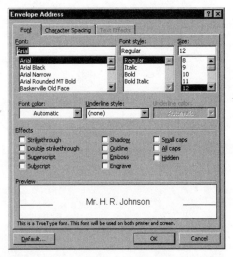

Figure 6 Use a dialog box like this to change the font formatting of envelope addresses.

Figure 7 The Envelope Size dialog box.

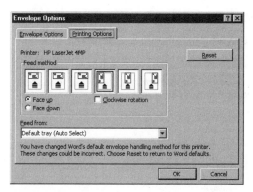

Figure 8 The Printing Options tab of the Envelope Options dialog box.

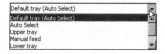

Figure 9 The Feed from menu.

To set printing options

1. Click the envelope icon in the Feed area of the Envelopes and Labels dialog box (**Figure 1**).

   or

   Click the Options button in the Envelopes and Labels dialog box (**Figure 1**), then click the Printing Options tab in the Envelope Options dialog box.

   The Printing Options tab of the Envelope Options dialog box appears (**Figure 8**).

2. Select the correct Feed method options to indicate the way envelopes are fed into your printer:

   ▲ Feed method icons graphically represent the way envelopes are fed into your printer.

   ▲ The Face up and Face down option buttons determine which side of the envelope is printed.

   ▲ The Clockwise rotation check box determines how your printer prints on envelopes inserted sideways.

3. If necessary, choose an option from the Feed from menu (**Figure 9**).

4. Click OK to save your settings and return to the Envelopes and Labels dialog box.

✔ Tips

■ The icons in the Feed method area change based on the other options set in that area.

■ If you're not sure how to set Feed method options, use the Envelopes and Labels dialog box to print on a plain sheet of paper. Examine the page to see how the envelope information was printed, then set Feed method options accordingly.

SETTING PRINTING OPTIONS

To print an envelope

1. Turn on your printer and insert an envelope into the appropriate feed location.

2. Click the Print button in the Envelopes and Labels dialog box (**Figure 1**).

   Word sends the information to the printer and prints in the background while you continue working.

✔ Tip

■ If you changed the contents of the Return address box as discussed on page 191, after step 2 above, Word asks if you want to save the new return address as the default return address (**Figure 10**). Click Yes or No as desired.

To save the envelope as part of the document

Click the Add to Document button in the Envelopes and Labels dialog box (**Figure 1**).

Word adds a new section to the document with the proper settings to print that section as an envelope (**Figure 11**). You can then use the Print command to print the envelope and document at the same time.

✔ Tip

■ I tell you about document sections in **Chapter 4** and about printing documents in **Chapter 6**.

Figure 10 If you make changes to the return address, Word offers to save it as the default.

Figure 11 An envelope added as a separate document section, viewed in Normal view.

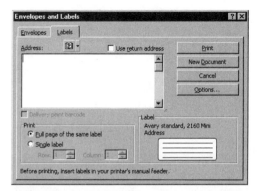

Figure 12 The Labels tab of the Envelopes and Labels dialog box.

Creating Labels

To create labels with Word, you must provide several pieces of information:

◆ **Address** is the address that should appear on the label.

◆ **Print options** enable you to specify whether you want a whole sheet of the same labels or, for a single label, the print position.

◆ **Label options** include printer information and the size of the label. Word supports most standard label products—including Avery labels—and enables you to set a custom label size if necessary.

To set the label address

1. Open the Envelopes and Labels dialog box.

2. If necessary, click the Labels tab to display its options (**Figure 12**).

3. Enter the name and address of the person to whom the label should be addressed in the Address box.

   or

   To print labels using the default return address, turn on the Use return address check box.

✔ Tips

■ If you are creating a label for a letter in the active document window, the Address box may already be filled in based on the inside address of the letter. You can "help" Word enter the correct address in this box by selecting the recipient's address before opening the Envelopes and Labels dialog box.

■ The default return address is stored in the User Information tab of the Options dialog box, which I discuss in **Chapter 14**.

To set Print options

In the Envelopes and Labels dialog box (**Figure 12**), select one of the Print option buttons:

- **Full page of the same label** prints a full page of labels using the information in the Address box.

- **Single label** prints just one label using the information in the Address box. If you select this option, you must specify the position of the label on the label sheet by entering values in the Row and Column boxes (**Figure 13**).

✔ Tip

- Use the Full page of the same label option with your return address to create pages full of return address labels for all your correspondence.

To set standard label options

1. Click the picture of the label in the label area or the Options button in the Envelopes and Labels dialog box (**Figure 12**) to display the Label Options dialog box (**Figure 14**).

2. Select the option button for your printer type. Then choose the appropriate option from the Tray menu (**Figure 15**).

3. Choose an option from the Label products menu (**Figure 16**).

4. Click to select one of the standard label products in the Product number list.

5. Click OK to save your settings and return to the Envelopes and Labels dialog box.

✔ Tip

- If you're not sure which Product number to select, consult the information on the box of labels.

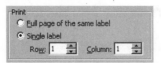

Figure 13 If you select Single label in the Envelopes and Labels dialog box, enter values for the label position.

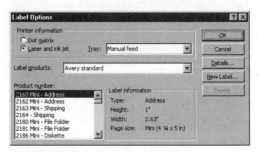

Figure 14 The Label Options dialog box.

Figure 15 Use the Tray menu to specify the feed location for your printer.

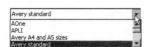

Figure 16 The Label products menu.

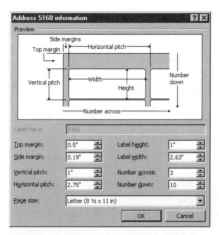

Figure 17 The Information dialog box for a specific label product.

To customize a standard label

1. Follow steps 1 through 4 on the previous page to select a label in the Label Options dialog box (**Figure 14**).

2. Click the Details button to display the Information dialog box for the label that you selected (**Figure 17**).

3. Set options in the dialog box to customize the label layout.

4. Click OK to save your settings and return to the Label Options dialog box.

5. Click OK to save your settings and return to the Envelopes and Labels dialog box.

✔ Tips

- The appearance of the Information dialog box (**Figure 17**) varies based on the label you selected in the Label Options dialog box (**Figure 14**).

- Don't change settings in a label's Information dialog box (**Figure 17**) unless your labels will not print properly with the default settings.

To create a custom label

1. Follow steps 1 through 4 on page 196 to select a label in the Label Options dialog box (**Figure 14**) that is similar to the one that you want to create.

2. Click the New Label button to display the New Custom laser (**Figure 18**) or New Custom dot matrix (**Figure 19**) dialog box.

3. Enter a name for the label layout in the Label name box.

4. Set measurement options for the label layout.

5. Click OK to save your settings and return to the Label Options dialog box. The name of the new label appears in the Product number list (**Figure 20**).

6. Click OK to save your settings and return to the Envelopes and Labels dialog box.

✔ Tip

■ The appearance of the New Custom dialog box (**Figures 18** and **19**) varies based on the label you selected in the Label Options dialog box (**Figure 14**).

To print labels

1. Turn on your printer and insert label stock into the appropriate feed location.

2. Click the Print button in the Envelopes and Labels dialog box (**Figure 12**).

   Word sends the information to the printer and prints in the background while you continue working.

✔ Tip

■ I tell you more about Printing in **Chapter 6**.

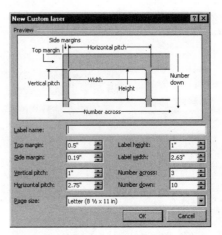

Figure 18 The New Custom laser dialog box lets you create custom laser and ink jet printer labels.

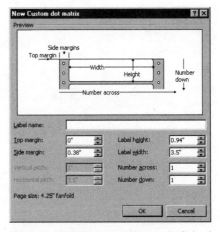

Figure 19 The New Custom dot matrix dialog box lets you create dot matrix printer labels.

Figure 20 The labels you create appear in the Product number list in the Label Options dialog box.

MAIL MERGE 12

Mail Merge

Word's mail merge feature enables you to create mailing labels, form letters, and other documents based on database information. This feature merges *fields* or categories of database information with static text to produce merged documents.

Mail merge uses two special kinds of documents:

◆ A **main document** contains the information that remains the same for each version of the merged document. In a form letter, for example, the main document would contain the text that appears in every letter.

◆ A **data source document** contains the information that changes for each version of a merged document. In a form letter, the data source would contain the names and addresses of the people to receive the letter.

The results of a mail merge can be sent directly to the printer or saved as a separate file on disk.

✔ Tips

■ You can use a single main document with any number of data source documents. Similarly, you can use a data source document with any number of main documents.

■ You can create a data source document with Word as I explain in this chapter or with another program, such as Microsoft Excel or FileMaker Pro.

■ Word's mail merge feature also includes powerful query and conditional functions. These advanced features are beyond the scope of this book.

The Mail Merge Helper

Word's Mail Merge Helper (**Figure 1**) steps you through the process of creating or identifying the main and data source documents and merging the files.

To open the Mail Merge Helper

Choose Tools > Mail Merge (**Figure 2**).

or

Click the Mail Merge Helper button  on the Mail Merge toolbar.

✔ Tip

■ The Mail Merge toolbar appears automatically when you open a main or data source document.

To use the Mail Merge Helper: an overview

1. Open the Mail Merge Helper (**Figure 1**).

2. Choose an option from the Create menu (**Figure 4**).

3. If desired, edit the main document's contents. Then return to the Mail Merge Helper.

4. Choose an option from the Get Data menu (**Figure 10**).

5. If desired, edit the data source document's contents. Then return to the Mail Merge Helper.

6. If necessary, edit the main document's contents to include fields from the data source document. Then return to the Mail Merge Helper.

7. Click the Merge button to display the Merge dialog box (**Figure 32**).

8. Set options as desired.

9. Click the Merge button to merge the documents.

Figure 1 The Mail Merge Helper.

Figure 2
To open the Mail Merge Helper and begin a mail merge, choose Mail Merge from the Tools menu.

✔ Tips

■ I provide details for all of these steps throughout this chapter.

■ To use the Mail Merge Helper for an existing main document, open the main document first, then follow all of these steps except step 2.

THE MAIL MERGE HELPER

Figure 3 An example of a main document for a form letter.

Creating a Main Document

A main document has two components:

◆ **Static text** that does not change. In a form letter, for example, static text would be the information that remains the same for each individual who will get the letter.

◆ **Mail merge fields** that indicate what data source information should be merged into the document and where it should go. In a form letter, the static text *Dear* might be followed by the field *«FirstName»*. When merged, the contents of the FirstName field is merged into the document after the word *Dear* to result in *Dear Joe, Dear Sally*, etc.

You can see both of these components in **Figure 3**.

Normally, a main document can be created with one or two steps:

◆ Enter the static text first, then insert the fields when the data source document is complete. This method is useful when you use an existing document as a main document.

◆ Enter the static text and insert the fields at the same time when the data source document is complete. This method may save time and prevent confusion when creating a main document from scratch.

✔ Tips

■ You cannot insert fields into a main document until after the data source has been created and associated with the main document.

■ You enter and edit static text in a main document the same way you do in any other Word document.

To create a main document

1. Open a document on which you want to base the main document.

   or

   Create a new document.

2. Open the Mail Merge Helper (**Figure 1**).

3. Choose an option from the Create menu (**Figure 4**):

   ▲ **Form Letters** are letters customized for multiple recipients.

   ▲ **Mailing Labels** are labels addressed to multiple recipients.

   ▲ **Envelopes** are envelopes addressed to multiple recipients.

   ▲ **Catalog** is a collection of information about multiple items.

4. A dialog box like the one in **Figure 5** appears.

   To base the main document on the document in the active window, click Active Window.

   or

   To create a main document from scratch, click New Main Document.

   The type and name of the main document appears in the Mail Merge Helper dialog box (**Figure 6**).

5. If you are creating a form letter, you can choose the document's name from the Edit menu within the Mail Merge Helper dialog box to add or edit the main document's static text (**Figure 7**).

✔ Tip

■ Do not add any static text at this point for mailing labels or envelopes. These main documents have special formatting needs that must be set up before you can add static text. I provide detailed instructions for completing mailing labels and envelopes later in this chapter and in **Chapter 11**.

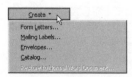

Figure 4
Use the Create menu to specify the type of main document to create.

Figure 5 Use this dialog box to specify whether you want to create a new main document from scratch or turn the document in the active window into a main document.

Figure 6 The type and name of the main document appears in the Main document area of the Mail Merge Helper dialog box.

Figure 7 A form letter without merge fields.

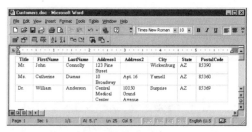

Figure 8 A data source document with three records.

Creating a Data Source

A data source document has two components:

- **Fields** are categories of information. In a form letter, for example, *LastName* and *City* might be two fields. Each field has a unique name which identifies it in both the main document and data source document.

- **Records** are collections of information for individual items. In a form letter, the John Smith record would include all fields for John Smith—his name, address, city, state, and postal code.

Word sets up a data source as a table (**Figure 8**), which makes it easy to work with data.

When you perform a mail merge, Word inserts the data from a data source record into a main document, replacing field names with field contents. It repeats the main document for each record in the source document (**Figure 9**).

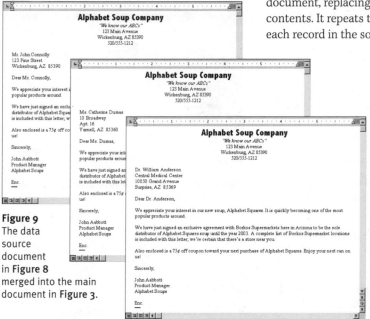

Figure 9
The data source document in **Figure 8** merged into the main document in **Figure 3**.

To create a data source

1. Create a main document as instructed earlier in this chapter. Make it the active document window.

2. If the Mail Merge Helper is not displayed, open it.

3. Choose Create Data Source from the Get Data menu (**Figure 10**) to display the Create Data Source dialog box (**Figure 11**). It lists commonly used field names for form letters, mailing labels, and envelopes.

4. Edit the Field names in header row list to include only the field names that you want in your data source document, in the order that you want them to appear:

   ▲ To remove a field name from the list, click to select it, then click the Remove Field Name button.

   ▲ To add a field name, enter it in the Field name text box, then click the Add Field Name button.

   ▲ To move a field name up or down in the list, click to select it, then click one of the Move buttons to the right of the list.

5. When you are finished, click OK.

6. A Save As dialog box appears (**Figure 12**). Use it to name and save the data source file.

7. A dialog box like the one in **Figure 13** appears next.

   Click the Edit Main Document button to add merge fields to the main document. I provide instructions a little later in this chapter.

   or

   Click the Edit Data Source button to add records to the data source document. I provide instructions on the next page.

Figure 10
Use the Get Data menu to set up a data source document.

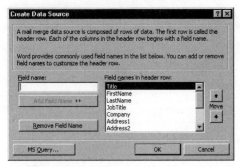

Figure 11 The Create Data Source dialog box.

Figure 12 Use a standard Save As dialog box to save the data source document.

✔ Tips

■ Field names cannot include spaces.

■ It's a good idea to save the data source file in the same folder in which you have saved or will save the main document. This makes it easy to find the data source document when merging the main document.

CREATING A DATA SOURCE

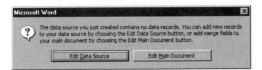

Figure 13 Use this dialog box to select a document to edit.

Figure 14 The name of the data source file appears in the Data source area of the Mail Merge Helper dialog box. You can use the Edit menu in the Data source area to edit the file.

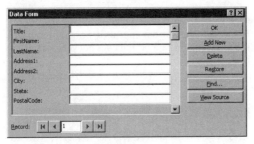

Figure 15 The Data Form dialog box.

To edit a data source

1. Click Edit Data Source in the dialog box that appears after you save a data source document for the first time (**Figure 13**).

   or

   Choose the name of the data source from the Edit menu in the Data source area of the Mail Merge Helper dialog box (**Figure 14**).

   or

   Click the Edit Data Source button 📝 on the Mail Merge toolbar.

   The Data Form dialog box appears (**Figure 15**).

2. Enter information for a specific record into each of the text boxes. You can press Tab to move to the next box or Shift Tab to move to the previous box.

3. To add another new record, click the Add New button and repeat step 2.

4. When you are finished adding records, click OK.

✔ Tips

- You can use other buttons in the Data Form dialog box (**Figure 15**) to scroll through, edit, delete, or search for records.

- Clicking the View Source button in the Data Form dialog box (**Figure 15**) displays the data source document in a Word document window (**Figure 8**).

EDITING A DATA SOURCE

To attach a data source to a main document

1. Make sure that the main document is open in the active document window.

2. Open the Mail Merge Helper (**Figure 1**).

3. Choose Open Data Source from the Get Data pop-up menu (**Figure 10**).

4. Use the Open Data Source dialog box that appears (**Figure 16**) to locate and open the file that you want to use as a data source for the main document.

5. If the main document does not contain any merge fields, a dialog box like the one in **Figure 17** or **18** appears.

   Click the Edit Main Document button (**Figure 17**) to add merge fields to a form letter or catalog, following the instructions on the next page.

   or

   Click the Set Up Main Document button (**Figure 18**) to set options and specify fields for mailing labels or envelopes, following the instructions on **page 208** or **209**.

✔ Tips

- It is not necessary to perform any of the above steps if you created the data source document using the Mail Merge Helper while the main document was in the active window.

- You can only attach one data source document to a main document at a time. Follow the above steps to attach a different data source to a main document that already has a data source attached.

Figure 16 Use the Open Data Source dialog box to select an existing data source document.

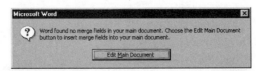

Figure 17 This dialog box appears if the main document is a form letter or catalog and does not yet contain any merge fields.

Figure 18 This dialog box appears if the main document is mailing labels or envelopes and has not yet been set up.

Figure 19 Position the insertion point where you want the field to appear.

Figure 20
The Insert Merge Field menu on the Mail Merge toolbar lists all the fields in the attached data source.

Figure 21 The field appears at the insertion point.

Completing a Main Document

Before you can perform a mail merge, you must complete the main document. What needs to be done depends on the type of main document you have created:

◆ Form letters must include all static text and merge fields.

◆ Mailing labels must include label options and merge fields.

◆ Envelopes must include envelope and printing options and merge fields.

◆ Catalogs must include all static text and merge fields.

To complete a form letter or catalog

1. If the main document is not open, open it. The Mail Merge toolbar appears above the document window (**Figure 7**).

2. Position the insertion point where you want to insert a merge field (**Figure 19**).

3. Choose a merge field from the Insert Merge Field menu on the Mail Merge toolbar (**Figure 20**). The field is inserted (**Figure 21**).

4. Repeat steps 2 and 3 for each merge field that you want to insert.

   Figure 4 shows an example of a main document with merge fields.

✔ Tip

■ Be sure to include proper spacing and punctuation as necessary between merge fields.

To complete mailing labels

1. Create or attach a data source to a mailing labels main document as instructed earlier in this chapter. When the dialog box in **Figure 18** appears, click the Set Up Main Document button.

2. Use the Label Options dialog box that appears (**Figure 22**) to select and set options for a label product.

3. Click OK to display the Create Labels dialog box (**Figure 23**).

4. Choose a merge field from the Insert Merge Field menu (**Figure 20**). The field is inserted in the Sample label box (**Figure 24**).

5. Repeat steps 3 and 4 for each merge field that you want to include on the label. When you're finished, it might look something like **Figure 25**.

6. Click OK to save your settings and return to the Mail Merge Helper.

✔ Tips

- I explain how to set options in the Label Options dialog box in **Chapter 11**. Consult that chapter for details when completing step 2.

- Be sure to include proper spacing and punctuation as necessary between merge fields.

- If you click the Close button in the Mail Merge Helper dialog box after step 6, you can see the main document that Word created for the mailing labels (**Figure 26**).

- Do not change the Word fields included in the mailing labels main document (**Figure 26**). Altering or removing a field can prevent the mailing labels from merging or printing properly.

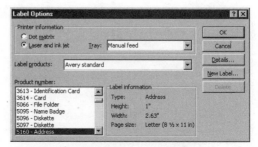

Figure 22 Use the Label Options dialog box to specify information about the label product.

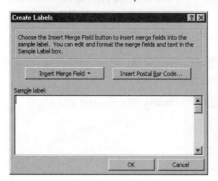

Figure 23 The Create Labels dialog box.

Figure 24 The field you select is inserted.

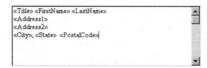

Figure 25 The merge fields for a name and address.

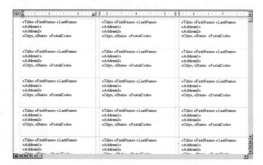

Figure 26 A mailing labels main document.

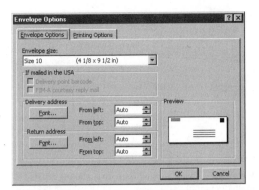

Figure 27 Use the Envelope Options dialog box to specify information about the envelope.

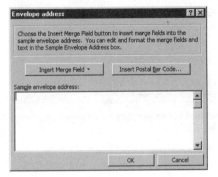

Figure 28 The Envelope Address dialog box.

Figure 29 An envelopes main document.

To complete envelopes

1. Create or attach a data source to an envelopes main document as instructed earlier in this chapter. When the dialog box in **Figure 18** appears, click the Set Up Main Document button.

2. Use the Envelope Options dialog box that appears (**Figure 27**) to select and set options for an envelope.

3. Click OK to display the Envelope Address dialog box (**Figure 28**).

4. Choose a merge field from the Insert Merge Field menu (**Figure 20**). The field is inserted in the Sample envelope address box (**Figure 24**).

5. Repeat step 4 for each merge field that you want to include in the envelope address. When you're finished, it might look like **Figure 25**.

6. Click OK to save your settings and return to the Mail Merge Helper.

✔ Tips

- I explain how to set options in the Envelope Options dialog box in **Chapter 11**. Consult that chapter for details when completing step 2.

- Be sure to include proper spacing and punctuation as necessary between merge fields.

- If you click the Close button in the Mail Merge Helper dialog box after step 6, you can see the main document that Word created for the envelopes (**Figure 29**).

- Do not change the Word fields included in the envelopes main document (**Figure 29**). Altering or removing a field can prevent the envelopes from merging or printing properly.

Merging Documents

The last step in performing a mail merge is to merge the main and data source documents.

Word offers several ways to merge the documents:

◆ View merged data on screen. This enables you to spot potential problems before actually performing the merge.

◆ Merge to a new document. The resulting file can be saved, modified, or printed another time.

◆ Merge to a printer. This merges the documents directly to paper, labels, or envelopes to create final output.

◆ Merge to electronic mail. This merges the documents as individual e-mail messages.

◆ Merge to electronic fax. This merges the documents as individual faxes to be sent via your fax modem.

✔ Tip

■ You must have a MAPI-compatible e-mail or fax program, such as Microsoft Outlook or Microsoft Fax, to merge to electronic mail or fax.

To view merged data on screen

1. Open the main document.

2. Click the View Merged Data button ![icon] on the Mail Merge toolbar.

   The merge field names are replaced with the contents of the first record in the data source (**Figures 9**, **30**, and **31**).

✔ Tip

■ You can scroll through the records in the data source while viewing merged records by clicking various buttons on the Mail Merge toolbar: First Record ![icon], Previous Record ![icon], Next Record ![icon], and Last Record ![icon].

Figure 30 Viewing merged data for a mailing labels main document.

Figure 31 Viewing merged data for an envelopes main document.

MERGING DOCUMENTS

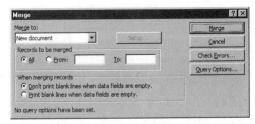

Figure 32 Use the Merge dialog box to set options for the merge.

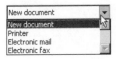

Figure 33
Choose the merge destination from the Merge to menu.

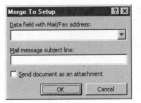

Figure 34
Use the Merge To Setup dialog box to set options specific for merging to e-mail messages and faxes.

To merge to a new document, printer, e-mail, or fax

1. Open the main document and click the Start Mail Merge button Merge... on the Mail Merge toolbar.

   or

   In the Mail Merge Helper dialog box (**Figure 1**), click the Merge button.

   The Merge dialog box appears (**Figure 32**).

2. Choose an option from the Merge to menu (**Figure 33**).

3. If you chose Electronic mail or Electronic fax in step 2, click the Setup button to display the Merge To Setup dialog box (**Figure 34**). Use the Data field with Mail/ Fax address menu to choose the data source field that contains the e-mail address or fax number. For an e-mail message, enter a message subject in the Mail message subject line box. Then click OK to return to the Merge dialog box.

4. To merge fewer than all records, enter starting and ending record numbers in the From and To edit boxes.

5. Select an option button in the When merging records area:

   ▲ **Don't print blank lines when data fields are empty** tells Word to omit the line a field would occupy if the field is empty. This is the default option and the best choice for creating form letters, mailing labels, and envelopes when the data source has empty fields.

   ▲ **Print blank lines when data fields are empty** tells Word to print a blank line when the field that would occupy that line is empty.

6. Click the Merge button.

Continued on next page...

MERGING DOCUMENTS

Continued from previous page.

7. If you are merging to a new document, Word creates the new document and displays it as the active window. You can edit, save, or print the document.

or

If you are merging to a printer, Word displays the Print dialog box (**Figure 35**). Set print options as desired and click the Print button.

or

If you are merging to e-mail or fax, Word creates and sends the e-mail messages or faxes using your MAPI-compatible e-mail or fax program.

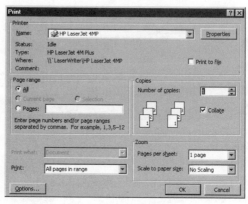

Figure 35 The Print dialog box.

✔ Tips

■ To quickly merge to a file, click the Merge to New Document button on the Mail Merge toolbar.

■ To quickly merge to a printer, click the Merge to Printer button on the Mail Merge toolbar. Use the Print dialog box that appears (**Figure 35**) to set printing options and click the Print button.

■ I tell you more about the Print dialog box in **Chapter 6**.

■ If you have trouble merging to e-mail or fax, check your e-mail or fax configuration to make sure it is properly set up.

WEB PAGES

13

Web Pages

The World Wide Web has had a bigger impact on publishing than any other communication medium introduced in the past fifty years. Web pages, which can include text, graphics, and hyperlinks, can be published on the Internet or an intranet, making them available to audiences 24 hours a day, 7 days a week. They can provide information quickly and inexpensively to anyone who needs it.

Word 2000 has built-in Web page creation, modification, and interaction tools. With Word, you can build and publish Web pages and open links to other Web pages and sites.

✔ Tips

- This chapter provides enough information to get you started using Word to create Web pages. Complete coverage of Web publishing, however is beyond the scope of this book.

- To learn more about the World Wide Web and Web publishing, check these Peachpit Press books:

  - ▲ *The Little Web Book* by Alfred and Emily Glossbrenner.

  - ▲ *Home Sweet Home Page* and *The Non-Designer's Web Book* by Robin Williams.

- Web pages are normally viewed with a special kind of software called a *Web browser*. Microsoft Internet Explorer and Netscape Navigator are two examples of Web browsers.

- To access the Internet, you need an Internet connection, either through an organizational network or dial-up connection. Setting up a connection is beyond the scope of this book; consult the documentation that came with Windows or Internet access software for more information.

- To publish a Web page, you need access to a Web server. Contact your organization's Network Administrator or Internet Service Provider (ISP) for more information.

- A *hyperlink* (or *link*) is text or a graphic that, when clicked, displays other information from the Web.

- An *intranet* is like the Internet, but it exists only on the internal network of an organization and is usually closed to outsiders.

Creating a Web Page

Word offers three ways to create a Web page:

◆ The **Blank Web Page** template lets you create a Web page from scratch, using appropriate formatting options.

◆ **Web page templates** enable you to create Web pages, complete with internal links, based on a variety of predesigned formats.

◆ The **Web Page Wizard** lets you create a Web site, complete with graphic elements and links, for a specific purpose.

◆ The **Save as Web Page** command lets you save a regular Word document as HTML. This encodes the document and saves it as a Web page.

✔ Tips

■ When you create a Web page using a Web page template or the Web Page Wizard, Word's menus automatically change to offer only those options that apply to a Web page.

■ *HTML (or HyperText Markup Language)* is a system of codes for defining Web pages. For more information about HTML, be sure to check out *HTML 4 for the World Wide Web: Visual QuickStart Guide* by Elizabeth Castro.

■ I tell you how to save a regular Word document as a Web page file near the end of this chapter.

■ You can use the File menu's Open command (**Figure 1**) to open an existing Web page so you can edit it with Word. I explain how to open files in **Chapter 2**.

Figure 1
The File menu includes commands for creating, saving, and previewing Web pages.

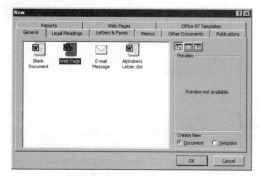

Figure 2 The General tab of the New dialog box enables you to create a blank Web page.

Figure 3 A blank document window for a Web page.

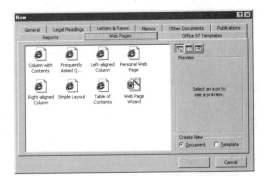

Figure 4 The Web Pages tab of the New dialog box offers Web page templates and the Web Page Wizard.

Figure 5 This example shows the default Web page created with the Personal Web Page template.

To use the Blank Web Page template

1. Choose File > New (**Figure 1**).

2. In the New dialog box that appears, click the General tab to display its options (**Figure 2**).

3. Click the Web Page icon to select it.

4. Click OK. Word creates a blank new Web page (**Figure 3**).

5. Enter and format text in the document window as desired to meet your needs.

✔ Tip

- I explain how to enter and format text for a Web page a little later in this chapter.

To use a Web Page template

1. Choose File > New (**Figure 1**).

2. In the New dialog box that appears, click the Web Pages tab to display its options (**Figure 4**).

3. Click an icon for the desired template to select it.

4. Click OK. Word creates a blank new Web page (**Figure 5**).

5. Edit placeholder text as desired to customize the Web page for your needs.

✔ Tips

- I explain how to edit and format text for a Web page a little later in this chapter.

- The blue underlined text that appears on Web pages are hypertext links. I tell you more about links later in this chapter.

To create a document with the Web Page Wizard

1. Choose File > New (**Figure 1**).

2. In the New dialog box that appears, click the Web Pages tab to display its options (**Figure 4**).

3. Click the Web Page Wizard icon to select it.

4. Click OK.

5. Follow the steps in the Web Page Wizard dialog boxes that appear (**Figures 6** through **13**) to create the Web pages.

6. When the wizard is finished, the home page appears (**Figure 14**). Edit placeholder text and enter new text as desired on each Web page to customize them for your needs.

✔ Tips

- If you select one of the two frame options in the Navigation screen of the Web Page Wizard (**Figure 8**), the Frame toolbar appears automatically with the home page (**Figure 14**). You can use this toolbar to create and modify navigation frames.

- Although the Web Page Wizard displays just the first or home page for a site, it creates multiple Web pages. You can use the Window menu to switch from one Web page to another for editing.

- I tell you about themes and links later in this chapter.

Figure 6 The Start screen of the Web Page Wizard explains what the Wizard will do.

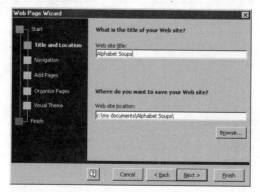

Figure 7 The Title and Location screen prompts you to enter a title for the Web site. The location for the site is entered automatically based on the site title.

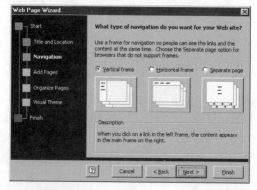

Figure 8 The Navigation screen offers three options for creating navigational links.

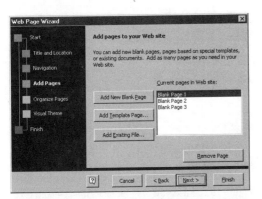

Figure 9 The Add Pages link enables you to add blank pages, template pages, or existing page files. You can also remove selected pages.

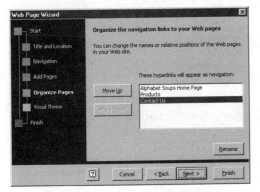

Figure 10 The Organize Pages screen enables you to rename the pages and to change their order.

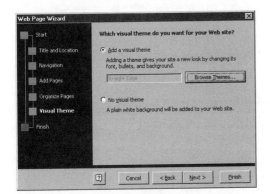

Figure 11 The Visual Themes screen lets you specify whether you want a special look for the pages.

Figure 12 Clicking the Browse Themes button in the Visual Themes screen (**Figure 11**) displays the Themes dialog box, which you can use to select a theme.

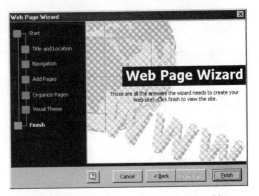

Figure 13 The Finish screen tells you that Word is finished gathering information and prompts you to click the Finish button.

Figure 14 The home page created by the Web Page Wizard with the settings shown in **Figures 6** through **13**.

Editing & Formatting Text

You can add, edit, delete, and format text on a Web page the same way you add, edit, delete, or format text in a regular Word document.

✔ Tip

- I cover editing text in **Chapter 2** and formatting text in **Chapters 3** and **4**. For more detailed instructions, consult those chapters.

To add text

1. Position the insertion point where you want to add the text.

2. Type the text that you want to add.

To edit text

1. Select the text that you want to change (**Figure 15**).

2. Type in the replacement text.

   The selected text is deleted and the replacement text is inserted in its place (**Figure 16**).

To delete text

1. Select the text that you want to delete (**Figure 17**).

2. Press Backspace.

   The selected text is deleted (**Figure 18**).

To format text

1. Select the text you want to format.

2. Use the menu commands, toolbar buttons, or shortcut keys to apply the desired formatting.

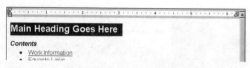

Figure 15 Select the text you want to replace.

Figure 16 The text you type replaces the selected text.

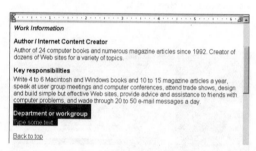

Figure 17 Select the text you want to delete.

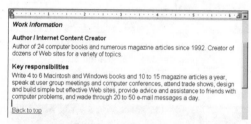

Figure 18 When you press Backspace, the text disappears.

Figure 19
The Format menu.

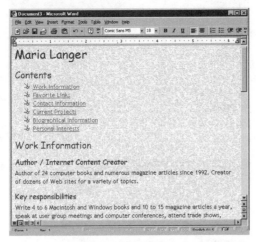

Figure 20 A Web page with the Cactus theme applied.

Themes

Word's Themes feature enables you to apply predefined formatting to text. It's similar to the Style Gallery feature I discuss in **Chapter 4**, but it includes special formatting appropriate for Web pages, such as background colors or patterns, body and heading styles and colors, hyperlink colors, bullets, horizontal lines, and table border colors.

✔ Tip

- You can use Themes with any Word document—not just Web pages.

To apply a theme

1. Choose Format > Theme (**Figure 19**).

2. In the Theme dialog box that appears (**Figure 12**), select the theme that you want to apply. The theme's elements appear in the Sample of theme area.

3. Set check box options as desired:

   ▲ **Vivid Colors** applies brighter colors to text and graphics.

   ▲ **Active Graphics** applies animation to some graphic elements.

   ▲ **Background Image** applies a background image to the page.

4. Click OK. The theme you selected is applied to the document (**Figure 20**).

✔ Tip

- To see graphic animation, you must view the Web page with Web browser software.

To remove a theme

1. Choose Format > Theme (**Figure 19**).

2. In the Theme dialog box (**Figure 12**), select (None).

3. Click OK. Any applied theme is removed.

APPLYING THEMES

Working with Pictures

You can insert pictures into Web pages by pasting them in or using commands under the Insert menu. Once a picture has been inserted, you can select it and change various settings for it using buttons on the Picture toolbar (**Figure 21**).

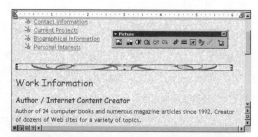

Figure 21 When you insert and select a picture, the Picture toolbar appears.

✔ Tips

- I explain how to use Insert menu commands to add pictures to Word documents and how to select and resize pictures in **Chapter 8**.

- You can choose Insert > Picture > From File to insert images used in themes. You can find the images on the following path: C:\Program Files\Common Files\ Microsoft Shared\Themes\ (**Figure 22**).

Figure 22 The Themes folder contains a folder for every installed theme.

To set word wrap & alignment

1. Double-click the picture for which you want to set word wrap and alignment options.

2. In the Format Picture dialog box that appears, click the Layout tab to display its options (**Figure 23**).

3. Click to select a Wrapping style icon:

   ▲ **In line with text** (**Figure 24**) turns off wrapping.

   ▲ **Square** (**Figures 25** and **26**) and **Tight** wrap text around the picture. (Tight is not available for pictures on Web pages.)

   ▲ **Behind text** (**Figure 27**) and **In front of text** (**Figure 28**) place the object in a different layer than text so either the text obscures the object or the object obscures the text.

4. If desired, select a Horizontal alignment option:

   ▲ **Left** (**Figures 25**, **27**, and **28**) positions the picture on the left side of the window.

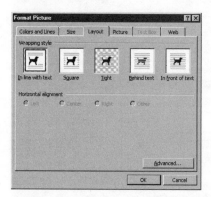

Figure 23 The Layout tab of the Format Picture dialog box.

Figure 24 An in line image appears in the same line as text. There is no text wrapping.

Figure 25 This image has Square wrapping and Left alignment turned on.

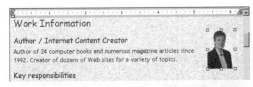

Figure 26 This image has Square wrapping and Right alignment turned on.

Figure 27 This image has Behind text wrapping and Left alignment turned on.

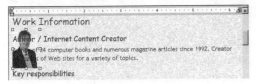

Figure 28 This image has In front of text wrapping and Left alignment turned on.

Figure 29 The Web tab of the Format Picture dialog box.

▲ **Center** centers the picture in the window.

▲ **Right** (**Figure 26**) positions the picture on the right side of the window.

▲ **Other** enables you to position the picture where you want by dragging it.

5. Click OK. The picture shifts its position accordingly.

✔ Tips

■ The options available in step 4 vary depending on the Wrapping style feature selected in step 3.

■ Not all text wrapping options are supported by all Web browsers.

To specify alternative text

1. Double-click the picture for which you want to set word wrap and alignment options.

2. In the Format Picture dialog box that appears, click the Web tab to display its options (**Figure 29**).

3. Enter the text you want to display in place of the picture in the Alternative text box.

4. Click OK.

✔ Tip

■ Alternative text displays in a Web browser in place of a picture while the picture is loading or if a viewer has the automatic display of images turned off.

SPECIFYING ALTERNATIVE TEXT

221

Hyperlinks

A hyperlink is text or a graphic that, when clicked, displays other information. Word enables you to create two kinds of hyperlinks:

- A link to a *URL* (*Uniform Resource Locator*), which is the address of a document or individual on the Internet. There are three main types of URLs:

  ▲ **http://** links to a Web page on a Web server.

  ▲ **ftp://** links to a downloadable file on an FTP server.

  ▲ **mailto:** links to an e-mail address.

- A link to a Word document on your hard disk or network.

By default, hyperlinks appear as colored, underlined text (**Figure 36**).

✔ Tip

- Word can automatically format URLs as hyperlinks. Simply type the complete URL; when you press (Spacebar) or (Enter), Word turns the URL into a hyperlink. You can set this option in the AutoFormat dialog box, which I tell you about in **Chapter 4**.

To insert a hyperlink

1. Position the insertion point where you want the hyperlink to appear.

   or

   Select the text or picture that you want to convert to a hyperlink (**Figure 30**).

2. Choose Insert > Hyperlink (**Figure 31**) or press (Ctrl)(K).

   or

   Click the Insert Hyperlink button on the Standard toolbar.

   The Insert Hyperlink dialog box appears (**Figure 32**).

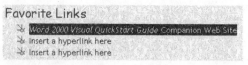

Figure 30 Select the text that you want to use as a hyperlink.

Figure 31 Choose Hyperlink from the Insert menu.

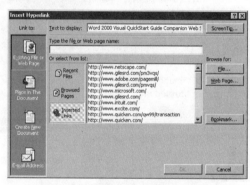

Figure 32 The Insert Hyperlink dialog box. This illustration shows a list of recently inserted links.

INSERTING HYPERLINKS

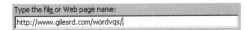

Figure 33 Enter the URL for the link location.

Figure 34 Word keeps track of recently opened files...

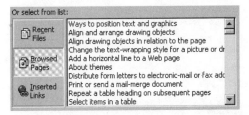

Figure 35 ...as well as recently browsed Web pages.

3. If necessary, enter the text that you want to appear as a link in the Text to display box.

4. Enter the complete URL or pathname for the Web page, e-mail address, or file to which you want to link in the Type the file or Web page name box (**Figure 33**).

or

Click one of the buttons along the left side of the URL or file list to display a list of Recent Files (**Figure 34**), Browsed Web Pages (**Figure 35**), or Inserted Links (**Figure 32**). Click to select one of the listed items.

or

Click the File button and use the Link to File dialog box that appears to locate and select a file on disk or accessible via network.

or

Click the Web Page button and use Internet Explorer to locate and select a Web page file on an intranet or the Internet.

5. Click OK to save your settings and dismiss the Insert Hyperlink dialog box.

The hyperlink is inserted.

or

The selected text turns into a hyperlink (**Figure 36**).

Favorite Links

⭐ *Word 2000 Visual QuickStart Guide* Companion Web Site
⭐ Insert a hyperlink here
⭐ Insert a hyperlink here

Figure 36 A link appears as underlined text.

To follow a hyperlink

1. Position the mouse pointer on the hyper-link. The mouse pointer turns into a pointing finger (**Figure 37**).

2. Click once.

   If the hyperlink points to an Internet URL, Word launches your Web browser, connects to the Internet, and displays the URL.

   or

   If the hyperlink points to a file on your hard disk or another computer on the network, the file opens.

✔ Tip

- The Web toolbar appears when you follow a link (**Figure 38**). You can use this toolbar to navigate to linked pages on your computer, your local area network, or the Web.

To remove a hyperlink

1. Drag to select the hyperlink (**Figure 39**).

2. Choose Hyperlink from the Insert menu (**Figure 31**) or press Ctrl K.

   or

   Click the Insert Hyperlink button 🔘 on the Standard toolbar.

3. In the Edit Hyperlink dialog box that appears (**Figure 40**), click the Remove Link button.

4. Click OK.

✔ Tips

- Removing a hyperlink does not delete the text or image that appears in the document window—just the link.

- You can also use the Edit Hyperlink dialog box (**Figure 40**) to change the URL or pathname for a linked file.

Figure 37 When you point to a hyperlink, the mouse pointer turns into a pointing finger.

Web toolbar

Figure 38 The Web toolbar appears when you follow a link.

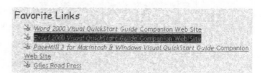

Figure 39 Drag to select the link.

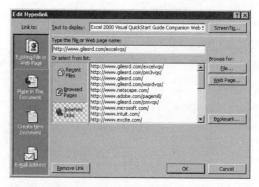

Figure 40 The Edit Hyperlink dialog box looks and works just like the Insert Link dialog box—but it includes a Remove Link button.

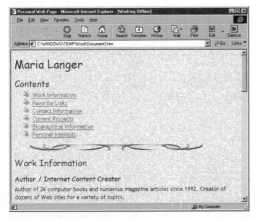

Figure 41 The Web Page Preview command displays the current document as a Web page with your Web browser software.

Figure 42 The Save As dialog box when you save a Web page.

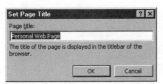

Figure 43
Use the Set Page Title dialog box to specify a document title.

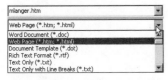

Figure 44 The Save as type menu determines what format the document will be saved in.

Working with Web Page Files

Word's File menu (**Figure 1**) offers several options for working with Web page files.

◆ Preview Web pages with your Web browser.

◆ Save Web pages created with a Web page template or the Web Page Wizard.

◆ Save Web page files as regular Word documents.

◆ Save regular Word documents as Web pages.

To preview a Web page

Choose File > Web Page Preview (**Figure 1**).

Word launches your Web browser program and displays the current document as a Web page (**Figure 41**).

To save a Web page

1. Choose File > Save As or File > Save As Web Page (**Figure 1**) to display the Save As dialog box (**Figure 42**).

2. Enter a name and select a location for the file.

3. To change the page title, click the Change Title button. Then use the Set Page Title dialog box that appears (**Figure 43**) to enter a new title for the page and click OK to return to the Save As dialog box.

4. Make sure Web Page is selected from the Save as type menu (**Figure 44**).

5. Click Save.

   Word saves the file. Each picture within the file is also saved as an individual GIF format graphic file (**Figure 45**).

Continued on next page...

PREVIEWING & SAVING WEB PAGES

Continued from previous page.

✔ Tips

- The name of a Web page file should not contain any spaces and should end with the *.htm* or *.html* file name extension to be properly recognized as a Web page file. If you're not sure which extension to use, ask your network administrator or ISP.

- When copying Web pages to a directory on a Web server, be sure to include the Web page file and all of its image files.

- The Change Title button only appears in the Save As dialog box (**Figure 42**) if the document was created with a Web page template or the Web Page Wizard or you chose File > Save As Web Page in step 1.

- To save a Web page as a regular Word document file, follow steps 1 and 2 above. Then choose Word Document from the Save as type menu and click Save.

- I provide more information about using the Save As dialog box in **Chapter 2**.

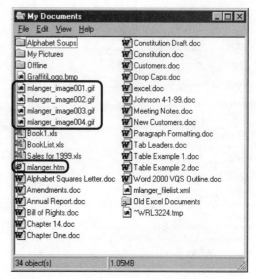

Figure 45 A Web page's images are saved with the Web page file.

SETTING OPTIONS

14

Figure 1
Choose Options from
the Tools menu.

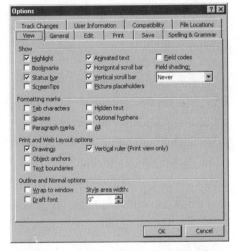

Figure 2 The View tab of the Options dialog box.

The Options Dialog Box

Word's Options dialog box offers ten categories of preferences that you can set to customize the way Word works for you:

◆ **View** options control Word's on-screen appearance.

◆ **General** options control general Word operations.

◆ **Edit** options control editing.

◆ **Print** options control document printing.

◆ **Save** options control file saving.

◆ **Spelling & Grammar** options control spelling and grammar checker operations.

◆ **Track Changes** options control the track changes feature.

◆ **User Information** options contain information about the primary user.

◆ **Compatibility** options control a document's compatibility with other applications or versions of Word.

◆ **File Locations** options specify where certain Word files are stored on disk.

✔ Tip

■ Word's default options are discussed and illustrated throughout this book.

To open the Options dialog box

Choose Tools > Options (**Figure 1**). The Options dialog box appears, displaying its most recently accessed tab (**Figure 2**).

View Options

The View tab of the Options dialog box (**Figure 2**) offers options in four categories: Show, Formatting marks, Print and Web Layout options, and Outline and Normal options.

Figure 3 The Field shading menu.

Show

Show options determine what Word elements appear on screen:

◆ **Highlight** displays text highlighting.

◆ **Bookmarks** displays document bookmarks by enclosing their names in square brackets. If displayed, the bookmarks do not print.

◆ **Status bar** displays the status bar below the window.

◆ **ScreenTips** displays comments in yellow boxes when you point to annotated text.

◆ **Animated text** displays animation applied to text. Turning off this option displays animated text the way it will print.

◆ **Horizontal scroll bar** displays a scroll bar along the bottom of the window.

◆ **Vertical scroll bar** displays a scroll bar along the right side of the window.

◆ **Picture placeholders** displays graphics as empty boxes. Turning on this option can speed up the display of documents with a lot of graphics.

◆ **Field codes** displays field codes instead of results.

◆ **Field shading (Figure 3)** enables you to specify how you want fields shaded:

▲ **Never** never shades fields.

▲ **Always** always shades fields.

▲ **When selected** only shades a field when it is selected.

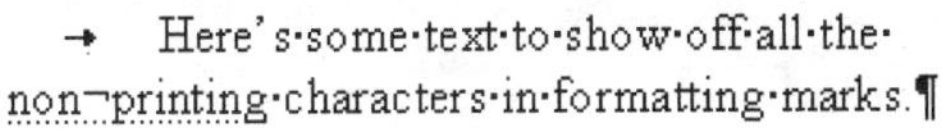

→ Here's·some·text·to·show·off·all·the·
non¬printing·characters·in·formatting·marks.¶

Figure 4 Formatting marks revealed!

Formatting marks

Formatting marks options determine which (if any) nonprinting characters appear on screen (**Figure 4**).

◆ **Tab characters** displays right-pointing arrows for tab characters.

◆ **Spaces** displays tiny dots for space characters.

◆ **Paragraph marks** displays backwards Ps for return characters.

◆ **Hidden text** displays a dotted under line under text formatted as hidden.

◆ **Optional hyphens** displays a hyphen with an angle on the end for optional hyphen characters.

◆ **All** displays all formatting marks. Turning on this option is the same as turning on the Show/Hide ¶ button ¶ on the Standard toolbar.

Print and Web Layout options

Print and Web Layout options determine what screen elements appear in Print Layout and Web Layout views.

◆ **Drawings** displays objects created with Word's drawing tools. Turning off this option can speed up the display and scrolling of documents with many drawings.

◆ **Object anchors** displays the anchor marker indicating that an object is attached to text. An object's anchor can only appear when the object is selected, this check box is turned on, and formatting marks are displayed. You must turn on this option to move an anchor.

◆ **Text boundaries** displays dotted lines around page margins, text columns, and objects.

◆ **Vertical ruler** displays a ruler down the left side of the window. This option is available in Print Layout view only.

VIEW OPTIONS

Outline and Normal options

Window options determine which window elements are displayed.

◆ **Wrap to window** wraps text to the width of the window rather than to the right indent or margin.

◆ **Draft font** displays most character formatting as bold or underlined and displays graphics as empty boxes. Turning on this option can speed up the display of heavily formatted documents.

◆ **Style area width** enables you to specify a width for the style area. When set to a value greater than 0, the style area appears along the left side of the window and indicates the style applied to each paragraph in the document (**Figure 5**). You may find this feature useful if you use styles in your documents.

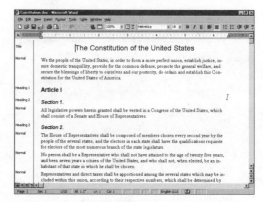

Figure 5 The style area displayed in Normal view.

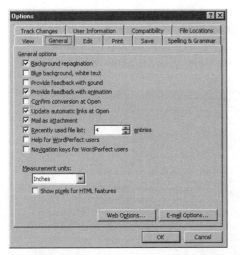

Figure 6 The General tab of the Options dialog box.

General Options

General options (**Figure 6**) control the general operation of Word. There are four categories: General options, Measurement units, Web Options, and E-mail Options.

General options

General options control many different Word features:

◆ **Background repagination** paginates documents automatically as you work.

◆ **Blue background, white text** displays the document as white text on a blue background—like old versions of WordPerfect software.

◆ **Provide feedback with sound** plays sound effects at the conclusion of certain actions or with the appearance of alerts.

◆ **Provide feedback with animation** displays special animated cursors while waiting for certain actions to complete.

◆ **Confirm conversion at Open** displays a dialog box that you can use to select a converter when you open a file created with another application.

◆ **Update automatic links at Open** automatically updates linked information when you open a document containing links to other files.

◆ **Mail as attachment** enables you to attach a file to an e-mail message using a File menu command. This option is only available if a compatible e-mail program is installed on your computer.

◆ **Recently used file list** enables you to specify the number of recently opened files that should appear near the bottom of the File menu. This feature is handy for quickly reopening recently accessed files.

Continued on next page...

Continued from previous page.

◆ **Help for WordPerfect users** provides Word instructions when you press a WordPerfect for DOS shortcut key. When this check box is turned on, *WPH* appears in the status bar at the bottom of the window.

◆ **Navigation keys for WordPerfect users** changes the functions of [Esc], [Home], [End], [Page Up], and [Page Down] so they work as they do in WordPerfect.

Measurement units

Measurement units enables you to set the units on the ruler and elsewhere in Word.

◆ **Measurement units** enables you to select the measurement unit used throughout Word. Options are Inches, Centimeters, Millimeters, Points, and Picas (**Figure 7**).

◆ **Show pixels for HTML features** changes the default measurement in dialog boxes to pixels when working with Web features.

Web Options

Clicking the Web Options button displays the Web Options dialog box (**Figures 8** through **12**), which has five different tabs of options relating to the Web. Although these options are advanced and far beyond the scope of this book, here's a quick overview of each tab:

◆ **General** options (**Figure 8**) control the coding and appearance of Web pages you create and view with Word.

◆ **Files** options (**Figure 9**) control file naming and locations and the default editor for Web pages.

◆ **Pictures** options (**Figure 10**) control the file formats of images and the resolution of the target monitor.

◆ **Encoding** options (**Figure 11**) control how a Web page is coded when saved.

Figure 7
The Measurement units menu.

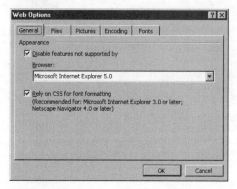

Figure 8 The General tab of the Web Options dialog box.

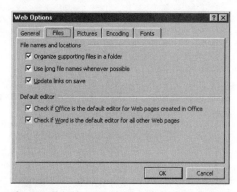

Figure 9 The Files tab of the Web Options dialog box.

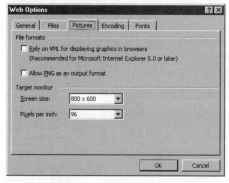

Figure 10 The Pictures tab of the Web Options dialog box.

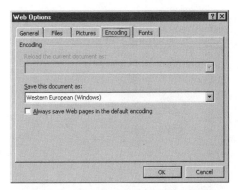

Figure 11 The Encoding tab of the Web Options dialog box.

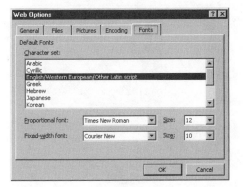

Figure 12 The Fonts tab of the Web Options dialog box.

◆ **Fonts** options (**Figure 12**) control the character set and default fonts.

E-mail Options

Clicking the E-mail Options button displays the E-mail Options dialog box (**Figures 13** and **14**), which has two different tabs of options relating to the E-mail. These options are advanced and far beyond the scope of this book, but here's a quick overview of each tab:

◆ **E-mail Signature** (**Figure 13**) enables you to enter and save text that can appear at the bottom of every e-mail message you write.

◆ **Personal Stationery** (**Figure 14**) enables you to specify the themes and font appearance used in e-mail messages you write.

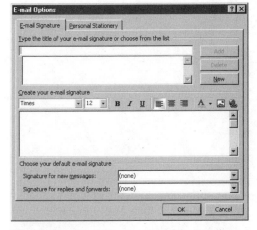

Figure 13 The E-mail Signature tab of the E-mail Options dialog box.

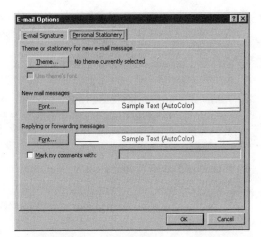

Figure 14 The Personal Stationery tab of the E-mail Options dialog box.

GENERAL OPTIONS

Edit Options

Edit options (**Figure 15**) control the way certain editing tasks work. There are two categories of options: Editing options and Click and type.

Editing Options

Editing options control the way text is edited and selected.

◆ **Typing replaces selection** deletes text when you start typing. If you turn this check box off, Word inserts typed text to the left of any text that was selected before you began typing.

◆ **Drag-and-drop text editing** allows you to move or copy selected text by dragging it.

◆ **Use the INS key for paste** enables you to press the Ins key to access the Paste command.

◆ **Overtype mode** replaces characters, one at a time, as you type. This is the opposite of insert mode.

◆ **Use smart cut and paste** adds or removes spaces as necessary when you delete, drag, or paste text. This feature can save you time when editing text.

◆ **Tabs and backspace set left indent** increases or decreases the left indent when you press Tab or Backspace . Be aware: This feature can cause undesired paragraph formatting changes.

◆ **Allow accented uppercase in French** enables Word's proofing tools to suggest accent marks for uppercase characters for text formatted as French.

◆ **Picture editor** lets you select a program to edit pictures. The only option on this menu is Microsoft Word.

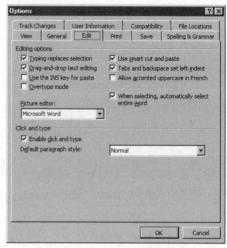

Figure 15 The Edit tab of the Options dialog box.

- **When selecting, automatically select entire word** selects entire words when your selection includes the spaces after words. This feature makes it impossible to use the mouse pointer to select multiple word fragments.

Click and type

Click and type affects the way Word's click and type feature works. This feature, which was not covered in this book, enables you to click anywhere on a page in Print Layout view and type to position text there.

- **Enable click and type** turns on the click and type feature.

- **Default paragraph style** specifies the default paragraph style for any text typed with the click and type feature.

Print Options

Print options (**Figure 16**) control the way documents print. There are four categories: Printing options, Include with document, Options for current document only, and Default tray.

Printing options

Printing options let you specify how the document content is updated and printed:

♦ **Draft output** prints the document with minimal formatting. This may make the document print faster, but not all printers support this option.

♦ **Update fields** automatically updates Word fields before you print. This feature prevents you from printing a document with outdated field contents.

♦ **Update links** automatically updates information in linked files before you print. This feature prevents you from printing a file with outdated linked file contents.

♦ **Allow A4/Letter paper resizing** automatically adjusts the paper size for documents created with another country's standard paper size (such as A4, which is used in Europe) to your standard paper size (which is Letter in the US).

♦ **Background printing** allows your printer to print Word documents in the background while you continue to work with Word or other programs. With this option turned off, you would have to wait for a document to finish printing before you could continue working.

♦ **Print PostScript over text** prints any PostScript code in a converted Word for Macintosh document (such as a digital watermark) on top of document text instead of underneath it. This option only works with PostScript printers.

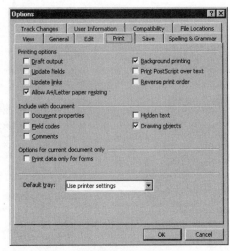

Figure 16 The Print tab of the Options dialog box.

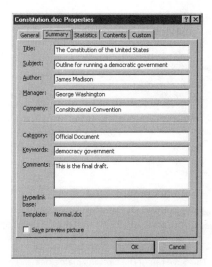

Figure 17 The Summary tab of the Properties dialog box.

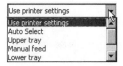

Figure 18 The Default tray menu.

◆ **Reverse print order** prints documents in reverse order—last page first. This might be useful if your printer stacks output face up.

Include with document

Include with document options enable you to print or suppress specific information from the document:

◆ **Document properties** prints the document's summary information on a separate page after the document. This information is stored in the Summary tab of the Properties dialog box (**Figure 17**), which you can display by choosing File > Properties.

◆ **Field codes** prints field codes instead of field contents.

◆ **Comments** prints reviewer comments on a separate page after the document.

◆ **Hidden text** prints text formatted as hidden.

◆ **Drawing objects** prints objects drawn with Word's drawing tools.

Options for current document only

As the name implies, options for current document only affect the way the active document prints:

◆ **Print data only for forms** prints just the information entered in fill-in forms—not the form itself.

Default tray

The Default tray menu (**Figure 18**) enables you to select a default printer feed location.

PRINT OPTIONS

Save Options

Save options (**Figure 19**) control the way files are saved to disk. There are two categories: Save options and File sharing options.

Save options

Save options enable you to set file saving preferences for all files that you save.

- ◆ **Always create backup copy** saves the previous version of a file as a backup copy with the original. Each time the file is saved, a new backup copy replaces the old one.

- ◆ **Allow fast saves** speeds up saving by saving only the changes to an existing file. If you turn off this check box, Word saves the entire file; this takes longer but results in slightly smaller files. This option is not available when the Always create backup copy option is enabled.

- ◆ **Prompt for document properties** displays the Properties dialog box (**Figure 17**) when you save a file for the first time. You can use this dialog box to enter and store information about the file.

- ◆ **Prompt to save Normal template** displays a dialog box that enables you to save or discard changes you made to the default settings in the Normal template. With this check box turned off, Word automatically saves changes to the Normal template.

- ◆ **Embed TrueType fonts** stores any True-Type fonts used in the document with the document. This enables others to view the file with the TrueType fonts that you used to create it, even if those fonts are not installed on their computers.

- ◆ **Embed characters in use only** stores only the TrueType font characters and styles that you used in the document. This can decrease the size of the document file. This option is only available when the Embed TrueType fonts check box is turned on.

Figure 19 The Save tab of the Options dialog box.

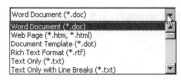

Figure 20 The Save Word files as menu.

Figure 21 If a file requires a password to open, this dialog box appears when you attempt to open it.

Figure 22 If a file requires a password to modify, this dialog box appears when you attempt to open it.

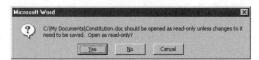

Figure 23 When a file is set to Read-only recommended, Word lets you decide whether you want to open it as read-only.

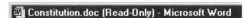

Figure 24 The words *Read-Only* appear in the title bar of a document you open as a read-only document.

◆ **Save data only for forms** saves the data entered into a form as a single, tab-delimited record that you can import into a database file.

◆ **Allow background saves** saves documents in the background while you continue working with Word.

◆ **Save AutoRecover info every** enables you to set a frequency for automatically saving a special document recovery file. Word can use the AutoRecover file to recreate the document if your computer crashes or loses power before you get a chance to save changes.

◆ **Save Word files as** enables you to choose a default format for saving Word files. The pop-up menu (**Figure 20**) offers the same options found in the Save As dialog box.

◆ **Disable features not supported by Word 97** turns off all Word 2000 features that are not supported by Word 97. This enhances the compatibility between these two file types.

File sharing options

The File sharing options affect only the current document.

◆ **Password to open** enables you to specify a password that must be entered to open the file (**Figure 21**).

◆ **Password to modify** enables you to specify a password that must be entered to save modifications to the file (**Figure 22**).

◆ **Read-only recommended** displays a dialog box (**Figure 23**) that recommends that the file be opened as a read-only file. If the file is opened as read-only, the words *Read-Only* appear in the title bar (**Figure 24**). Changes to the file must be saved in a file with a different name or in a different disk location.

SAVE OPTIONS

Spelling & Grammar Options

Spelling & Grammar options (**Figure 25**) control the way the spelling and grammar checkers work. There are two categories of preferences: Spelling and Grammar.

Spelling

Spelling options control the way the spelling checker works:

◆ **Check spelling as you type** turns on the automatic spelling check feature.

◆ **Hide spelling errors in this document** hides the red wavy lines that Word uses to identify possible spelling errors when the automatic spelling check feature is turned on. This option is only available when the Check spelling as you type option is enabled.

◆ **Always suggest corrections** tells Word to automatically display a list of suggested replacements for a misspelled word during a manual spelling check.

◆ **Suggest from main dictionary only** tells Word to suggest replacement words from the main dictionary—not from your custom dictionaries.

◆ **Ignore words in UPPERCASE** tells Word not to check words in all uppercase characters, such as acronyms.

◆ **Ignore words with numbers** tells Word not to check words that include numbers, such as MariaL1.

◆ **Ignore Internet and file addresses** tells Word not to check any words that appear to be URLs, e-mail addresses, file names, or file pathnames.

◆ **Custom dictionary** displays the name of the currently selected custom dictionary. This is the dictionary file to which words are added when you add words to the dictionary during a spelling check. You can

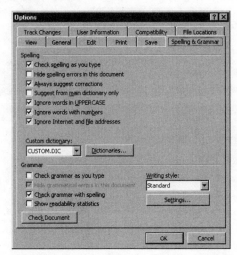

Figure 25 The Spelling & Grammar tab of the Options dialog box.

Figure 26 The Custom Dictionaries dialog box.

use the menu to select a different custom dictionary if desired.

◆ **Dictionaries** enables you to create, edit, add, and remove custom dictionaries. Click this button to display the Custom Dictionaries dialog box (**Figure 26**), which lists all the custom dictionary files open in Word. Then:

▲ To activate a dictionary file so it can be used by the spelling checker, turn on the check box to the left of its name in the Custom dictionaries list.

▲ To change the language of the selected dictionary file, choose a language from the Language menu.

▲ To create a new custom dictionary, click the New button and use the dialog box that appears to name and save the new dictionary file.

▲ To edit the selected dictionary, click the Edit button to open it in Word. Then make changes and save it.

▲ To add a dictionary to the Custom dictionaries list, click the Add button and use the dialog box that appears to locate and open the dictionary file. This feature makes it possible to share dictionary files that contain company- or industry-specific terms with other Word users in your workplace.

▲ To remove a dictionary from Word, select the dictionary and click the Remove button. This does not delete the dictionary file from disk.

Grammar

Grammar options control the way the grammar checker works:

◆ **Check grammar as you type** turns on the automatic grammar check feature.

◆ **Hide grammatical errors in this document** hides the green wavy lines that Word uses to identify possible grammar errors when the automatic grammar check feature is turned on. This option is only available when the Check grammar as you type option is enabled.

◆ **Check grammar with spelling** performs a grammar check as part of a manual spelling check.

◆ **Show readability statistics** displays readability statistics (**Figure 27**) for a document at the conclusion of a manual spelling and grammar check. This option is only available when the Check grammar with spelling option is enabled.

◆ **Writing style** enables you to select a set of rules for the grammar checker. Use the menu to select one of five options (**Figure 28**).

◆ **Settings** enables you to customize the rules for the grammar checker. Click this button to display the Grammar Settings dialog box (**Figure 29**). Choose the set of rules that you want to modify from the Writing style menu (**Figure 28**), then use the options in the dialog box to set the style's rules. You can use the Reset All button to reset all writing style rule sets to the default settings.

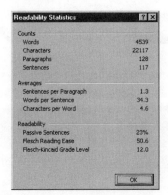

Figure 27 The readability statistics for the Constitution of the United States.

Figure 28 The Writing style menu.

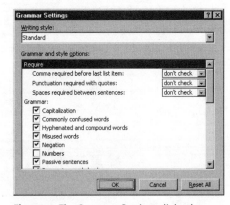

Figure 29 The Grammar Settings dialog box.

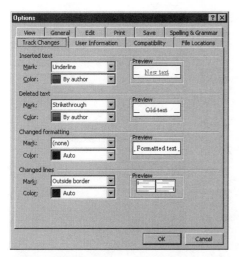

Figure 30 The Track Changes tab of the Options dialog box.

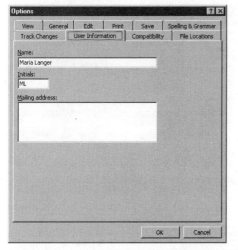

Figure 31 The User Information tab of the Options dialog box.

Track Changes Options

The Track Changes options (**Figure 30**) control the way the change tracking feature works. For each option, you can change the mark and color that Word uses to display document changes. The Preview areas show formatting samples.

◆ **Inserted text** controls the appearance of text that is inserted into the document.

◆ **Deleted text** controls the appearance of text that is deleted from the document.

◆ **Changed formatting** controls the appearance of text which has been reformatted.

◆ **Changed lines** controls the appearance and location of margin marks beside changed lines of text.

User Information Options

The User Information options (**Figure 31**) store information about the primary user of that copy of Word. This information is used by a variety of features throughout Word.

◆ **Name** is the user name. This information is filled in when you install Word. Word uses this information for the comments and track changes features.

◆ **Initials** is the user initials. This information is also filled in when you install Word, based on the user name. Word uses this information for the comments and track changes features.

◆ **Mailing address** is the user's mailing address. This is used as the default return address for the envelopes and labels feature.

Compatibility Options

Compatibility options (**Figure 32**) control the internal formatting of the current Word document for compatibility with other applications or versions of Word.

◆ **Font Substitution** enables you to specify a font to be used in place of a font applied in the document but not installed on your computer. (This happens most often when you open a file that was created on someone else's computer.) Click this button to display the Font Substitution dialog box (**Figure 33**). You can then select the missing font name and choose a substitution font from the Substituted font menu. The menu will include all fonts installed on your computer. To permanently apply the substituted font to text formatted with the missing font, click the Convert Permanently button. If the document does not contain any missing fonts, Word does not display the Font Substitution dialog box.

◆ **Recommended options for** enables you to select a collection of compatibility rules for a specific application. Choose an option from the menu (**Figure 34**).

◆ **Options** enables you to toggle check boxes for a variety of internal formatting options. These options are automatically set when you choose one of the rule sets from the Recommended options for menu, but you can override them as desired.

◆ **Default** applies the current dialog box settings to all documents created with the current template from that point forward.

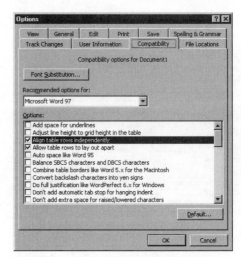

Figure 32 The Compatibility tab of the Options dialog box.

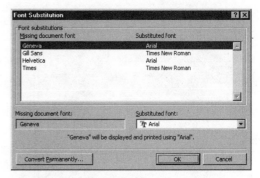

Figure 33 The Font Substitution dialog box.

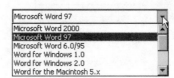

Figure 34 The Recommended options for menu.

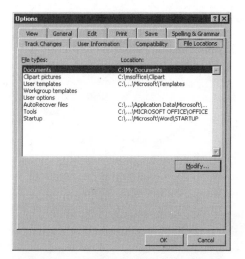

Figure 35 The File Locations tab of the Options dialog box.

Figure 36 The Modify Location dialog box.

File Locations Options

File Locations options (**Figure 35**) enable you to set the default disk location for certain types of files. This makes it easier for Word (and you) to locate these files.

To set or change a default file location

1. Click to select the name of the file type for which you want to set or change the file location (**Figure 35**).

2. Click the Modify button.

3. Use the Modify Location dialog box that appears (**Figure 36**) to locate and open the folder in which the files are or will be stored.

4. Click OK.

The pathname for the location appears to the right of the name of the file type.

MENUS & SHORTCUT KEYS

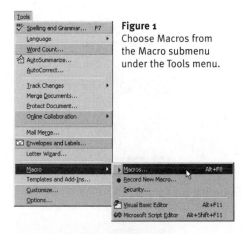

Figure 1
Choose Macros from the Macro submenu under the Tools menu.

Figure 2
Select Word commands from the Macros in menu.

Figure 3 Select the ListCommands macro.

Figure 4
The List Commands dialog box enables you to select which commands to list.

Menus & Shortcut Keys

This appendix illustrates all of Word's full menus and provides a list of shortcut keys—including some that don't appear on menus.

To use a shortcut key, hold down the modifier key (usually Ctrl) and press the keyboard key corresponding to the command. For example, to use the Save command's shortcut key, hold down Ctrl and press S.

✔ Tips

- I tell you all about using menus and shortcut keys in **Chapter 1**.

To create a document that lists all menu commands & shortcut keys

1. Choose Tools > Macro > Macros (**Figure 1**) to display the Macros dialog box.

2. Select Word commands from the Macros in menu (**Figure 2**).

3. Select ListCommands in the Macro name list (**Figure 3**).

4. Click the Run button.

5. In the List Commands dialog box that appears (**Figure 4**), select Current menu and keyboard settings.

6. Click OK.

File Menu

Ctrl N	New
Ctrl O	Open
Ctrl W	Close
Ctrl S	Save
F12	Save As
Ctrl P	Print
Alt Ctrl I	Print Preview

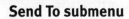

Send To submenu

Edit Menu

Ctrl Z	Undo
Ctrl Y	Repeat
Ctrl Y	Redo
Ctrl X	Cut
Ctrl C	Copy
Ctrl V	Paste
Del	Clear
Ctrl A	Select All
Ctrl F	Find
Ctrl H	Replace
Ctrl G	Go To

View Menu

Alt Ctrl N	Normal
Alt Ctrl O	Outline

Toolbars submenu

Insert Menu

Ctrl	Alt	F	Footnote
Ctrl	Shift	F5	Bookmark
Ctrl	K		Hyperlink

AutoText submenu

Picture submenu

Format Menu

Ctrl	D	Font
Shift	F3	Change Case
Alt	Ctrl	K	AutoFormat
Ctrl	Shift	S	Style

Background submenu

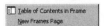

Frames submenu

Tools Menu

| F7 | Spelling and Grammar |

Language submenu

| Shift | F7 | Thesaurus |

Track Changes submenu

Online Collaboration submenu

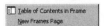

Macro submenu

Alt	F8	Macros
Alt	F11	Visual Basic Editor
Alt	Shift	F11	Microsoft Script Editor

Table Menu

Help Menu

F1	Microsoft Word Help
Shift F1	What's This?

Insert submenu

Delete submenu

Select submenu

Alt Clear	Table

AutoFit submenu

Convert submenu

Window Menu

TABLE, WINDOW, & HELP MENUS

INDEX

INDEX